18.95

THE
PUBLIC IVYS

Also by Richard Moll

Playing the Private College Admissions Game

P^{THE}UBLIC IVYS

A Guide to America's Best
Public Undergraduate Colleges
and Universities

Richard Moll

VIKING

VIKING
Viking Penguin Inc., 40 West 23rd Street,
New York, New York 10010, U.S.A.
Penguin Books Ltd, Harmondsworth,
Middlesex, England
Penguin Books Australia Ltd, Ringwood,
Victoria, Australia
Penguin Books Canada Limited, 2801 John Street,
Markham, Ontario, Canada L3R 1B4
Penguin Books (N.Z.) Ltd, 182–190 Wairau Road,
Auckland 10, New Zealand

First published in 1985 by Viking Penguin Inc.
Published simultaneously in Canada

LIBRARY OF CONGRESS CATALOGING IN PUBLICATION DATA
Moll, Richard.
  The public ivys.
  Includes index.
  1. State universities and colleges—United States—
Directories.   2. State universities and colleges—United States—
Handbooks, manuals, etc.   I. Title.
L901.M63   1985   378.73   83-40659
ISBN 0-670-58205-0

Grateful acknowledgment is made to the following for permission to reprint copyrighted material:

Alcalde Magazine: A selection from the January 1982 Alumni Magazine, reprinted with permission of *Alcalde* magazine, published by The Ex-Students' Association of the University of Texas.

The University of North Carolina Press: A selection from The First State University, by William S. Powell. Copyright © 1972 by The University of North Carolina Press. Used with permission of the publisher.

Printed in the United States of America by
R. R. Donnelley & Sons Company, Harrisonburg, Virginia
Set in Baskerville

To my nephew Tom

a representative of the brightest
and best of a college generation

and

to Guidance Counselors throughout
the high schools of America—our most
unrewarded and overworked professional group

Acknowledgments

This second book was more difficult to produce than the first—more research, more travel, more time. A California mudslide outside my front door did not expedite the project. So thanks—not just for guidance and encouragement, but for patience—to my editors, Martha Kinney and William Strachan; to my agent Molly Friedrich; to my employer, the University of California at Santa Cruz; to my UCSC associate Joe Allen, who so effectively and cheerfully stood in when book matters kept me from the office; to my selfless typist, Jane Gomez; and to my family and friends, who seemed to understand when time and tensions pressured.

Thanks also to those colleagues and staffs at the Public Ivy institutions who provided data, arranged interviews, and assisted in so many ways—in particular:

University of California, Berkeley	Bob Bailey, Bob Brownell
University of Colorado	Jana Lynn
Georgia Tech	Jerry Hitt
University of Illinois	Gary Engelgau
Miami University (Ohio)	Chuck Schuler
University of Michigan	Cliff Sjogren
New College (Florida)	Roberto Noya
University of North Carolina	Richard Cashwell
Penn State	Don Dickason
University of Pittsburgh	Jeff Bolton
SUNY-Binghamton	Geoff Gould
University of Texas	Shirley Binder

University of Vermont	Jeff Kaplan
University of Virginia	Larry Groves,
	Jean Rayburn
University of Washington	Tim Washburn
William and Mary (Virginia)	Gary Ripple
University of Wisconsin	David Vinson

Contents

Introduction:
The Time Has Come

Every spring the mails bring nasty, sometimes venomous, letters to college admissions directors and deans from a handful of the rejected candidates' shout-before-they-pause fathers. The mails also bring plaintive, often moving pleas from the kids assigned to the waiting list, and a tiny handful of thank-you's from the admitted. Also in the mailbag are gracious, rather effusive notes from the secondary schools—particularly the private ones—recording the recent college admissions season's successes, thanking the college at hand, and urging a visit to the school in the fall to smile at the upcoming batch of new seniors who will soon be mounting at the starting gate.

The letters from power-play dads and earnest teenagers will probably never change. (Mothers seem to be most active prior to the announcement of the colleges' decisions. Thank God for the mothers, who so frequently chair the family's college search with patience and intelligence.) But the letters from the secondary schools are changing. Because the times are changing. A little prep school in Michigan says it all with the following observation in its annual spring message to colleges: "One notable difference in this year's college placements was due almost entirely to economics and may call for a new category on our placement list: 'Accepted at first choice college (usually private and more selective) but attending another that costs less.' I have no doubt whatsoever that you too are painfully aware of this trend and share our real concerns."

The message is clear: even the parents with ready cash are wondering if Olde Ivy is worth two to three times the price of a thoroughly respectable public institution. Granted, most parents of the highest-achieving high school students seem willing to kill to put the money together for Stanford,

Yale, Amherst, Cal Tech, and a little club of other high-prestige private institutions. But that list of colleges isn't very long now and is shrinking fast. Twelve to fifteen thousand dollars for a second- or third-level private college is considered out of the question by more and more Americans, given the competing demands for their dollar today. Although students pursue admission to the most costly private universities to "know they could have gone," more and more often the matriculation deposit is paid at the less expensive public institution of similar quality and rising prestige.

The *Chronicle of Higher Education,* every college administrator's *New York Times,* has been repeating this theme. A headline on page one in the spring of 1982 read: "Swing from Private to Public Colleges Noted in Applications for Fall." The article said there would undoubtedly be a further increase in the population of college students in the public sector, which already enrolled 78 percent of the total. In the same journal, half a year later: "Private Colleges Report 16,000 Fewer Freshmen." "The largest, most pervasive losses of first-year students were at less selective liberal arts colleges. . . . It is clear that the sluggish economy, combined with federal cuts in student aid and the threat of deeper cuts, is forcing new students to abandon their plans to attend independent colleges. Instead, they are postponing their higher education or, more often, are opting for less expensive, government-run institutions." Not long after, in the *Chronicle:* "40,962 Fewer Students Enrolled at Private Institutions This Fall; Early Data Show 27,506 More Students at Public Colleges."

The news crept out of the academic journals and into public view. Front page, *New York Times,* September 1982: "Aid Uncertainties Spur Enrollment in Public Colleges: Private Universities Lag." The article said: "Some public colleges have been flooded with late applications from students who suddenly found they could not afford to attend their first-choice private colleges. And some private colleges are still soliciting applications long after the deadline to try to keep their enrollments at last year's levels." Several weeks later, the *Times* continued: "Most admissions directors interviewed said that they had not yet had time to track down where the missing students (who had paid deposits for fall enrollment but did not matriculate) went, but most assumed that at least some went to public institutions where the costs were lower. The movement of some middle-class students from private to public colleges has been apparent for the last year or so . . . 'About 60 percent of our students have usually gone to private schools,' said Luis R. Fritsche, a counselor at Great Valley Senior High School in Walvern, PA. 'This year the figure dropped to 40 percent. More students are ending up at Penn State, West Chester and other public institutions.' "

A quickened drift from the private to the public sector of higher education because of price, a perceived decline in financial aid, and an uncertain economy, is not the only barometer of the times. There are deeper problems affecting enrollment in academe. A seminar announcement in 1982 from the American Association for Higher Education carried this banner: "THE ENROLLMENT CRISIS"—followed by a jolting summary:

- "A 23 percent drop in college-aged people will occur over the next 15 years.
- Even small enrollment decreases will produce large college revenue reductions.
- 100 to 400 colleges and universities will close because of enrollment problems over the next 20 years."

These factors obviously create anxiety among admissions officers, who now know all the dreary demographic predictions by heart. An article in the *Wall Street Journal* predicted that "by 1994, there will be at least 37 percent fewer graduating high school seniors than in 1980 in such Northeastern states as New York, Pennsylvania, New Jersey, Massachusetts and Connecticut. The number will plummet 45 percent in Rhode Island and 59 percent in Washington, D.C. Mid-western states, including Michigan, Illinois and Ohio, also will be hard hit with declines exceeding 30 percent."*

But the "baby bust" that produced this bleak situation created subtleties of perhaps even greater consequence. One is that the sharpest decline in births during the post-baby-boom period was among affluent whites, and every highly selective college in America is predominantly white. To maintain even the percentage of teenagers who *now* proceed to college would require increased attendance by blacks, Hispanics, and other underrepresented minorities. Although that movement has accelerated since the late sixties, current cuts in federal, state, and institutional financial aid threaten to reduce the number of minority students attending colleges and universities.

Many institutions hope to fill the gap created by too few "traditional" students by admitting an increasing number of older students, particularly re-entry women. Clearly, there are many older prospective students—women whose education was cut short by marriage and family, men and women who need re-tooling to respond to changing job demands and a changing society. But colleges need two to four part-time enrollees to make up for the loss of one full-time student, and only the urban institutions have the potential to develop this "new" student body. In addition to these demographic woes college admissions officers face declining budgets in these

Wall Street Journal, December 14, 1982.

tough economic times. No wonder their outlook grows grimmer each year.

Meanwhile, out in the marketplace, today's teenagers have pulled an about-face. The high school seniors of the eighties seem to have different values from their counterparts of the sixties and seventies. They are not demonstrating against a war; they are busy preparing for high-tech employment. Going to college to develop marketable skills is an obsession. Students have moved to the right politically. Altruism has moved down the scale of priorities, making big money has moved up. Studying the humanities and social sciences is considered a luxury; to survive, one majors in engineering, business, or computer science. According to the College Board, whose Student Descriptive Questionnaire is filled out by 90 percent of the students taking the SAT, the freshman class of 1983 could be described as follows: most students, but especially women, want high-paying jobs and technological training; they plan to avoid the liberal arts and low-paying fields such as art or teaching. The College Board also noted that computer science as an intended major had tripled in popularity since 1978, and women in 1982 accounted for over half of the intended business majors. This is a 36 percent increase in a decade.

A list of best-selling books on campus published in the *Chronicle of Higher Education* gives further insight to the new teenager. Gone from the college bookstores' best-seller lists are the familiar titles read by the earlier generations of students: *The Greening of America, Future Shock, The Prophet,* and the how-to pop psychology books like *How to Be Your Own Best Friend.* In their place are *The Official Preppy Handbook, 101 Uses for a Dead Cat,* and *What Color Is Your Parachute?*

Different times, indeed! An extraordinarily practical generation of prospective college students who, instead of the customary question about what percentage of students get into graduate school, ask admissions officers about the average starting salary last year of the graduating seniors in computer engineering. There is a dramatic decrease in the number of high school graduates, particularly the ones most likely to attend college full-time. Also, these students express a genuine apprehension regarding the merits of America's long-established bent toward a liberal arts education. And there is among many parents a reluctance or inability to sacrifice, as their own parents often did, for expensive college costs.

Directly or indirectly, all of these changes contribute to the growth and importance of the public college sector. Among a number of unique idiosyncrasies of the eighties, an accelerated turn to public education, particularly among America's "established class," will surely have the longest lasting consequences. This turn of events has had repercussions inside academe, often in quite sensitive areas. The Reverend Timothy S. Healy, president of Georgetown University, was explicit in an address to the American Association of State Colleges and Universities:

There are two areas where tempers are fraying thin between public and private colleges. . . . The first is the most obvious, to draw and keep students. As the long foreseen drop in the age cohort begins to bite, it can stir real panic. . . . Private institutions will claim that they are in an unfair competition, since the tax supported public colleges can attract students at low rates, while privates must peg price close to cost. So they will labor to make public colleges raise tuition, or to change the flow of public dollars into tuition support programs for private colleges. . . . The second area where rub begets resentment is access to the private philanthropic dollar for public institutions. . . . Private colleges feel that philanthropy is their bag and that foundations, corporations, and individuals ought to limit their gifts to institutions that do not receive substantive help from state and local governments. Public colleges deny this vehemently.

While these new rivalries stir officialdom, fresh traditions are taking root in the healthier-than-ever public sector of higher education. One development has been inevitable: the emergence of a national pecking order, a perceived hierarchy of who is best among public colleges and universities. As in the private sector, with its reputed "best"—the Ivy League, the Seven Sisters, and a handful of others—an elite in the public sector has evolved, relatively unnoticed. These Public Ivys are beginning to surface.

Educators have yet to develop a cogent, fair method of ranking colleges. The nation's perceived "best" colleges in the private sector are those in the Ivy League. Yet, this fraternity of eight (Brown, Columbia, Cornell, Dartmouth, Harvard, Pennsylvania, Princeton, and Yale) was not elevated as the result of accrediting agencies' careful scrutiny. Instead, the Ivy League officially emerged as a sports league, inaugurated and named surprisingly recently—in 1954. There are some curious members of this elite club, all of whom profit enormously from the halo effect of the league's title. Take Cornell, for example. Cornell is a strange amalgam of private and public. Some divisions are state supported, some are privately supported. Cornell's admissions policies, not to mention its administration and funding, are quite different from one segment to the next. Rather than Cornell, why aren't Johns Hopkins, Duke, Rice, or Stanford in the Ivy League? These institutions seem closer to Yale and Harvard in tone and purpose. It is odd indeed that an athletic schedule along with a little tradition has promoted a public consensus of "the nation's best."

The Seven Sisters seem to have emerged from oral tradition alone. Granted, they share early beginnings, a common purpose of creating for women the quality of education that men could find at Harvard, Yale, or Princeton. But why seven, particularly now that the league has been aborted by Vassar's coeducation and Radcliffe's near-disappearance into the conglomerate called Harvard? Why—then or now—not Connecticut College, Wheaton, Skidmore, or Mills as part of the elitist Sisters? Perhaps as a reaction to the questionable yet popular acceptance of the Ivy League and the Seven Sisters as the top of the nation's pecking order, more than a few attempts have been made through the years to rank colleges. But there is little agreement on what the criteria can and/or should be.

A typical approach to ranking colleges is to decry the competition's criteria and conclusions first, and then proceed to make strongly stated conclusions based on equally questionable methodology. For example, the combined prefaces to the *Gourman Reports: A Rating of Undergraduate Programs in American and International Universities* (1967, 1977, and 1980) set an inviting stage with high-sounding language, but it is fuzzy at best:

> Past and recent studies have not helped us to gain a better judgement on the very serious questions about our undergraduate institutions. . . . I record here that surveys or books based upon ambiguous evidence continue to produce the false images among schools. The myth supplies the emotional and volitional drive that gives the institution a cohesion and enables it to put its energies into play. The false image has been handed down throughout the decades in order to persuade the public to preserve the reputations of the respective schools. . . . Many surveys in the past and present have deliberately eschewed a "sophisticated methodology framework" in favor of a "simple analytical account," but this does not deal adequately or in any depth with numerous interconnected issues of procedure and policy which have to be faced and dealt with by the decision-makers in the colleges and universities.

The author then reveals his own broad categories of criteria: "standards and quality of instruction," "scholastic work of students," and the like, and proceeds to rank institutions. But the listings—by discipline, by athletic/academic balance, et cetera—are somehow noteworthy by their exceptions. William and Mary, Middlebury, Barnard, Wellesley, SUNY-Binghamton, Davidson, Vassar, Colorado College, Connecticut College, and Bowdoin, for example, are nowhere to be found. How could these stellar colleges fail to make a single list? The author's answer: they hadn't been reviewed and rated! "Too small," said he.

And there is the sensational approach to rating colleges, certain to capture headlines. One author ranked colleges by the percentage of graduates who had made the Social Register. Sure enough, the papers picked it up, and there probably were more than a few believers.

All efforts to rate undergraduate education have not been sensational and/or ill-advised. Perhaps the best example is the extensive research conducted by the Higher Education Research Institute in Los Angeles. Its president, Alexander W. Astin, has become a near-celebrity with his articles, lectures, and talk show appearances, as the national recorder of each new American college freshman class's personal and political values, aspirations, social and family background, and academic strengths and weaknesses. His annual "student characteristics" announcements are widely anticipated and always dependable.

Equally well-publicized have been Astin's college and university ratings based on student selectivity. But there has been a problem: Astin and his cohorts have featured standardized test results as *the* insight to the quality of a student body. His college ratings, therefore, are generated by the ratio of high-scoring students (on the SAT or equivalent tests) to the total student body. Astin first ranked institutions in 1965 on the basis of the college destinations of National Merit Scholars (always chosen with a heavy bias toward SAT performance); in 1973 and 1977 he broadened his review to include average test scores of an institution's entire freshman class. Although his tabulations were broadly publicized and considered a badge of success to the "winners," there was sound criticism of his methodology. The influential dean of admissions at Stanford responded in 1979: "This Astin survey makes test scores more important than they actually are. In fact, a forthcoming survey of several major private institutions indicates there are very few schools where test scores are the most important factor in admissions. This is particularly true for the most popular schools. Any one of the top 20 schools in the nation could 'stack' its ranking on the Astin-Solomon scale simply by using test scores alone as the basis of admission."

Whether or not it relies too heavily on test scores, the Astin report always gives parents and educators something to think about. Fortunately, researcher Astin and his colleagues seem never satisfied with the criteria utilized in their previous study. They try to create ways to more accurately judge undergraduate institutions. One of their latest surveys incorporated "reputational" ratings by faculty members across the land who were asked to judge departments of other universities in their own academic disciplines. Most prior studies indicated that faculty rather automatically gave high points to the undergraduate programs of institutions famous for their *graduate* offerings in particular disciplines. Astin commented in an article in *Change Magazine:* "This finding suggests at least two conclusions: either those institutions that excel in graduate education also provide exemplary training at the undergraduate level, or a strong halo effect is operating. If the latter is true, raters *assume* that the most renowned graduate schools also provide an excellent undergraduate education, even though different characteristics might contribute to successful bachelor's level experiences."

Indeed, Astin and his research staff found the "halo effect" to be very strong in influencing faculty rankings of undergraduate programs. The questionnaires included a number of institutions on the business school list which didn't offer business at all. Princeton emerged in the top-ten-of-the-nation winners for business as a result of the faculty vote, even though a major program in business at Princeton doesn't exist!

One other Astin discovery in the 1977 report was perhaps predictable:

> It is also worth noting that every (most selective) institution is privately controlled and operates a residential undergraduate program (many have required residence for freshmen). The fact that no public institutions are among the most selective in the country is no doubt attributable in part to the large size of most public institutions. While it is probably true that the top students in many large public institutions are just as intellectually capable as the best students in the selective private colleges, the low end of the ability distribution is almost always larger at the more widely accessible public institutions. Thus the *average* score (selectivity) is inevitably lower at most public institutions.

My prediction is that Astin's findings regarding public versus private college selectivity will soon be dated. Brown, Williams, Princeton, Duke, and their small band of first cousins will remain highly selective. But the runner-up list of highly selective private colleges will be nudged aside, one by one, by the quickly rising prestige of the public colleges—a small group of publics, that is. Price will play a prominent role in this changing of the guard, but other factors, like the vogue for technical training, changing perceptions of what "prestige" is all about, demographic trends, and transparent quality of offerings, will also figure strongly.

It is probably obvious by now that my bias leans toward the more subjective analysis of institutions. No one characteristic or conglomerate of objective characteristics—percentage of Ph.D.s on the faculty, endowment per student, mean SAT scores of entering freshmen, starting salaries of graduating seniors, or number of Nobel Prize winners—can substantiate a "best" rating when people and places and funds can change abruptly.

So how do we rate or recognize the best institutions? Which of the growing number of significant public institutions are working their way up to "Ivy"? And what does the designation "Ivy" connote? For starters, a great deal of prestige. Second and inseparable from the first, a presupposition of exceptional quality in programs, teaching, facilities, and total undergraduate experience. Third, a crowd attempting to storm the front gates or very selective admissions standards. Fourth, an avowed mission to develop the "whole person," usually via liberal arts emphasis and a consequent de-emphasis of vocational programs and skills. And finally, the resources to match ideas with materials and manpower, and then maintain the quality.

In short, what "Ivy" has come to mean translates into the following criteria for nominating a comparable public school list: (1) admissions selectivity; (2) a quality undergraduate experience and importance accorded the liberal arts; (3) money, from whatever source, to assemble personal, academic, and physical strength—and the resourcefulness to manage funds wisely; (4) the prestige, the mythology, and the visibility that enhance the place and the name.

Let's consider the criteria in detail.

1. Admissions selectivity (particularly for freshmen)

Study after study indicates that the most selective institutions are the most prestigious, and those that muster greatest alumni loyalty. Thus, concentration on freshman admissions becomes key. But this is a frustrating area to review, and apples are often inescapably compared to oranges. Some selective public institutions use objective data (test scores and grade point averages) exclusively, while others combine the objective with the subjective (personal strengths, recommendations, and essays). Some have severe quotas for out-of-staters, while others welcome large numbers of out-of-staters to assure "balance." On the whole, though, the Public Ivys share high SATs and even higher high school GPAs, large out-of-state contingents, disappointingly low ethnic diversity, and a surprising degree of subjective analysis in the admissions process.

2. A quality undergraduate academic program and experience, and the importance accorded liberal arts

This is another difficult area to judge conclusively, particularly in the larger institutions. A faculty roster can be impressive indeed, the percentage of Ph.D.s high, the national awards exhaustive. But are the famous professors in the classroom? If so, can they *teach?* Whom *does* an institution put up front? Scholars good at titillating undergraduate minds? And how about class size? If a genius is up front who has the natural knack of clearly and inspiringly translating complicated equations or theories to students, who cares about class size? Granted, the availability of personnel and facilities for individual guidance in the academic arena is important. Perhaps it is "environment for learning," then, that is more important to assess than which institution has won the most Guggenheim Awards and how many hours per week the winners teach undergraduates.

But "environment for learning" can hardly be charted; it has to be felt, experienced. It is the result of a magic mix of accomplished scholars creating atmosphere; an inherently curious student body, with just enough individual assistance in the learning process to promote the self-confidence to proceed; the physical resources to comfortably accommodate and equip all phases of the process; the staff, both academic and administrative, to keep all the parts meshing; and the peripheral environment (housing, extracurriculars, fun spots) to provide appropriate relief (but not near-total distraction, as winning teams or an exciting city can sometimes do). The whole package is compromised, it seems to me, if core areas of knowledge are eliminated or minimized, if learning missions are dictated by that which "prepares" one for a specific goal—to be a career officer or a career nurse or a career anything—and if there is the promise and/or expectation of rewards or success. Elitist or not, this view of Ivy tilts toward the priority of learning, not living.

3. Resources

Economic times are tough all over, but particularly for higher education. The taxpayer's revolt that started with Proposition 13 in California has become contagious. The resulting nationwide cutback in educational funding, state by state, has reached epidemic proportions. And the problem does not stop with the states. Significant federal revenues have been cut by the Reagan administration. An editorial in the June 1982 issue of *Nature* records the consequences of budgetary retrenchment in higher education accurately:

> The easiest response is to conserve fuel, cut down on office staffs and maintenance, defer new building or expensive new computers or other instruments, to shave the number of faculty evenly across the board—and to avoid fights. But that does not maintain quality. To maintain quality a school must cut out the fat (weak departments) or do away with tenure—both of which can lead to embittered fights on campus and also lawsuits. Another course is to raise tuition fees at state schools above the traditional nominal level. But while this raises revenue, it discourages applicants and contradicts the very idea that state schools are meant to

embody high quality education for everyone. None of these remedies is pleasant, let alone conducive to an unperturbed environment for study.

Let's step back for a moment to consider the magnitude of higher education in this country, all of which costs money. There are approximately 3,000 institutions of higher learning in the United States.* Some of the most *costly* majors that colleges offer continue to be, or are becoming, very popular: computer science, premedicine, all forms of engineering. The faculty must be well paid and nurtured; between 1970 and 1980, however, faculty salaries did not begin to keep pace with inflation, as "real" salaries dropped 21 percent while teaching loads and layoffs increased. The student body, in our "accessible" public school system, must be financed according to financial need: roughly 50 percent of those who attend college qualify for federal and/or state aid on the basis of need. The heart of the university is research, involving both students and faculty; the federal government funds 69 percent of all basic research in America, over half of which is conducted on college campuses. (The federal investment in campus-based research in 1979 totaled $3.6 billion.) Good research and sound teaching require top equipment and laboratories; one-quarter of the existing campus plant-space in the United States needs renovation now, at an estimated cost of $50 billion.

Despite this compelling scenario of legitimate need, money for higher education is drying up at both the federal and state levels. Student charges—tuition/board/room—are skyrocketing, therefore, as public funds for higher education fail to keep pace with inflation. According to the *Chronicle of Higher Education,* "The energy-rich states and some growth-oriented Sunbelt areas were able to keep up with double-digit inflation, but for most of the others it was a losing race. Among the hardest hit were Washington, Oregon, and Idaho, where the housing slump has affected the lumber industry, and Michigan, Ohio, and Pennsylvania, where reduced automobile production has caused widespread factory layoffs. The largest gains were in states rich in oil, gas, and coal: Alaska, Wyoming, Texas, North Dakota, Oklahoma, Montana, and Louisiana."*

The resources of a state university from within its own public boundaries are mercurial, depending on a myriad of political and environmental circumstances, most of which can change almost overnight. And often state legislatures vote budgets for higher education that are several months

*The data in this section was reported in the American Council of Education's *Higher Education and National Affairs* newsletter, November 12, 1982.
Chronicle of Higher Education, p. 10, October 21, 1981.

retroactive, leaving college administrators ulcerous regarding present and future planning. Individual states rise and fall on the list of most-generous-to-higher-education, depending on local moods and leadership, on new priorities, and, of course, on economic circumstances. In 1982–1983, state support of public colleges and universities varied from as little as $1,943 per student in New Hampshire to as much as $6,608 in Wyoming and $12,712 in Alaska. North Dakota's legislature earmarked more than 20 percent of its total revenues for higher education, more than any other state. In Massachusetts, higher education claimed only 5 percent of the state's total tax revenue.

Table 1 is an analysis of state funds for higher education, pinpointing the dramatic differences among states and some dramatic changes within individual states.

There are sources of funding for public higher education, of course, beyond federal and state monies and direct student tuition. More and more, public institutions are looking for private support. "In the four-year period from 1975 to 1979, public universities increased the total amount of their revenue from private gifts and grants by 49 percent, compared with a 41 percent increase at private universities . . . Support per student from private funds during this four-year period increased 72 percent at public research universities and 55 percent at private research universities."*

Private monies are not new to the public sector. Some state institutions have been very successful in generating funds from loyal alumni and/or foundations; others have profited from extraordinary exploitation of their own natural resources. The University of Texas at Austin, for example, is noteworthy on both fronts: at last count, UT was second only to Harvard (and ahead of Yale, Princeton, and Stanford) in market value of endowment, bolstered by oil sales. (A comparison of public versus private endowments, institution by institution, appears in the appendix.)

The realized wealth of an institution, regardless of the source of funds, can perhaps best be judged by dividing available monies by student body size. The tiny college with a moderate endowment often affords more per student than the huge institution with a sizeable endowment. But subtleties of apportionment can foil a quick fix on endowment per student, particularly the undergraduate. If a research institution is strapped with extraordinary expenses for the medical school, or if the expensive particle physics facilities are for graduate students alone, or if government research grants are used only to serve the professor in the lab, what does charted wealth matter to the quality of education for the freshman or sophomore?

---

*The *Chronicle of Higher Education,* February 24, 1982, quoting a report from the UCLA Graduate Information Service.

Unfortunately apportionment, from one institution to the next, is nearly impossible to sort out and compare. How does one chart undergraduate benefits when some faculty members become graduate-oriented but are expected to teach a course or two at the undergraduate level every other semester? Or when monies for libraries include large professional school purchases? Or when laboratories are built which only incidentally permit undergraduate usage? It is obviously easier to get a handle on monies available per student at William and Mary, primarily an undergraduate institution, than at the massive University of Michigan, with its multitude of graduate students and research faculty.

An effort has been made to evaluate the Public Ivys' resources. But monies available per undergraduate may not be the most important factor. The key issue is often how creatively the available monies are used to accommodate the undergraduate in his or her college environment. Some "rich" institutions do it poorly. Some "poor" institutions do it well.

4. Image, prestige

Mysterious as college folklore is in source and transmission, questionable as it is in accuracy, the popular image of an institution is *very* important to a student's desire to attend, to a parent's comfort in investing a seeming fortune, to a faculty member's decision to teach or do research. Image and the consequent level of prestige can, and too often do, mean more than the *reality* of a college in building and maintaining institutional strength.

In the private college sector, a student admitted to Yale does not say "no, thank you" and attend Bucknell; a student admitted to Duke does not turn it down for Sweetbriar; a student admitted to Oberlin does not defer in favor of Knox. Rarely can one *prove* the qualitative difference that has dictated the choice, but the pecking order is clear, the prestige factor considerable, and the appeal of the more famous name irresistible. The phenomenon of folklore has not passed unnoticed in my choice of Public Ivys.

Who is in the best position to evaluate colleges? In my view, high school guidance counselors and college advisors are uniquely suited to do so. With a minimum of personal bias (that is, compared to parents, teenagers' friends, college admissions officers, alumni, and faculty), they keep up with, and interpret, individual institutions' offerings, strengths, weaknesses. They guide their better students to institutions that can sometimes disappoint, or to institutions that can surprisingly overwhelm and please.

Table 1. How the States Rank on 7 Scales

	1983-84 appropriations (a) Amount	Rank	Appropriations per capita (b) Amount	Rank	Approp. per $1,000 of personal income (c) Amount	Rank	2-year change (d) Per cent	Rank	10-year change (e) Per cent	Rank	2-year change less inflation (f) Per cent	Rank	10-year change less inflation (g) Per cent	Rank
Alabama	$ 410,038,000	20	$103.91	27	$11.67	16	+ 9%	35	+147%	32	– 1%	35	+ 10%	32
Alaska	150,752,000	39	340.30	1	20.85	1	+23%	3	+544%	1	+12%	3	+186%	1
Arizona	336,080,000	29	116.25	23	11.09	20	+10%	33	+147%	31	0%	33	+ 10%	31
Arkansas	197,321,000	35	85.64	40	9.87	28	+ 7%	41	+169%	20	– 2%	41	+ 19%	20
California	3,150,376,000	1	128.19	13	8.83	35	– 5%	49	+172%	19	–14%	49	+ 21%	19
Colorado	366,747,000	26	119.66	22	9.90	27	+20%	5	+161%	23	+ 9%	6	+ 16%	23
Connecticut	273,706,000	31	87.17	38	6.15	46	+19%	9	+128%	37	+ 9%	10	+ 1%	37
Delaware	77,792,000	45	129.65	11	10.64	24	+ 8%	40	+132%	35	– 2%	40	+ 3%	35
Florida	956,258,000	5	91.66	37	8.06	38	+19%	10	+176%	18	+ 9%	11	+ 23%	18
Georgia	570,170,000	13	101.06	33	10.18	26	+14%	21	+161%	24	+ 4%	22	+ 16%	24
Hawaii	181,560,000	38	181.92	3	15.17	5	+17%	13	+217%	7	+ 7%	14	+ 41%	7
Idaho	101,007,000	42	103.60	28	10.94	22	+ 6%	43	+148%	30	– 3%	43	+ 10%	30
Illinois	1,106,007,000	4	96.58	35	7.73	41	+ 8%	39	+101%	46	– 2%	39	+ 11%	46
Indiana	503,484,000	16	91.76	36	8.89	34	+ 4%	46	+116%	42	– 5%	46	+ 4%	42
Iowa	372,128,000	25	127.75	14	11.88	14	+16%	16	+158%	25	+ 5%	17	+ 14%	25
Kansas	306,473,000	30	126.96	15	10.88	23	+10%	31	+181%	17	0%	32	+ 25%	17
Kentucky	400,529,000	21	108.60	26	11.97	13	+18%	12	+205%	10	+ 7%	13	+ 36%	10
Louisiana	503,086,000	17	115.04	24	10.26	25	+11%	30	+217%	8	+ 1%	30	+ 41%	8
Maine	76,653,000	46	67.48	49	6.29	45	+15%	18	+ 92%	49	+ 4%	19	– 15%	49
Maryland	437,028,000	19	102.37	29	8.14	37	+13%	26	+153%	29	+ 3%	27	+ 12%	29
Massachusetts	451,423,000	18	78.47	43	5.38	48	+24%	2	+155%	28	+13%	2	+ 13%	28
Michigan	887,471,000	7	97.35	34	8.54	36	+ 5%	44	+ 91%	50	– 5%	45	– 15%	50
Minnesota	612,209,000	11	147.77	6	13.07	10	+12%	28	+165%	22	+ 2%	28	+ 18%	22
Mississippi	345,370,030	28	134.54	9	16.80	2	+15%	17	+206%	9	+ 5%	18	+ 36%	9
Missouri	363,689,000	27	73.49	47	6.98	44	+12%	27	+101%	45	+10%	5	– 11%	45
Montana	103,617,000	41	128.88	12	12.73	12	+24%	1	+182%	16	+13%	1	+ 25%	16
Nebraska	193,925,000	36	121.81	20	11.35	18	+ 7%	42	+185%	14	– 3%	42	+ 27%	14
Nevada	75,360,000	47	85.93	39	7.02	43	+14%	19	+183%	15	+ 4%	20	+ 26%	15
New Hampshire	41,141,000	49	43.35	50	2.93	50	+ 5%	45	+136%	34	– 5%	44	+ 5%	34
New Jersey	531,891,000	15	71.77	48	5.31	49	+14%	20	+106%	44	+ 4%	21	+ 8%	44

State	Appropriation (thousands)[a]	Rank	Per $1,000 personal income[c]	Rank	Per capita[b]	Rank	2-yr increase[d]	Rank	10-yr increase[e]	Rank	2-yr adjusted[f]	Rank	10-yr adjusted[g]	Rank
New Mexico	187,600,000	37	137.23	8	14.83	6	+9%	34	+242%	6	0%	34	+52%	6
New York	2,166,908,000	3	123.74	18	9.66	30	+17%	15	+120%	40	+6%	16	-2%	40
North Carolina	864,658,000	9	143.73	7	15.23	4	+14%	22	+201%	11	+4%	23	+34%	11
North Dakota	108,725,000	40	161.55	4	14.12	7	0%	48	+243%	5	-9%	48	+52%	5
Ohio	883,761,000	8	81.91	42	7.41	42	+20%	8	+156%	27	+9%	9	+13%	27
Oklahoma	389,167,000	23	121.16	21	11.22	19	+20%	7	+305%	4	+9%	8	+80%	4
Oregon	272,969,000	32	102.12	31	9.61	31	+8%	38	+121%	39	-2%	38	-2%	39
Pennsylvania	902,253,000	6	75.91	46	5.83	47	+10%	32	+110%	43	0%	31	-7%	43
Rhode Island	97,651,000	44	102.63	30	9.16	32	+17%	14	+130%	36	+6%	15	+2%	36
South Carolina	392,471,000	22	122.15	19	13.82	9	+9%	36	+166%	21	-1%	36	+18%	21
South Dakota	53,070,000	48	76.14	45	7.81	40	-7%	50	+97%	47	-15%	50	-13%	47
Tennessee	387,738,000	24	83.33	41	9.14	33	+9%	37	+157%	26	-1%	37	+14%	26
Texas	2,282,342,000	2	149.38	5	12.84	11	+20%	6	+356%	2	+9%	7	+103%	2
Utah	198,060,000	2	126.72	16	14.10	8	+14%	24	+198%	13	+4%	25	+33%	13
Vermont	40,343,000	50	77.88	44	7.92	39	+19%	11	+119%	41	+8%	12	+3%	41
Virginia	617,283,000	10	112.66	25	9.84	29	+13%	25	+199%	12	+3%	26	+33%	12
Washington	566,477,000	14	132.66	10	11.01	21	+14%	23	+125%	38	+4%	24	0%	38
West Virginia	199,319,000	33	101.85	32	11.41	17	+4%	47	+144%	33	-5%	47	+8%	33
Wisconsin	595,843,000	12	125.23	17	11.69	15	+12%	29	+96%	48	+2%	29	-13%	48
Wyoming	100,780,000	43	198.39	2	16.64	3	+22%	4	+328%	3	+11%	4	+90%	3
Total U.S.	$25,390,809,000		$115.29		$10.45		+12%		+173%		+2%		+21%	

(a) Reported by M. M. Chambers of Illinois State University as state tax funds appropriated for operating expenses and scholarship programs for higher education. Amount of appropriations may be reduced later in some states because of shortfall in revenues. Not included are appropriations for capital outlay or money from sources other than state taxes. Included are appropriations for annual operating expenses even if appropriated to some other agency of the state for ultimate allocation to institutions of higher education. Pre-allocated state taxes whose proceeds are dedicated to any institution of higher education are included. Also included are state tax funds appropriated for scholarships and statewide governing or coordinating boards.

(b) State appropriations divided by the Census Bureau's population estimates for 1982.

(c) State appropriations divided by personal income, in thousands of dollars, reported by the Commerce Department for 1983.

(d) Increase in appropriations for 1983-84 over 1982-83, as reported by M.M. Chambers.

(e) Increase in appropriations for 1983-84 over 1973-74, as reported by M.M. Chambers.

(f) Two-year increase in appropriations adjusted for inflation of 9.8 per cent, as indicated by the Labor Department's Consumer Price Indexes for June 1983 and June 1981.

(g) Ten-year increase in appropriations adjusted for inflation of 125.2 per cent, as indicated by the Labor Department's Consumer Price Indexes for June 1983 and June 1973.

Chronicle of Higher Education, October 26, 1983.

Through it all they gain a sense of the good, better, and best colleges. They're influenced, of course, by the prestige hierarchy, but a big name doesn't remain big for long if a guidance counselor's best kids are disappointed at that college, time after time.

Secondary school guidance counselors across the nation have been helpful consultants to me for this project, as have many college admissions officers, faculty, college candidates, and parents. With their advice, I have assembled a list of prototypes of "the best" in public undergraduate education—the Public Ivys, and a list of worthy runners-up.

The Public Ivys: (1) the multicampus University of California, featuring Berkeley; (2) Miami University of Ohio, in Oxford; (3) the University of Michigan at Ann Arbor; (4) the University of North Carolina at Chapel Hill; (5) the University of Texas at Austin; (6) the University of Vermont at Burlington; (7) the University of Virginia at Charlottesville; and (8) the College of William and Mary in Williamsburg, Virginia.

Each of the following Ivy profiles resulted from a campus visit that lasted several days and included a range of interviews with students, faculty, and staff to learn about academic programs, student life, and resources; a review of the admissions situation; an immersion in local history, lore, and artifacts; and an attempt to become at least tourist-familiar with the college town and area. There was, in other words, an attempt to "get a feel for the place" as college candidates are urged to do, beyond what the guidebooks list. I tried to view each institution in terms of what an undergraduate might experience, constantly on guard against the graduate or professional school "halo effect." Also, presupposing all eight Ivy-prototypes were superior, I let local representatives guide me to their strongest virtues—programs, people, buildings and arrived at my own conclusions thereafter. Thus, there is intended unevenness in these chapters, partly to relieve monotony for the reader, but largely because some campuses seemed more distinctive in resources than in history and tradition, others had more compelling campus beauty than unique academic programming, and some had particularly colorful or assertive students and staff.

America enjoys a wealth of variety in higher education. But the top of the private sector has typically been considered the best and the most prestigious. The naming of the Public Ivys belatedly begs for a turning point in that tradition. This "other sector" has come fully of age—although the quality has often been there, public perception has not matched it. I can only hope prospective students, their parents, secondary school and college personnel, and observers of higher education will appreciate these institutions as much in the reading as I did in the analysis.

The Public Ivys

University of California
The System, featuring Berkeley

Miami University
Oxford, Ohio

University of Michigan
at Ann Arbor

University of North Carolina
at Chapel Hill

University of Texas
at Austin

University of Vermont
at Burlington

University of Virginia
at Charlottesville

William and Mary College
Williamsburg, Virginia

University of California

Berkeley

Atmosphere

The University of California, or "Cal," is Berkeley. And although Berkeley alumni are reluctant to acknowledge it, Cal is also eight other campuses: Davis, Irvine, Los Angeles, Riverside, San Diego, San Francisco, Santa Barbara, and Santa Cruz. Although the branches were founded over the stretch of a century—from Berkeley in 1868 to Irvine, San Diego, and Santa Cruz all in 1965—the nine campuses of UC, unlike any other state's university system, share so much in common, including overall quality of faculty, students, and resources, that *collectively* they qualify as Public Ivy.

True, there are differences among them. UC San Francisco, for example, is almost exclusively given to the health sciences and graduate level instruction. And among the eight which admit freshmen and undergraduate transfers, there are marked differences in size, tone, emphasis, and location. Nonetheless, qualitative similarities rule: all eight share the same undergraduate admissions policy and practice, all are governed by a common board of regents, all struggle together (and then, among themselves) for a bigger slice of the state's diminished financial pie.

But only one campus *thinks* it is "Cal." And Berkeley makes a good case. It was first. Although not the largest (UCLA wins on that count), UCB annually tops the others in awards and honors to faculty, in admissions selectivity within UC guidelines, and in national public esteem. Berkeley has the only UC bookstore that can sell Cal T-shirts and get away with it.

But one wonders if Berkeley can also get away with transferring the well-deserved and oft-stated puffery regarding incomparable graduate and

University of California at Berkeley

1) Size of Student Body

Undergraduate __21,267__ Graduate __8,743__ Total __30,010__

2) 1983 Freshman Class Profile

Class Size __6,330__   % Men __54__   % Women __46__
Percent of Applicants Admitted __58__
Average SATs: Verbal __526__   Math __608__
High School Class Rank: Top Tenth __87__ % Top Quarter __97__ %
   Geographical Distribution (% of class):
In-State __90__ % Middle Atlantic __3__ % New England __1__ %
West __95__ % Middle West __1__ % South __0__ %
Minority Students __34__ % of Class
Financial Aid __30__ % of Class

3) Retention of Students

__61__ % of freshmen graduate in four years
__68__ % of freshmen graduate in five years

4) Ten Most Popular Majors of Graduating Seniors, 1983

1. Political Science
2. English
3. Electrical Engineering
4. Business Administration
5. Psychology
6. History
7. Architecture
8. Economics
9. Computer Science
10. Civil Engineering

5) The Financial Picture (1982–83)

Annual Campus Budget	$ 416,059,718
1983–84 Tuition and Fees for State Residents	$ 1,361
1983–84 Tuition and Fees for Out-of-State Residents	$ 4,721

Revenues

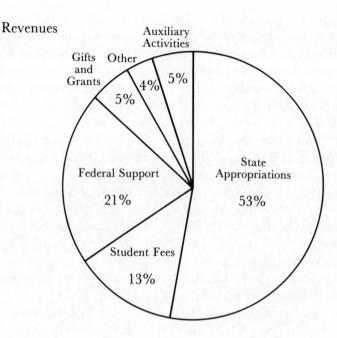

Expenditures

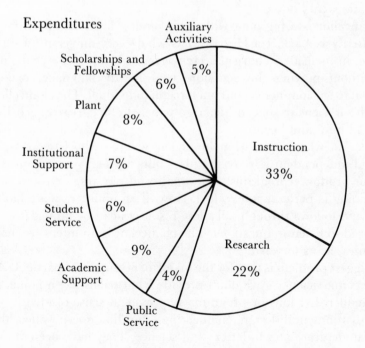

professional school ratings to the undergraduate colleges and programs. This is halo effect in the extreme. In fact, there may be an Emperor's Clothes problem here. "Emperor" is the right term, for Berkeley may be the closest thing in America to a European university: graduate and professional school emphasis coupled with a "let the undergraduates tag along if they can survive the race without undue coddling and won't interfere with the *real* business of the organization" mentality.

The European versus the American concept of university sparks considerable discussion at Berkeley. While the administration must pay tribute and attention to the latter, the publish-or-perish faculty seem committed to the former, and the undergraduates suffer the squeeze in the middle. Undergraduate students are clearly not a priority at research-oriented UCB, and their awareness of that shows. But few would leave, for leaving would bruise self-esteem and sacrifice Cal on the resume. Student staying power is strong at Berkeley—as strong as the complaints.

The best spokesman for the full Berkeley picture is, of course, the chancellor, Ira Michael Heyman.

The men in administration at Berkeley always look like they've just had lunch at the Princeton Club. There is a uniform: blazer, gray slacks, blue button-down shirt, great freedom with ties. Chancellor Heyman flaunts his freedom and wears bows.

The chancellor is a big man with a big smile—a big laugh, in fact, with head tilted way back. Ira Heyman has what every university wants, and few have, in its leader: charisma. He speaks right up, says what's on his mind without playing the occasion, uses bawdy language, makes thoughtful, balanced comments, and is a forceful individual. The chancellor threw himself on a cushy sofa in his large paneled office, rearranged the pillows around him, and began.

"For the kid who knows what he or she wants—who is aggressive and witty and independent—we're the place. But we *live*, you see, on the ratings of our graduate programs. The quality of our research and our graduate training is perhaps unexcelled. Now, if an undergraduate has a precise goal and follows through, all these resources can be tapped."

He paused to listen to questions. The chancellor is an intent listener. He nods, smiles, leans forward.

"Our biggest problem is that for the majority of our kids—particularly those in letters and science—we don't provide what seems like a home. A few of our smaller divisions or programs *do* provide a sense of identity— chemistry, environmental design, engineering—but that doesn't affect the 16,000 or so undergraduates in letters and science. They have been out to sea for quite some time at Berkeley. Even their academic programs do not provide consistency or identity. The proposed major dangles down into their lives the first two years, but we have no basic program as tangible and complete as Harvard's, for example. We're trying to address ourselves to the undergraduate problem, as you'll see in everything you read around here, but it's a damn large sea to harness."

After helping himself to more coffee, he continued. "How can we change the sense of anonymity here? Kids have big classes in the first two years, largely with teaching assistants as the point of focus, TAs who are unevenly trained by the departments. It couldn't be less like what my own kid is experiencing—and loves—at Williams College in the East.

"We'd probably have a more cohesive undergraduate unit if everyone was just admitted to the freshman class, rather than immediately to natural resources, or engineering, or chemistry, or some other separate unit. But we have to fit students to resources and we have to have control. The whole thing seems rather impossible to administer, don't you think?"

Admissions policy? Chancellor Heyman let loose one of his throw-back-the-head laughs before starting a well-informed discussion of Berkeley's (and the University of California's) much maligned undergraduate admissions policy. "As you well know, we abide by the California Master Plan, invented by Clark Kerr, which mandates us to admit only the top 12.5 percent of the students leaving secondary school. And we admit by the formula—a combination of SATs and/or Grade Point Average—that all other UC campuses employ. But we can play with it, because Berkeley has far more applicants eligible by formula than we can accommodate. So we end up admitting about 40 percent of the class from the applicants who are at the top of the formula calculation, and the rest by whatever factors we pick and choose within the remaining group minimally eligible by formula. Then all those who Berkeley chooses *not* to retain, we redirect to other University of California campuses. They almost always are admitted to their second or third choice campus.

"But even in admissions we're not particularly consistent. Engineering picks its own freshmen and transfers, for example. Do they employ the same criteria as the admissions office? Who knows? All I know is that it is idiotic to be as detailed with picking and choosing as the current UC admissions formula requires. It is so rigid that the brilliant or lopsided kid who may have missed taking one prerequisite or who may have a low grade in the one subject he hates can get passed by. But considering the enormity of California and this multicampus university system, our admissions policy is probably not all bad."

The chancellor nearly knocked his coffee cup off the table uncrossing his long legs and rearranging his pillows. He covered with another jolly laugh.

"I do know that we end up with a goddamn diverse group, with a

hunk who are brilliant and relatively dedicated. Yes, the faculty gripes
about deficient writing skills and underpreparation in general, and we all
wish that we had as many blacks and browns as we have Asians, but all
in all, it's a damn fine student body. And we're recruiting hard now to
make it even finer. I just wish we could provide them more a sense of
'home' once they arrive here.

"Budget cutbacks and support for the university? Well, Jerry Brown,
the governor, was emotionally engaged with the university. He was a man
of interesting and provocative ideas, but a poor manager, and he just didn't
do much. But we can't complain—he clearly went to bat for the University
of California in his last couple of years, in a difficult era of financial con-
straint. Recently, we have been counting on a budget drop of approximately
1 percent per year. Almost all of that has been felt in capital cutbacks: we
haven't built up the computer the way we should have at Berkeley, and
other equipment needs seem to take the gaff first when the budget is down.
All I hope for is a gradual return to a steady state and that looks more
promising now.

"To help the cause, I'm spending about 25 percent of my time in
private fund-raising. We now say we're 'state assisted,' and the alumni and
others must help make up the difference. Since 1973 we've been recasting
this whole goddamn thing regarding alums, other private resources, and
development campaigns. I intercede when I can be useful. I only hope our
alumns prove to be as loyal as Harvard's and Yale's. I think they are."

The chancellor's secretary was badgering him to head to the faculty
club for his luncheon meeting, twice postponed. Walking out of the top
executives' California Hall, which feels less like a granite mausoleum than
it looks, he underlined his major theme again: "Sure, there are episodic
and anecdotal gripes here among faculty and students alike. I hear all that
crap, but read the questionnaires that our undergrads fill out indicating
that they have high regard for the teaching here, and most would return
if they had it to do over again. So we're good—but that can't cloud the
weakness of a kid's not finding an identity at Berkeley until sometime in
the junior year when he settles into a major. Those with a sense of loyalty
at Berkeley are those who stumble upon a home early: a fraternity or
sorority or cooperative, in some cases, but more often a small division or
program."

The Campus

Those who visit Berkeley looking for a college home usually come to
a jolting halt at the main entry to campus, off Bancroft Way (a lively and
cosmopolitan street featuring everything from Magnin's and preppy men's

shops to the ever-crowded Espresso Roma, the Guggenheim-inspired University Art Museum, raucous fraternities, and religious organizations), to gape at the happenings in Sproul Plaza, one of Berkeley's official "free speech areas." It is circus without an admission charge. A microphone singles out which political or social cause will be heard next—nearly every cause is here—but the sounds are usurped by the sights: the sixtyish lady walking her bike, wrapped in orange with huge fake purple flowers stuck under her opera helmet, hugging a miniature poodle, spiked leather straps on her ankles, silver slivers on her ears; a young man in a black formal jacket playing a spinet piano, on wheels, with a bucket for contributions perched on top, treble end; a smiling fellow in an automated wheelchair, head steadied by an anchored chain, whirling from one onlooker to the next to engage in some sort of game he supports with one hand; a few stripped-to-the-waist tan athletic bodies topped by short hair; considerably more stripped-to-the-waist pale thin bodies topped by cascades of long hair; fully clothed, fast-moving Asians; students wading and splashing in a fountain named for a dog who, for years, "hung out here"; and pounds of leaflets being passed out to protest one United States policy or another, to support one Latin American government-of-the-people or another, to publicize the coming rally, dance, cause, or cure.

Across the bridge behind elegant Sather Gate, once the point of entry to Berkeley, a well-manicured, busy, compact, rolling green campus unfolds. It totals 1,200 acres.

A campus tour group of prospective students and parents at Berkeley can be as interesting as the campus scanned. Two sets of Asian parents, not together, always walked ahead of our pack, turning back to ask questions about math, science, and graduate school placement. One not-exactly-sober-for-11-A.M. alum talked over the guide, telling his slightly embarrassed teenage daughter how it used to be and how it *should* be now. Three individual candidates asked quiet questions about admissions, class size, housing, and cost—all three fit the "nerd" category. The guide was good: a senior, one day's beard, supreme energy, and diplomacy in responding to the tricky, varied questions ("Sure, we have big classes, but if the guy up front is a Nobel or a Pulitzer, do you care?" Actually, some of our teaching assistants are a bit more fluent in their native language than in English, but that is the exception, not the rule.")

One can't leave Berkeley's vast, modern Student Union (a lively monument to Clark Kerr's chancellorship) without noticing how daring a structure it is in Berkeley's constant run of somber block buildings, tile roofs, structures of sameness. The Disneyesque Union with its flying banners and ornaments and inviting boutique signs screams relaxation, away from the academics, and surely Disney would have loved the fantasy active 'round-the-clock in Sproul Plaza, next to the Union. But not all prospective students' parents who visit the campus do. The fellow with rings in his nipples caused particular consternation—but the guide marched on, pretending not to notice, gleefully telling the story of how the fountain is named for Ludwig, the mutt, who lived there for years but decided to move on. The group passed two theaters and rows of eateries adjacent to the Union as it headed through Sather Gate to the more somber part of campus, guided by rows of weird plane trees.

The huge Life Sciences Building was described as a "combination of Roman Gothic and Aztec Indian" by the undergraduate guide with confidence, and "once the largest academic building in America."

Visiting a huge "typical" classroom was probably a mistake. Not only was it large, but the entry and the room itself were filthy. "Yes, it's large. But we have small classes, too. My poli sci classes average 30 to 40," the guide explained. "You just have to fend for yourself at Berkeley. We keep being told it's like a European university—and I guess that's true. You can get lost in the shuffle, but not if you're determined to avoid it. Profs all have office hours—*real* profs, not just TAs."

Most visitors to Berkeley, thinking they will find an urban university, are surprised by the beauty of Strawberry Creek, which meanders through campus, and by the well-manicured lawns and flowers (particularly the majestic lily of the Nile) and magnificent trees.

Berkeley's urban forest is reputed to be among the more remarkable plant collections in the state, featuring three hundred tree species, including Tasmanian blue gum eucalyptus, California laurels, California buckeyes, tall redwoods, willows, elderberrys, maples, and magnificent live oaks, some approaching three centuries in age. The tear gas that floated over UCB in the sixties and early seventies killed a number of valuable trees, and recent budget cuts have resulted in a decline of plant maintenance. Nonetheless, Berkeley's show of nature is splendid.

Close by is the main Doe Library, designed by John Galen Howard (1864–1931), who also designed Sproul Hall, California Hall, the Sather Gate, the Sather Tower, a host of other academic buildings, and the lovely Hearst Greek Theater. Howard taught at Berkeley for three decades and was founder of the School of Architecture. Attached to Doe is a small, elegant addition called the Bancroft Library, which houses rare books and special collections; recently there was a superb display of California authors' letters of protest to their editors and publishers, including outraged notes from John Steinbeck. All told, Berkeley lists its holdings at nearly six million volumes. "Somehow, Doe Library brings to life the halls of knowledge. Students just love this place," the guide extolled.

On the well-trimmed walkways, up and down Sather Tower, past magnificent old South Hall (Berkeley's oldest building, 1874), one keeps spotting the primary mode of campus transportation: "Humphrey Go-Barts," small, peppy little busses that cart people to main campus points and connect to BART, the Bay Area's rapid transit system.

Nearly dwarfed by the impressive new engineering facility on one corner of campus is the Hearst Mining Building (John Galen Howard, 1907), another gift to Berkeley from the well-heeled publishing family, this one with a working mine beneath the stately, small Classical gem above, which is complemented by a circle drive with pool and foliage.

Nearby is a boxy structure housing Berkeley's well-regarded chemistry division. The tour group entered the theaterlike main lecture hall, which has television cameras suspended liberally throughout so students can see the experiments taking place way down front. The guide blurted out, "Some turkey got into the room before we did," and he was right. Scrawled in huge letters on the blackboard down front was "Fuck off Nazi Punks—Death to Reagan." Somehow the group was unmoved, then, in hearing that the entire "stage" rotates so one experiment can quickly follow another.

Close to the outdoor Hearst Greek Theater, where Charter Day and other official ceremonies and a few rock concerts are held, are the two attractive, cozy faculty clubs (men's and women's, both open to the other group now) and the large Cowell Hospital (whose director says that any medical problem can be handled on campus, short of major surgery). The handsome California Memorial Stadium is in the distance, next to Berkeley's famous, bustling International House.

Sighting the stadium excited the guide, but no more so than had walking through Doe Library. "Did you all know that Joe Kapp of the Minnesota Vikings is our new coach now? We're *ready!*" There is strong fan support at Berkeley for football, even though the teams haven't been stellar lately. The new football coach, an evangelist for varsity athletics and Burt Reynold's co-star in the movie "The Longest Yard," is creating even more enthusiasm. But the push at UCB is less toward being the spectator than becoming the recreational participant. The one large structure nearing completion at Berkeley is a new recreational athletic facility, featuring an Olympic-size pool. The $19 million complex has been financed largely through students' self-imposed fees.

Circling back toward the Union, the tour guide motioned toward two more sporting phenomena at Berkeley: all over town, parking garages topped with green tennis courts, always full; and, another example of the Hearst largesse, the elegant Women's Gymnasium with its black-marbled swimming pool walls and its mammoth decorative urns (once cement, now fiberglass made to *look* like cement, a change necessitated by earthquake precautions).

The guide pointed toward Bancroft Way, saying large complexes of dorms existed a block or so away. Not much was said on this issue, as Berkeley doesn't have much to brag about. University-operated residence halls have spaces for 3,250 students, 65 percent of which are reserved for new students. But only 15 percent of the student body can be accommodated in university facilities; several thousand are turned away each year and must fend for themselves. Many of those who make it into campus housing, including freshmen, do so through a lottery system conducted each spring for fall slots. The tour ended in front of modern, drab Barrows Hall, a social science enclave, with the guide pointing to a symbol of Berkeley: the broad glass walls at Barrows where computer printout lists are posted at registration to indicate which students have made it into a class and which have not.

Student Life

A "representative group of Berkeley undergraduates" was assembled by the director of admissions for a candid discussion of UCB. The contingent that gathered was sizable, but, according to them, "atypical" because there were no fraternity or sorority members, a majority of minorities, no jocks, and *all* were on scholarship or work-study. Nonetheless, these students were quite different from each other. Their campus involvements varied from Korean students' or Chicano students' organizations to Community Health Center, Chinese Evangelical Fellowship, Women's Jail Group, ASUC (Associated Students of the University of California), to "survival— pure and simply, survival," and "a concerted effort *not* to get involved in any organization at this place."

This was a lively, outspoken group . . . and not very positive. "The Greeks, who are growing in strength at Berkeley as the nation becomes more conservative, are guilty of racial discrimination, nepotism, favoring the rich, and such blatant anti-semitism that one fraternity recently placed a horse head on the porch of a Jewish organization's office, a la *Godfather*." (Regrettably, there was no one present to defend the system. Later, the administration's Greek adviser, who happens also to be an Episcopal rector, said the Greeks at Berkeley had seen tremendous growth between 1973 and 1978, but the increase was tapering off as the student body became more diversified, and "undergraduates openly question whether being in the Greek system will profit them any." Although the Greek numbers are significant at Berkeley—about 3,100 members in twenty-nine fraternities and seventeen sororities—the members could care less about politics or social issues, according to the adviser, and thus have not become a campus force. They have great parties, some offer excellent housing, and regrettably, their "fun" is a bit more malicious than it used to be, said the reverend. Unlike on some other campuses, the UCB fraternities and sororities have not become coed. At Berkeley, the Greek system is just one more option.

When asked which few adjectives best summarized Berkeley, the student group let words fly, but only a few drew consensus.

FREEDOM. "You can study *anything*, any way you want to here—or you can choose not to study at all."

"There is respect for freedom here, both in academic and social circles. But right now the town is more liberal than the university. It used to be the reverse."

"Yeah, we're known for our freedom, but you still had best not cross a professor regarding his or her point of view. And the administrators are the most inflexible of all. I don't think we're quite as liberal as we're reputed to be. There are very few outspoken progressives around here any more."

"You're right: the L.A. influence is creeping in, although Reagan would still be hooted out of Sproul Plaza."

COMPETITIVENESS. "There is too much grading by the curve here, which breeds incredible rivalries. Add to that some outright discrimination by faculty toward women and minorities in certain departments, and you have a tough situation for some."

"There are *huge* lectures, so it all becomes impersonal and cutthroat."

"Now wait a minute. A good professor friend of mine has office hours twice a week, and *no* one comes to see him. Yes, we have large lectures—though usually followed by small seminars—but you can't bitch about how impersonal it is if you don't take the initiative to talk to the professors who really want to see you!"

"Hey, I've had Latin classes with three students in them. If all the rest of you weren't flocking frantically to business and engineering and computer science, you *too* could have small classes."

"The whole thing is made hopeless by the bozo TAs who are allowed to move straight from the classroom to *teaching* without any standards whatsoever. They may know their stuff, but they can't communicate it."

"You see, because of 'the times,' there is even more pressure—you know, the job market, the economy. Everyone seems to want to get into a corporation eventually—that makes them killers on this level. And some of the minority students are the most guilty—twice the killers."

PROFESSIONALISM. "There are often brilliant minds teaching, counseling."

"Not true in my major. What's yours?"

OPPORTUNITY. "Everything is available to us here, in the classroom and out. And if you can't keep up, there is a really good Student Learning Center to help you out."

"Berkeley may have *too* much opportunity. I often don't know which way to turn."

The one-liners from this crowd shot by quickly. Rarely did one student wait for the other to finish. The Asian women were particularly active, outspoken, and negative. Two white men enjoyed competing with each other in biting cynicism, offset by the thoughtful graduate student in classics who reflected generously on his undergraduate years at Berkeley. The most sensitive and articulate spokesperson was a woman in a wheelchair (there are approximately two hundred and fifty students in wheelchairs at Berkeley); her cool, authoritative balance always brought the others to silence.

The group responded to what they would do "to make Berkeley a better place." Most agreed they would lop off a few thousand students in order to create smaller classes, better housing, and a more viable community. And all agreed the financial crunch was beginning to show: "last hired, first fired" for those holding on-campus jobs; inadequate computer facilities; desperate need for expanded housing; and inadequate funding for all phases of affirmative action.

"Berkeley is becoming more and more elitist," said one Hispanic woman who chose to stare at the wall behind her for most of the discussion, turning to the group only to make a few sour contributions. No one seemed to notice or object.

Academic Programs and Staff

Moses Hall is not far from the impressive Sather Tower, or the "Campanile," the 308-foot obelisk that was erected in 1914, modeled after St. Mark's campanile in Venice; it serenades the campus with forty-eight carillon bells, manually played, three times daily. A recently retired professor of philosophy, housed in Moses within earshot of the bells, had been described as a local "romantic" who had been at Berkeley dozens of years and could put the present in context with the past. One might expect a mellow, white-haired fellow with pipe and an officeful of memorabilia. No. A huge man gestured from under a file cabinet—it was on his back, careening down the hall in a do-it-yourself office move. The professor appeared, unencumbered, shortly thereafter—safe, robust, very sweaty, well-tanned, bald, smiling with an uncanny resemblance to Mr. Clean. He wasted no time sharing his views about Berkeley's academic scenario.

"The prestige of Berkeley is the prestige of its graduate schools. And the prestige of its graduate schools means the prestige of its faculty. This is a place where we don't have to use texts authored by others. Professionally, we're tops. *Tops.*" He glanced out the small-paned leaded windows, paused, and continued.

"But you're here to talk about the undergraduate division. And that's a problem. The lower division, you see, has always been something of an orphan. No one really pays much attention to the freshmen and sophomores; we pay a *little* attention to juniors and seniors because they are majoring in something. If they're good, the quality of the faculty rubs off on them. But I think it's drivel to take a freshman or sophomore and put him at the feet of one of our Nobel Prize winners, thinking something wonderful will happen. It's just a waste of everyone's time. I think it's even a waste of time to put freshmen in seminars—they're not ready. We're really not set up to accommodate anyone short of the junior year."

The seasoned professor wiped sweat from his face, fished for a book he had written about undergraduate education, glanced out the window at the forest of green overhanging Strawberry Creek, and struck again with candor.

"A good faculty, you see, is an *obstacle* to reform in undergraduate higher education. If they're good, they just can't bother with youngsters and unintelligible notions like interdisciplinary studies. I say leave educational reforms to the administrators—they're paid to do it, and here at Berkeley they make all the appropriate noises. But I don't know why the hell we keep putting scientists in these administrative, reforming roles— those who have learned by rote, rather than the theologians and the philosophers who have traditionally theorized about education and have done a pretty good job.

"Advising of undergraduates? Another problem. I don't think much of peer advising, which seems fashionable now, but if there is no one else to do it, bring on the peers. The real issue at Berkeley is whether a student can make it on his own or not. If he can, there are great riches here.

"Remember that we've always had 50 percent of our undergraduates who just got by, who just existed, who just made it through. And that's still the case. But now we spend thousands on remedial training to bolster students who probably shouldn't be here in the first place, given the nature of Berkeley. Our lower group has just changed its face. Berkeley has not."

He was anxious to get on with his move. Would his tough-talk regarding undergraduate education be echoed around campus? Yes . . . a chock-full-of-news quarterly, funded by the Office of Undergraduate Affairs, confirmed much that the students and the retiring professor had said.

The Fall 1981 issue of *Teaching at Berkeley* focused on problems associated with the increased numbers of lower division students: "The purpose is to stimulate discussion about new directions the campus might take to make education more rewarding intellectually and less traumatic personally for freshmen and sophomores." A follow-up issue was promised with proposed solutions.

The "problems" issue indicated that over half of UCB's undergraduates are now "lower division," up considerably from four years earlier, due largely to a declining number of transfers to the junior year. "One obvious consequence of the shift in enrollments has been a shortage of nearly everything believed to be necessary for a quality lower division education . . . increased enrollment pressures on required and introductory courses; . . . increased impersonality and greater student diversity . . . ; inadequate numbers of suitable classrooms; a need for more and better-trained TAs; increased pressures on advising, counseling, and tutoring services—all of which are used more extensively by lower division students."

The *Teaching at Berkeley* authors had a story to tell with convincing factual documentation. They indicated that in two brief years, there was an increase of over 2,000 freshman and sophomores enrolled in UCB classes, and also mentioned that two-thirds of all American colleges and universities have fewer than 2,500 students in total, close to the number represented by UCB's increase in the lower division alone. Within two years, the average class size in lower division courses rose by ten, from fifty-three to sixty-three. Offerings of courses at Berkeley had not grown with the increase in freshmen/sophomore population. During the three quarters of the 1980–1981 academic year, 15,300 students were refused courses they wanted at registration.

A primary problem regarding course registration difficulties at Berkeley is that the students have narrowed their fields of interest and have grown inflexible. According to *Teaching at Berkeley:*

> It is not only the increased numbers of freshmen and sophomores which make for oversubscribed courses at Berkeley, it is the very narrow range of fields in which today's young people aspire to major and the few "gatekeeping" courses which serve as the sine qua non to those majors . . . In the past few years, a familiar

pattern has emerged: a student applies for admission to the School of Business Administration and is rejected. The student then tries Economics, Statistics, Computer Science, and then anything he or she can find. The route varies, but the process is the same. The student becomes frantic . . . The process of gaining admission to a major has become in many cases more stressful and uncertain than the process of getting into the University itself.

Regardless of the frustrations, Berkeley students stay put. They have the lowest two-year attrition rate of any UC campus—approximately 15 percent—and 81 percent of the UCB seniors graduating recently said "yes" when asked, "If you had it to do over, would you come to Berkeley again?" On the other hand, only 48 percent of the freshmen and 59 percent of the graduating seniors said they were either "satisfied" or "very satisfied" with their total experience at Berkeley. The *Teaching at Berkeley* authors put all these contradictory figures together convincingly:

Students who find their own needs and learning style not compatible with what this school offers face a difficult dilemma . . . They may be miserable and/or unsuccessful here, but to transfer to another, less prestigious school seems by definition to be a sign of personal failure—in their own eyes as well as those of family and friends . . . Once in the door, any decision to leave carries the stigma of academic incompetence, however undeserved.

Berkeley can talk candidly about its problems. Resolving them creates equally upfront discussion. But once there is consensus regarding solutions, where will the money come from? the human resources? the leadership in a decentralized, proud-by-division complex?

As promised, a later issue of *Teaching at Berkeley* (Spring 1982) contained snippets of advice given by a parade of professors and consultants on strengthening lower division education. The list of recommendations was lengthy: advance registration concepts; a common intellectual experience for freshmen and sophomores; more seminars; creating a diversity of lower division programs to parallel the increasingly diverse student body; devising means of introducing freshmen and sophomores to faculty research and creative work in the context of existing courses; and designing special courses organized by theme rather than by department. Also recommended: guaranteeing students an on-campus living experience at some point in their academic careers; expanding the Summer Bridge program and tailoring orientation programs to different groups of students; adopting a pass/

no pass grade option for first year students; launching an early "buddy system" for peer advising; abolishing undergraduate major titles that sound like careers (e.g., business administration); finding alternatives to large lectures; expanding advisory services to area high schools so incoming students will be better prepared for Berkeley work. And the list goes on . . .

A first step toward bringing order out of the wealth of ideas for undergraduate reform was the creation of the Division of Freshman and Sophomore Studies. One professor tapped to get the program off the ground was a black marathon runner (3 hr. 30 min.), whose office in the Department of History and Afro-American studies is stuffed with books, papers, and a ten-speed bicycle where chairs should be. He'd earned his Ph.D. in religious studies at Yale.

"I knew I'd be ambivalent returning to a place where I had once studied, because the university has grown so large. But living in the Bay Area was irresistible.

"What we lack at Berkeley now is an undergraduate ethos. It was probably here once, but it must have flown out the window in the turbulent sixties. Students now just find themselves adrift—they're responsible, on the whole, for their own education. Those who are enterprising—academically street-wise, let's say—make it. *If* they're successful in getting to the heart of the faculty and the library, they find remarkable resources. Even though we have structured support—half the students take advantage of the Student Learning Center, for example—the place changed when the letters and science faculty formally decided to give up advising and hand it over to 'professionals.' "

This professor had a comforting, searching manner. A good counselor, one would think.

"I have student office hours, but they don't come. Unfortunately, students here seem to think that the professor can be approached only when he's on the podium. That's what I mean—no undergraduate ethos. An astounding number of students don't know a single teacher. On the other hand, large size creates large opportunities—500 courses, 100 majors—and that's a big plus. But we're so departmentalized that I'm not sure you could say a college exists at Berkeley. We *are*, however, starting small programs that, in time, may make a difference to the feel of the place. We're trying to revive faculty interest in advising with a specific program where a teacher and fifteen freshmen get together informally on a regular basis. It is off to a mildly successful start. The peer advising program is off to a wonderful start: the upperclassmen are really enthusiastic about it, and they're the key. In time, we just hope more of a real fellowship will develop at Berkeley. It's hard—*I* had troubles here as a graduate student; I really don't think I could have made it as an undergraduate, in its present form."

Given all the talk about the role of undergraduate education at Berkeley—just as the chancellor had warned—it seemed important to gather clues directly from the Undergraduate Affairs Office.

The office is headed by another huge fellow in the common administrative uniform. But his cramped office wasn't very buttoned-down. It was aclutter with plastic trinkets, fake-fruit-handled ballpoint pens, artifacts from the nation's K-Marts, and even his old Indiana high school football trophy, painted gold! Bright yellows and blues, UC's colors, were everywhere.

The vice-chancellor for undergraduate affairs talked in colors as bold as the walls. A botanist, he is also a missionary who said his job had three parts: to rejuvenate undergraduate education, to improve undergraduate student life, and to improve Berkeley's affirmative action. All three depend, in his view, on strength in admissions.

"We don't compete with any other UC campus. Our points of reference are Stanford, Cal Tech, and the eastern Ivy League. Yes, our applicant pool will probably decline somewhat now, but less because of the demographics of California than the realities of self-selection—kids know it is useless to apply here if they don't have a 3.5 average. We've never been so selective, and probably are more selective than most of the elitist privates. Take electrical engineering, for example: they had 200 spaces for new freshmen last fall, hundreds of applicants, and *117* applicants with 4.0 averages! They couldn't really fish below a 3.9 GPA cutoff. What bothers me, though, is that we may be developing a private school profile: our students' parental income level is getting much higher, averaging well over $40,000 now, with 6 percent of last year's freshmen coming from families bringing in over $100,000. The more selective we are, the more we appeal to the better educated families. But, still, we tend to draw heavily from our own immediate area. Two-thirds of the undergraduate student body come from the nine counties of the Bay Area; one-third come from only fifty high schools; and we take less than 10 percent from out-of-state."

The phone in the vice-chancellor's office kept ringing. Most of the talk was related to affirmative action. But the outspoken vice-chancellor had other priorities on his mind.

"The Nerd Factor is one of our biggest problems at Berkeley. We get too many students through the rigid, statistical UC admissions formula who are technically bright as hell, but aren't much else. And that affects our community tone. To counter the situation, we're starting to recruit the well-rounded, bright kids ambitiously, like they were all top athletes. Our new "chancellor's scholarships"—and all the wining and dining that goes with awarding them—should help. But even without the new push, we're doing fine. The women here have the highest SAT math average in our history. Our student body is 21 percent Asian; some say that number could well climb to 35 percent by the end of the decade. And we have an altruistic crowd: Berkeley is the country's largest supplier of Peace Corps volunteers. Oh, by the way, we also produce more Ph.D.s than any other institution in the country. With more flexible admissons policies, we could draw an even *better* student body—more from rural areas, more ethnics, more balanced kids. As it is now, the chancellor and I have to pull a few in who are *essential* to the balance—not many, but a few."

He walked to the door to see what was causing a commotion outside, took another phone call, restacked some papers on his trinkets table, and talked about undergraduate education at Berkeley. He was rather blustery.

"*Over*rated? Are you kidding? If anything, our undergraduate training is underrated. We're easily the best public university in the nation in a large urban environment. Think about that for a minute—no one else comes close! And that makes us rather akin to a German university: in a city, not residential, the faculty does not nurture students—perhaps a little less humane than some other places, but those who can persist are big winners. European universities and Berkeley foster independence. Hell, at Stanford a student can't flunk a course, and can drop one just before the final examination—should *that* be what more than $15,000 per year buys? Students who want to be left alone can be here. Most are. That's Berkeley. And we're the stronger for it."

Admissions

In almost all of the University of California admissions offices (each UC campus runs an independent admissions shop, but with common guidelines), the primary task of the director of admissions is to process credentials; usually another administrator oversees "outreach," or the recruitment campaign.

At Berkeley, the head of outreach is another huge man, a black, same uniform, with the loudest and best laugh of all the administrative team, a jarring handshake, and a jaunty free-flowing manner that surely attracts. He needed no prodding to begin.

"If they're not assertive when they come, they sure as hell are when they leave. And it's our job to let the candidates know that will happen. Our image? That's a tough one. About every factor here is a turn-on for some, a turn-off for others. Take size, for example: some want a big place for the independence and opportunity it allows; others fear they will get lost in a place this large and complicated. Berkeley is like a huge candy store—who's going to help the kid pick out the right flavor? With a big appetite, he can have a ball: one recent student structured a major in magic, another combined physics with dramatic arts.

"To everybody out there we're prestigious, and most want a taste of the place. We don't have to sell Berkeley. Our only real rival is Stanford—we don't worry at all about UCLA. UC Davis, now and then, will steal a good one from us who wants a straighter place—or Santa Cruz for the one who wants a personalized liberal arts education. But the prestige can work against us, too; some good kids won't apply here for fear of rejection. And when the 'prestige' becomes 'elitism,' we're in trouble. It's a fine line to draw."

The outreach director kept a fast pace. He just kept talking, loudly.

"Some schools are big. And other schools are good. Berkeley is one of the few that are *both big and good*. Hell, our alums run the state. ["Better-known living alumni," as identified by Berkeley's Office of Public Affairs, include: Steve Bartkowski, Chief Justice Rose Bird, Governor Jerry Brown, Joan Didion, John Kenneth Galbraith, John W. Gardner, Philip Habib, Clark Kerr, Nancy Kissinger, Robert McNamara, Ed Meese, Gregory Peck, Cruz Reynoso, Glen Seaborg, Irving Stone, Robert Penn Warren, Senator Pete Wilson.] Our only problem is that in the rural areas of California and in the southern part of the state they still think we're teargassing through the late sixties. But as Berkeley goes, so goes the world. We addressed the disruption and resolved it; other places are still fighting the battles."

This fellow was one compelling cheerleader. He rose to walk around his office (which had drawn from the same bucket of canary yellow paint as the vice-chancellor's quarters).

"We're moving into new territories of recruitment now, and we're very much on our own. The UC Systemwide Office used to run this whole admissions thing, you know—centrally for all campuses. Then each campus opened a Relations with Schools Office to disseminate information. Now we're into *real* recruiting, and no one is going to tell us what to do. Systemwide, for example, slapped our wrists for using the term 'Cal' in recruitment literature for fear of offending the other UC campuses. We just gave them the finger and proceeded. This *is* Cal, damn it, and I don't care what the hell the rest of them think."

The big laugh boomed. It was as jarring as the original handshake.

"Yeah, we're a little nervous about the demographic projections. And that is one reason we're more active. We're chasing minority kids and the highest-ranking majority kids. Our new chancellor's scholarships will help lure the latter away from Stanford and the Ivies—the chancellor is helping by giving an annual dinner for the principals of our top forty feeder schools. Even *he* is helping to recruit the very best. Can you imagine? The big man from the sky heading out to high schools? I guess you might say we're developing the Eastern model in admissions now—alums helping, faculty helping, and targeting the top schools. This all started with the minority effort, but it has grown well beyond that now."

The director of admissions himself—awesome size, same blazer, same yellow walls, but different building—was as assertive.

"Why does Berkeley belong in the eight Public Ivys? Well, I'll tell ya—but I'm not willing to restrict it to the publics. Berkeley deserves top position in any damn league you want to talk about. And I mean that. Our only restriction here is our state: little, if any, out-of-state recruiting is allowed, partly because California's money has been running short lately. And we've also declined in the number of good transfers available. But these elements don't detract from our still being The Best. What makes us best? The faculty. Granted, the graduate schools dominate, but all that quality can't help but filter down. About one-third of the faculty have had some connection with Harvard along the way. And did you know we hand out more degrees annually than any other campus in the world? Over ten thousand per year. And our placement in graduate schools and jobs is probably about the best around. (OK, I've only seen *our* figures—I haven't seen the others. But ours are damn hard to beat.) And ou administration plays hardball, keeps us on our toes all the time. In my view, we only need to look around our own state to judge if we're the best in the nation. The University of California *is* the best in the nation; if Berkeley is the best of that league—well, there you have it. We don't even compete with a place like the University of Virginia. Can't imagine they count for much."

This director has the reputation of not holding back. He was giving the full dose. . . .

"Nobels teach undergraduates here. Who else can say that? Oh, we do have our minor shortcomings. We're poor in campus research and documentation, as you may have found. One reason is that we're so damned decentralized, there is no office to draw all the data together from individual parts. And that decentralization hurts the admissions effort: housing, financial aid, outreach, and admissions should be in one unit. As it is, we're all over the place, reporting to different bosses. To the public we must look uncoordinated as hell. And there is an unsettled feeling at Berkeley now because seven—seven!—strategic administrative posts are being vacated through retirement, resignation, etcetera, so everyone, at least for the moment, is busy running for office."

The pace did not slacken. "But the chancellor's doing a hell of a job—has probably tripled the endowed chairs, for example. We may have suffered a little from state funding neglect while all the other UC campuses were being built or strengthened during the sixties and seventies. But the world doesn't expect nine Berkeleys, and they're not going to get them. UCB does what it does best."

The director deferred to the Office of Student Research for statistics regarding admissions. But finding that office is something of a chore. Berkeley has kept a series of World War II "temporary" buildings and has painted them earth brown to camouflage them, greatly assisted by fast-growing pines. But the buildings house a host of important academic and administrative offices. The research office is tucked away, buried in papers and numbers. Its leader is a jolly little fellow, full of insights as well as statistics.

"There are student academic gypsies, you know—the *brightest*, who head wherever the action is. *Now* it happens to be in business and engineering, and they're flocking to it." The research chief talked about UCB's tone. "There are microclimates here. You can join a world at Berkeley and never come out. Some microclimates are subtle, understated, but *strong*—the Computer Center, for example. Its citizens hardly ever come out. And co-ops are a way of life here. Fraternities are a way of life here. There are many Berkeleys, maybe too many."

Whichever Berkeley one seeks, admissions-by-formula is the key to entry. The grades in high school prerequisite courses are all that count in the formula: four years of English, three years of mathematics, one year of history, two years of foreign language, one year of natural science, and several advanced courses in areas selected by the student. In-staters can gain admission to the UC system by attaining a 3.3 or higher GPA in the required courses, by scoring 1100 or higher on the SATs and 1650 or higher on three achievements (with no one being below 500), or, should both of these routes fail, by an "eligibility index" using a sliding scale to juxtapose GPA and standardized test scores. Out-of-staters must qualify by GPA (3.4 or higher in the required courses) or by standardized test scores (an 1100 combined SAT and a total of 1730 on three achievements, with no one below 500). Ninety-four percent of each UC campus's new class is selected by this formula. Six percent of each class is admitted by "special action," allowing some subjectivity in the admissions officers' review (this is how UCLA gets those teams!).

If a UC campus ends up with more candidates eligible by formula than can be admitted, the institution must fill half the class with those who score highest via the formula and fill the rest of the class by subjective picking and choosing among those who are formula-eligible (at Berkeley, priority is given to those from Northern California and the Bay Area, to underrepresented minorities, and to those with special talents, i.e., strong athletes, musicians, etc.).

The University of California admissions formula is rigid, prompting obvious inequities: giving greater weight than even the College Board recommends to standardized test scores, taking all GPAs at face value rather than analyzing them in the context of a high school's qualitative level, and overlooking entirely a candidate's "personal strengths" except among the 6 percent who enter via "special action." UC's admissions policies are under considerable fire at present. California traditionalists, however, feel the UC system is just fine.

Resources

The "First Annual Report by a Chancellor" appeared in *California Monthly*, Berkeley's pizzazzy alumni magazine, in 1980–1981. In Ira Heyman's assemblage of highlights of Berkeley's one hundred and seventh year, a clear theme, accompanying impressive accomplishment, was the need for expanded resources, particularly from the private sector.

The chancellor first outlined a "typical year" at Berkeley: winning one more Nobel Prize, winning the prestigious National Mathematical Institute to the Berkeley campus, leading the nation in Guggenheim fellowships, etcetera, etcetera.

Then the chancellor lamented Berkeley's financial plight. Although the University of California had built three new campuses and greatly expanded five others in the preceding two decades, Berkeley itself had only expanded slightly and had aged substantially. There was need for revitalization in the biological sciences, as most new advances were in DNA, and Berkeley was not keeping pace. Since ten of Berkeley's eleven Nobel laureates will have retired by the early 1990s, when nearly half of the current faculty will have reached retirement age, the task of faculty recruitment looms as a profound one reaching every one of Berkeley's sixty-five departments. The chancellor named the goal of seeking one hundred more endowed chairs by 1990, each requiring a minimum endowment of $300,000.

Chancellor Heyman pointed to the successes of the relatively new Office of Vice-Chancellor for Undergraduate Affairs in better accommodating lower level students on campus. He underscored the profound challenges that remain in this area. In sum, the chancellor outlined UCB's assessment of needs: $100 million in facilities and new equipment in the biological sciences alone; $30 million in endowed chairs; a yet-uncharted sum for dramatic improvement in underclass training.

> Once a state supported institution, Cal is today better described as state assisted, with nearly half of Berkeley's budget coming from non-state funds . . . Not since the turn of the century, when Phoebe Apperson Hearst's generosity contributed so mightily to the University's surge in excellence, has the support of alumni

and friends held such importance for the quality of scholarly enterprise at the University of California.

Another thoughtful spokesman regarding Berkeley's current strengths and needs was an assistant vice-chancellor for just about everything—involved with budgets and financial aid, the Educational Opportunity Program (EOP) and affirmative action, recreational sports, foreign students. He was athletic-looking and wore an open-necked blue shirt and a colorful belt; he looked like a Californian! The office was austere—an ex-boardroom in old Sproul Hall, drenched with fine oak and paneling, with huge doors and a first-row-first-balcony view of zany Sproul Plaza.

"Berkeley is a good choice for a Public Ivy," he said thoughtfully. "Diversity breeds excellence. Our diversity is actually less in the makeup and background of the faculty and the student body per se than in the social, cultural, political styles and postures that develop and integrate here. Why, we even have an active Young Republicans Club now!

"Once a reputation is there, it's there. Berkeley picked it up with scientific breakthroughs in the forties and fifties and has never lost the momentum. Faculty were probably recruited in the fifties and sixties for research first, to teach grad students second, and to teach undergrads third. That has created problems; but nonetheless, we wouldn't be what we are today had that list of priorities been different. Now we're trying to hold our own in the face of budget cutbacks. There have been reductions ever since Reagan was governor. Pre-Reagan, we were just asked, 'Do you have enough money to get the job done well?'; that changed in a hurry when Reagan came on board. Now we fight for the dollars. Too bad. The crunch has come just at the time that our top administration is genuinely interested in reforming undergraduate education and student life. The question is, simply, will there be the money to *do* that? If not, can graduate funds be diverted to undergraduate needs? That obviously would be a sensitive battle to initiate. But the undergraduates are a strong lobbying force for improving their own lot; for example, they're demanding much more money for counseling needs. This is a legitimate request. We have approximately 2,000 foreign students, 2,000 immigrants, 1,200 EOP students, and 700 athletes who often need special support services, not to mention the 'regular' kids who have needs too. In short, we're on the threshold of some tough battles regarding priorities without enough money to satisfy all. Something will have to give if undergraduate life is to improve."

Undergraduate life at Berkeley *will* improve if the current administration has its way and is successful in uncovering or reallocating resources. A new governor in California has already moved to improve the state's contribution to higher education in general and to the University of California in particular.

Meanwhile, the greatness of Berkeley is a given. It is written all over the rankings and award charts. In a recent issue of *California Monthly*, the editor said nonchalantly: "As you may have noticed, awards are so regular a part of life at Berkeley that they seem to fall naturally, like punctuation marks." Several pages back, the president of the California Alumni Association said, in a plea for donors, "Berkeley is one of America's three best universities, and its top public institution. That means a great deal to us Old Blues."

And well it should. In leaving Berkeley, it seems appropriate to document some of UCB's recent "winnings":

> In seventeen of the past nineteen years, Berkeley has been at the top of the nation's list in winning Guggenheim fellowships.
>
> In 1977 a survey by Everett Ladd, Jr., and Seymour Lipset, asking more than 4,000 faculty members to "name the five departments nationally in your discipline that have the most distinguished faculties," put Harvard at the top of the list, followed closely by UC Berkeley in the number 2 position. (Next in line were Stanford, the University of Chicago, the University of Michigan, and Yale.)
>
> Berkeley's Office of Public Information issued a news release in April 1982 that four more UCB professors had been elected to the National Academy of Sciences, considered one of the highest honors that can come to an American scientist. Berkeley's total of National Academy of Science members is second in the nation only to Harvard's.

High honors to UC Berkeley have rolled in for years and will continue. "That means a great deal to us Old Blues," they say around San Francisco Bay. It means a great deal to the rest of the nation, too.

Davis

A California guidance counselor remarked: "Surely among all the kids on the UC campuses, the ones at Davis call home the most." And that probably says it. Davis is Straight City—California's version of the Mid-

University of California at Davis

1) Size of Student Body

Undergraduate __13,830__ Graduate __5,141__ Total __18,971__

2) 1983 Freshman Class Profile

Class Size __3,908__ % Men __46__ % Women __54__
Percent of Applicants Admitted __89__
Average SATs: Verbal __496__ Math __559__
High School Class Rank: Top Tenth __100__ % Top Quarter ___ %
   Geographical Distribution (% of class):
In-State __87__% Middle Atlantic __1__ % New England __1__ %
West __92__ % Middle West __3__ % South __3__ %
Minority Students __14__ % of Class
Financial Aid __46__ % of Class

3) Retention of Students

__40__ % of freshmen graduate in four years
__62__ % of freshmen graduate in five years

4) Ten Most Popular Majors of Graduating Seniors, 1983

1. Biological Sciences
2. Engineering
3. Agricultural Economics
4. Economics

5. Psychology

6. Political Science
7. International Relations
8. Animal Sciences
9. Food Biochemistry and Sciences
10. Design

5) The Financial Picture (1982–83)

Annual Campus Budget	$ 366,837,506
Percent of Annual Budget from State Appropriation	49
1983–84 Tuition and Fees for State Residents	$ 1,353
1983–84 Tuition and Fees for Out-of-State Residents	$ 4,713

west. Not only does its Central Valley setting, fifteen miles west of the state capital in Sacramento, *look* like the flats of Illinois with lush growing fields, but the campus started as an agricultural station for Berkeley. And the tone is Midwestern too: the work ethic is strong, life seems uncomplicated, the environment is respected, people look healthy and smile, buildings are functional, disco-city diversions would be intrusive, conservatism is the rule.

UCD is popular, very popular—with parents, of course, as much as with loyal legions of students. As a result, Davis has grown quickly since becoming a comprehensive university in 1951. The students reputedly have a no-nonsense approach to their studies, eager to get ahead in the mainstream. There is considerable academic pressure. Although historically recognized for instruction and research in agricultural sciences and veterinary medicine, the campus has, within the last fifteen years, built a strong reputation in a broad range of disciplines, complemented by an extremely well-organized and active Work-Learn program. Undergraduates enter one of three colleges: the College of Letters and Science, the largest on campus, which offers the arts, social sciences, humanities, and the natural and physical sciences; the College of Agricultural and Environmental Sciences, which focuses on animal sciences, applied economic and behavioral sciences, food nutrition and consumer sciences, plant sciences and pest and disease management, and resource sciences; or the College of Engineering, which offers majors in aeronautical, agricultural, chemical, civil, electrical and computer, materials science, and mechanical engineering.

Strong and serious as Davis may be, life is not restricted to the crowded library. There is a sense of close community. The dorms can accommodate only 3,000 students, so most students live in the small, friendly town. Everybody does something in recreational or intramural sports, although there is a strong intercollegiate program also, with impressive NCAA Division II accomplishments in football. Everybody has a bike for local mobility, and everybody escapes to the Sierras for backpacking or to San Francisco for a taste of city life that Sacramento doesn't offer. But the campus quad itself is alive with causes, concerts—always something worth noticing. The Union is as overcrowded as the bikeways and the labs are. In short, life is balanced at Davis: calm, directed, and wholesome. Yes, there are those who would say "dull." Purposeful, nonetheless.

Irvine

Orange County is not just John Birch territory any more. Surrounding the rolling, rather arid 1,510-acre UC Irvine campus, in coastal foothills near Balboa Island and Newport Beach, is rapid growth: diverse residential communities, huge business and industrial complexes, and obvious wealth. The Irvine campus, founded in 1965, is a symbol of the change, the variety, the expansion of the area. True, as one disembarks at the "John Wayne Airport" nearby, old images persist—but they don't fit this energized corner in the University of California system.

UCI seems to have a little bit for everybody, neatly and rather conservatively structured. There are five undergraduate schools: Biological Sciences, Fine Arts, Humanities, Physical Sciences, and Social Sciences. Interdisciplinary and professional studies are offered in the Department of Information and Computer Science, the Program in Social Ecology, the School of Engineering, and the School of Management. In all, there are thirty-four undergraduate majors available, but over seventy concentrations: for example, a student can major in English but concentrate in creative writing.

Although many of the students at Irvine commute, compromising the vibrance of on-campus social life, there is spirit here. How many student bodies would come up with "Anteaters" as the team mascot? And speaking of sports, UCI isn't doing badly: in its first fifteen years, Irvine captured a total of sixteen NCAA team championships—fifteen in Division II and one in Division I.

On-campus housing is growing—again, with imagination. The "Today Show" recently zeroed in on an Irvine innovation: an eighty-space recreational vehicle park where students (or student groups) can rent space during the school year with water, electrical, and sewage hookups provided by the university. A variety of dorm arrangements are available, accommodating approximately one-third of the student body.

UCI's charismatic chancellor has said:

> The Irvine campus has all the opportunities associated with being one of the nation's top 100 research universities, along with a balance and strength of liberal arts and professional programs unusual for a campus of 10,000. But we strive for more. To me, an educational institution never arrives: it is always in the process of becoming and learning, and as a consequence of learning, of becoming something more.

UCI, along with its (in)famous county, is becoming "something more."

University of California at Irvine

1) Size of Student Body

Undergraduate __9,436__ Graduate __1,858__ Total __11,294__

2) 1983 Freshman Class Profile

Class Size __2,810__ % Men __49__ % Women __51__
Percent of Applicants Admitted ___
Average SATs: Verbal __459__ Math __552__
High School Class Rank: Top Tenth __44__ % Top Quarter __97__ %
  Geographical Distribution (% of class):
In-State __80__% Middle Atlantic __≤1__ % New England __≤1__ %
West __97__ % Middle West __≤1__ % South __≤1__ %
Foreign __2__ %
Minority Students __34__ % of Class
Financial Aid __45__ % of Class

3) Retention of Students

__31__ % of freshmen graduate in four years
__43__ % of freshmen graduate in five years

4) Ten Most Popular Majors of Graduating Seniors, 1983

1. Social Sciences
2. Social Ecology
3. Biological Sciences
4. Humanities
5. Fine Arts
6. Information and Computer Sciences
7. Physical Sciences
8. Engineering

5) The Financial Picture (1982–83)

Annual Campus Budget	$ 215,570,572
Percent of Annual Budget from State Appropriation	38.5
1983–84 Tuition and Fees for State Residents	$ 1,405
1983–84 Tuition and Fees for Out-of-State Residents	$ 4,765

Los Angeles

UCLA is not big, it is vast. The undergraduate student body alone numbers over 23,000. And yet, on entering any one of the campus gates from fashionable Westwood, next door to the stars' homes in Bel Air, one senses the potential of a unit—a college! Its rolling, tree-filled grounds, beautifully maintained, not only minimize huge complexes and hide the somewhat unsightly but also provide a wealth of surprises: a magnificent large sculpture garden (mercifully devoid of public defacement), a show-piece inverted fountain, bricked plazas, outdoor cafes, grand staircases. The adjacent college town of Westwood is equally compact, lively, well-maintained, tasteful, comprehensive. And all of this is within close range of the Santa Monica mountains, five miles from the Pacific, and a half hour from the heart of Los Angeles which—yes, admitting a terrible smog problem—is far more interesting, diverse, and pleasant than image would have it.

But the unexpected beauty of UCLA's campus and area cannot remove the anonymity the cityful of undergraduates feel here. Classes, particularly in the first two years, are huge, and graduate students as lecturers and graders abound. Since university housing (which gets high marks) can accommodate fewer than one-fifth of the undergrads, the majority commute, lost in the urban sprawl somewhere, showing up in Westwood for classes and athletic events, only to disappear again.

But UCLA can pull surprises. Their incredibly successful teams bring school spirit and loyalty into focus, nine campus newspapers stay in business, the arts thrive, the Greeks (twenty-five fraternities, eighteen sororities) provide minishelters from the anonymity, and the political action of the place seems spunkier than at many small, cohesive colleges.

Academically, anything goes. Because of size, a kaleidoscope of courses is offered—if one can beat the lines. A superb education is available at UCLA if the undergraduate can expend the time and patience to walk carefully through the maze.

There are five undergraduate schools and colleges offering seventy undergraduate majors and considerable flexibility, including self-designed majors. To complement the pervasive large-lecture experience, UCLA sponsors a number of special programs: the Freshman/Sophomore Seminar Program where classes are limited to fifteen students, and the Honors Collegium in the College of Letters and Science, for example. There are, of course, outstanding academic resources at UCLA: a system of nineteen libraries holding more than four million volumes, a superb art gallery, the Museum of Cultural History with the nation's largest collection of primitive art, television and movie production studios, etcetera.

University of California at Los Angeles

1) Size of Student Body

   Undergraduate __23,134__ Graduate __11,620__   Total __34,754__

2) 1983 Freshman Class Profile

   Class Size __6,537__   % Men __49__   % Women __51__
   Percent of Applicants Admitted __84__
   Average SATs: Verbal __484__   Math __561__
   High School Class Rank: Top Tenth _____ % Top Quarter __100__ %
      Geographical Distribution (% of class):
   In-State __96_____% Middle Atlantic __≤1__ % New England __≤1__ %
   West __97_____ % Middle West __≤1__ % South __≤1__ %
   Foreign __2_____ %
   Minority Students __46__ % of Class
   Financial Aid __38__ % of Class

3) Retention of Students

   __30__ % of freshmen graduate in four years
   __55__ % of freshmen graduate in five years

4) Ten Most Popular Majors of Graduating Seniors, 1983

   1. Economics   6. History
   2. Psychology   7. Mathematics
   3. Political Science   8. Art
   4. Engineering   9. Sociology
   5. English   10. Theatre Arts

5) The Financial Picture (1982–83)

Annual Campus Budget	$ 784,490,000
Percent of Annual Budget from State Appropriation	36
1983–84 Tuition and Fees for State Residents	$ 1,362
1983–84 Tuition and Fees for Out-of-State Residents	$ 4,722

Like its city, its curricular offerings, and its campus, UCLA's student body offers something of everything. On the surface, one sees the preppy or jockish Greeks lingering at campus boundaries. But the commuter population is, of course, the majority population here—and underrepresented minorities are quickly growing in number along with older and part-time students. Largely due to the economy and the consequent desire of students to cut costs by staying close to home, UCLA's applicant pool is growing swiftly, drawing on the miles of bodies in greater Los Angeles. Thus, the size and diversity in this largest of all UC institutions continues to build. But UCLA's quality is too often eclipsed in the public's mind by the impact of its quantity. The quality is there, and that grows too.

Riverside

At UC Riverside, founded in 1954, almost everything is small scale. UCR has the smallest University of California student body, a compact little campus, even a tiny viewbook for prospective students. And that is just the way they would like to keep it. Rumor has it that the students at UCR understate their college's merits or even publicly criticize the place *purposely* in an effort to keep enrollment low, to keep Riverside the sleeper of the UC system so they can have it all to themselves. On the truly negative side, Riverside has a smog problem, and some consider its semiarid location at the base of the Box Spring Mountains, an hour's drive east of Los Angeles, to be less than ideal.

What started as a citrus station is now a comprehensive university campus with thirty-three departments and over fifty majors. Still highly regarded in the sciences, with an abundance of graduate students creating a serious research environment, Riverside's programs span the spectrum from law and society to computer science to environmental sciences, with a popular biomedical science major in cooperation with the UCLA School of Medicine through which a student can earn the M.D. degree in seven years.

Riverside has succeeded in creating the most ethnically diverse student body within the University of California, and it houses an impressive 72 percent of its students in on-campus residence halls. UCR provides the small college feel at public university cost.

University of California at Riverside

1) Size of Student Body

  Undergraduate __3,357__   Graduate __1,349__   Total __4,706__

2) 1983 Freshman Class Profile

  Class Size __762__   % Men __51__   % Women __49__
  Percent of Applicants Admitted __67__
  Average SATs: Verbal __471__   Math __538__
  High School Class Rank: Top Tenth _____ % Top Quarter __100__ %
    Geographical Distribution (% of class):
  In-State __96__% Middle Atlantic __≤1__ % New England __≤1__ %
  West __98__ % Middle West __≤1__ % South __≤1__ %
  Minority Students __36__ % of Class
  Financial Aid __50__ % of Class

3) Retention of Students

  __36__ % of freshmen graduate in four years
  __46__ % of freshmen graduate in five years

4) Ten Most Popular Majors of Graduating Seniors, 1983

  1. Administrative Studies
  2. Biology
  3. Liberal Studies
  4. Psychology
  5. Political Science
  6. Biochemistry
  7. Sociology
  8. Computer Science
  9. Economics
  10. History

5) The Financial Picture (1982–83)

  Annual Campus Budget $ 90,387,857
  Percent of Annual Budget from State Appropriation   66
  1983–84 Tuition and Fees for State Residents $ 1,371
  1983–84 Tuition and Fees for Out-of-State Residents $ 4,731

San Diego

"If a kid is really bright, and very serious about science, math, and surfing, there is only one university to consider: UC San Diego," said a California high school guidance counselor recently in sharing impressions of UC campus differences. And that may well be so.

UCSD's roots are old: originally a nineteenth-century marine station at La Jolla, it was later named the Scripps Institution of Oceanography and then adopted in 1912 by the University of California. In the 1950s, graduate programs at UCSD expanded in the physical and natural sciences. But not until 1965 did the campus formally open to UC undergraduates. There has been very quick growth. Today, UCSD's popularity is soaring.

San Diego has four medium-size, rather self-sufficient colleges within the university. Although the colleges have their social differences, the choice of major does not restrict college choice. The four differ most in their general education requirements. *Muir College,* the largest, emphasizes "freedom with responsibility," another way of saying fewer exacting requirements than the other colleges. *Revelle College,* the oldest, is more traditionally structured: during the first two years, students spend one-third of their time in mathematics and the natural sciences, the other two-thirds in social sciences, humanities, foreign languages, and fine arts. *Third College,* committed to having a "multi-ethnic, multi-cultural" student body, stresses close cooperation among students and faculty in a broad academic program including science and math, social science and the humanities. *Warren College,* the newest of the four, has a flexible progam, but requirements in writing, math, computer science, and symbolic logic, plus the completion of a major and two minors.

UC San Diego, somewhat in the Berkeley tradition, brags about its graduate and professional school ratings. With six resident Nobels, a host of National Academy of Science members, and a tradition of teaching that has included such luminaries as Herbert Marcuse and Linus Pauling, there is good reason. The undergraduates have traditionally felt like extras here, but student enthusiasm is clearly on the upswing. Housing is inadequate after the freshman year, forcing most of the undergraduates away from campus and into wealthy, resorty La Jolla proper or San Diego. There is an empty feel to UCSD at times, partly because of the commuter majority and the uninspired architecture. Perhaps this explains San Diego's low undergraduate retention rate, compared to the other UC campuses. But the teams (water sports are the big ones here), the musical activities, the social and political clubs do keep moving.

University of California at San Diego

1) Size of Student Body

   Undergraduate __11,122__ Graduate __2,560__ Total __13,682__

2) 1983 Freshman Class Profile

   Class Size __2,328__ % Men __51__ % Women __49__
   Percent of Applicants Admitted __82__
   Average SATs: Verbal __510__ Math __580__
   High School Class Rank: Top Tenth __90__ % Top Quarter __100__ %
       Geographical Distribution (% of class):
   In-State __93__ % Middle Atlantic __1__ % New England __1__ %
   West __95__ % Middle West __2__ % South __1__ %
   Minority Students __28__ % of Class
   Financial Aid __33__ % of Class

3) Retention of Students

   __40__ % of freshmen graduate in four years
   __50__ % of freshmen graduate in five years

4) Five Most Popular Majors of Graduating Seniors, 1983

   1. Social Sciences
   2. Science and Mathematics
   3. Engineering
   4. Humanities
   5. Arts

5) The Financial Picture (1982–83)

Annual Campus Budget	$ 423,000,000
Percent of Annual Budget from State Appropriation	27
1983–84 Tuition and Fees for State Residents	$ 1,500
1983–84 Tuition and Fees for Out-of-State Residents	$ 4,860

The UC San Diego faculty is superb, the atmosphere serious. The spectacular, maverick library alone is worth a visit to campus. And 1,200 acres overlooking the Pacific Ocean, just thirty minutes from Mexico and fifteen minutes from one of California's most desirable cities, deserve very careful consideration indeed.

Santa Barbara

Santa Barbara in the late sixties and early seventies saw protest at the level of burning the local Bank of America and campus confrontations so severe that then-Governor Reagan closed the place down. But miracle of miracles, what a turnaround! Even the ex-governor might approve of UC Santa Barbara's current image: blue-eyed-blondes-at-the-beach taking time out for the books, a bit more time out for the booze.

And beach they do have. UCSB has a splendid location: 100 miles north of Los Angeles, 330 miles south of San Francisco, next door to a small town everyone loves. And they have two miles of Pacific coastline to themselves, with an ideal climate as a dividend. But it all looks better from a low-flying plane. Close up, the campus is rather scruffy, with a hodge-podge of styles and structures (including World War II barracks, now offices) and a rambling layout that makes a bike as necessary as a desk and lamp (there are 11,000 bicycles and seven miles of bike paths!). But the campus is incidental to the environment: the ocean, the lagoon, the nearby town are wonderful.

The academic offerings at Santa Barbara are strong: it is, after all, the University of California. And the program is also balanced: as many undergraduates major in the natural sciences and engineering as in social sciences and humanities.

The large College of Letters and Science offers a wide range of opportunity, with more than seventy majors including nineteen areas of interdisciplinary study. The College of Engineering lists undergraduate majors in chemical, electrical, computer, mechanical, environmental, and nuclear engineering. The College of Creative Studies provides an alternative approach for students who want to pursue advanced or independent work in the arts, literature, mathematics, and the sciences. Other organizations located at UCSB contribute considerably to the academic atmosphere: the Center for the Study of Democratic Institutions; the Institute for Theoretical Physics, which brings together physicists from all over the world; the Marine Science Institute; and UC's headquarters for the Education Abroad Program.

University of California at Santa Barbara

1) Size of Student Body

Undergraduate __14,744__ Graduate __2,009__ Total __16,753__

2) 1983 Freshman Class Profile

Class Size __4,443__ % Men __43__ % Women __57__
Percent of Applicants Admitted _73_
Average SATs: Verbal __472__ Math __540__
High School Class Rank: Top Tenth _____ % Top Quarter __100__ %
    Geographical Distribution (% of class):
In-State _95_____% Middle Atlantic _1_ % New England ___ %
West __96_____ % Middle West __1_ % South _____1_ %
Foreign _1_____ %
Minority Students _15_ % of Class
Financial Aid _32_ % of Class

3) Retention of Students

_52_ % of freshmen graduate in four years
_56_ % of freshmen graduate in five years

4) Ten Most Popular Majors of Graduating Seniors, 1983

1. Business Economics
2. Liberal Studies
3. Communications
4. Electrical Engineering
5. Mechanical Engineering
6. Political Science
7. Sociology
8. English
9. Biological Sciences
10. History

5) The Financial Picture (1982–83)

Annual Campus Budget	$ 122,348,422
Percent of Annual Budget from State Appropriation	50
1983–84 Tuition and Fees for State Residents	$ 1,362
1983–84 Tuition and Fees for Out-of-State Residents	$ 4,722

Most freshmen live in the nine on-campus residence halls; most sophomores, juniors, and seniors live in Isla Vista, a residential community
within a bike ride of campus. Isla Vista may have looked presentable when
it opened, but now it is a declining pre-fab village of privately owned
apartment houses looking something like a resort community gone broke.
Some students escape to housing in nearby Goleta or Santa Barbara itself,
several miles away.

UCSB is high on intramural and recreational sports, but it also sends
eleven men's and seven women's intercollegiate teams to NCAA Division
I competition. Two hundred fifty clubs and organizations, a strong vol-
unteer force in the local community, and a fine arts series round out campus
life.

Santa Cruz

As a prospective student's mother said at the end of the UCSC campus
tour, "Good grief—it looks like a huge national park with eight World's
Fair pavilions." It does. Santa Cruz has the reputation for "the most
beautiful campus in America"—2,000 acres of redwoods and former ranch-
land rolling pasture high above the Pacific with spectacular views of Mon-
terey Bay. Its eight small residential colleges (copying the Oxford/Cambridge,
Harvard/Yale concept), each strikingly different, are a visual treat in themselves. Add the proximity of Carmel and Big Sur to the south and Palo
Alto and San Francisco to the north, and there is considerable atmosphere
indeed.

But there are other components of the UCSC reputation. Santa Cruz
is "different"—granted, less different now than when it opened in 1965 as
the exceedingly popular flower child of the UC system, flaunting its
alternative-style education—but still "different." As the demands of a more
conservative public force UCSC to pull in its sails somewhat, some lament
the passing of a symbol of that rebellious time in American collegiate history
while others feel that a slightly tempered Santa Cruz will be a progressive,
small university of distinctive power, one perhaps closer to the model its
founders originally envisioned.

UC Santa Cruz seems to have been the twinkle in Clark Kerr's eye
before the president of the UC system became embroiled in controversy
resulting from Berkeley's Free Speech Movement. (He was ultimately,
sacrificially, fired by Governor Ronald Reagan, who honored a campaign
promise "to clean up the mess at Berkeley.") Kerr and his educational

University of California at Santa Cruz

1) Size of Student Body

Undergraduate _6,351_ Graduate _542_ Total _6,893_

2) 1983 Freshman Class Profile

Class Size _1,208_ % Men _50_ % Women _50_
Percent of Applicants Admitted _71_
Average SATs: Verbal _512_ Math _550_
High School Class Rank: Top Tenth _30_ % Top Quarter _71_ %
   Geographical Distribution (% of class):
In-State _86_ % Middle Atlantic _3_ % New England _5_ %
West _89_ % Middle West _2_ % South _1_ %
Minority Students _22_ % of Class
Financial Aid _39_ % of Class

3) Retention of Students

_25_ % of freshmen graduate in four years
_46_ % of freshmen graduate in five years

4) Ten Most Popular Majors of Graduating Seniors, 1983

1. Biology
2. Psychology
3. Literature
4. Environmental Studies
5. Art
6. Computer and Information Sciences
7. Economics
8. Politics
9. Sociology
10. Earth Sciences

5) The Financial Picture (1982–83)

Annual Campus Budget	$ 82,000,000
Percent of Annual Budget from State Appropriation	54
1983–84 Tuition and Fees for State Residents	$ 1,458
1983–84 Tuition and Fees for Out-of-State Residents	$ 4,818

guru friends thought the strong UC system would be even stronger if at least one campus focused on the undergraduate rather than on graduate and professional school students. Thus came Santa Cruz, with a limit of 10 percent graduate students, a liberal arts and science program, a faculty devoted to undergraduate teaching, and other "ideal" factors—not only the location but, more important, the personalized residential college system. Only the accident of opening in the late sixties brought the addition of the idiosyncrasies tagged "alternative," for which UCSC became well known—no grades, programs with trendy labels like "history of consciousness," do-your-own-thing majors—and the consequent rush of brilliant, affluent, suburban white students who were eager to experiment.

The core components of the Santa Cruz dream remain intact, and a scholarly chancellor from Cal Tech is accelerating straight academic rigor. UCSC still has small classes and liberal arts and sciences, but it now has opened a computer engineering program (capitalizing on the proximity of Silicon Valley and the electronics industry) and tracks in business and communications. The sciences are easily the most popular majors at UCSC now, and probably the most demanding. All undergraduates must take comprehensive examinations and/or complete a senior thesis to earn the bachelor's degree. Optional letter grades have been added to UCSC's Narrative Evaluation System (the faculty member writes a paragraph describing the student's performance in a course). The residential college system still creates the feel of a small private college in the context of a medium-size public university. There are no fraternities or sororities and no football team, although recreational sports are popular. Bright students still come, those who do not insist on having "vocational handles" on their studies, and Santa Cruz maintains an impressive record of graduate school entry.

The UCSC uniqueness, mainstreamed a bit, lingers on, partly because of the spectacular location and the "liberal" town, partly because it still attracts students who, as one high school guidance counselor put it, are a little more "organic" than the students elsewhere in the system, wanting demanding academics coupled with an emphasis on social conscience.

Miami University of Ohio

Atmosphere

It's a drab ride to Miami in southwestern Ohio. Corn. Wheat. Endless forgotten fields. Roadhouses. Fifties' tacky houses with immaculate lawns and wrought iron. Small hills to relieve the road ribbons. Tired gas stations, cafe and motel signs.

But lo, order and a manufactured kind of beauty pop out on the hill-plateau of Oxford (population 8,500), aptly named to house what mid-westerners call "The Yale of the West." (I remember it well from Indiana high school days; the bright and worldy would often apply to the top private colleges *and* Miami.) Trees and shrubs well groomed. A brick main street. Immaculate everything. "Modified Georgian" college buildings, old and new, trying so very hard to look Virginia, not Ohio.

This is surely what midwestern parents dream of: a replica of *their* college experience of the midfifties. The Williamsburg look. Order. No cars! Academics tilted toward "training for leadership." The minority frat and sorority members holding the majority of influential positions on campus. Pep squads and a new stadium for very serious, rather successful football. And endless monograms on shetland and cashmere sweaters.

The building that houses the admissions office somehow escaped the Williamsburg look. Grey Gables, a delightful limestone structure, was home to college presidents for a span, then it became a guest house, then a restaurant, and finally it was moved from the center of campus to make way for new dorms; it is now the reception hall for prospective students. The cozy building is not alone responsible for the "welcome!" spirit at Miami.

The admissions staff have that hey-how-*are*-ya? genuineness that mid-westerners not only do well but do honestly. Individuals rarely make lasting impressions here, for they don't differ much from the last or the next. Groups make statements, provide impressions and tone. It's life by

Miami University
Oxford, Ohio

1) Size of Student Body

   Undergraduate __13,423__ Graduate __1,447__   Total __14,870__

2) 1983 Freshman Class Profile

   Class Size __3,375__   % Men __43__   % Women __57__
   Percent of Applicants Admitted __78__
   Average SATs: Verbal __500__   Math __560__
   High School Class Rank: Top Tenth __40__ % Top Quarter __75__ %
      Geographical Distribution (% of class):
   In-State __77__% Middle Atlantic __5__ % New England __2__ %
   West __1__ % Middle West __90__ % South __2__ %
   Minority Students __3__ % of Class
   Financial Aid __35__ % of Class

3) Retention of Students

   __60__ % of freshmen graduate in four years
   __69__ % of freshmen graduate in five years

4) Ten Most Popular Majors of Graduating Seniors, 1983

   1. Marketing
   2. Accountancy
   3. Finance
   4. Systems Analysis
   5. Elementary Education
   6. Psychology
   7. Mass Communication
   8. Political Science
   9. Zoology
   10. Art

5) The Financial Picture (1982–83)

Annual Campus Budget	$ 106,477,010
1983–84 Tuition and Fees for State Residents	$ 2,220
1983–84 Tuition and Fees for Out-of-State Residents	$ 4,270

Revenues

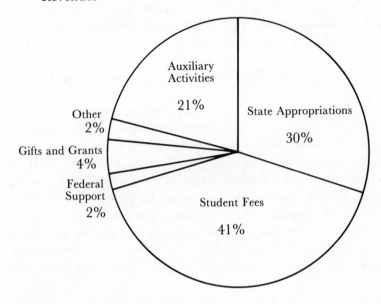

Expenditures

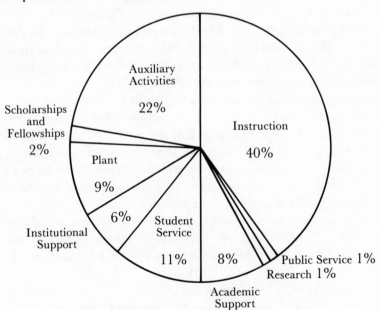

consensus. The warmth prevails, and an earnest let's-get-the-job-done attitude. The humor is basic; the personal idiosyncracies, if there, are submerged; and the national collegiate cynicism somehow passed this place by. There is family at Miami, the old kind where people stick together.

The admissions staff is a family, nodding in agreement with each other, smiling, rarely jarring. They look alike, speak alike, and become one.

"You're at the right place for Ivy," said a young admissions officer. "We've tried very hard to *look* Ivy—students and campus alike, even the town. And for some reason, all the world thinks we're private, not public. We're currently viewed as selective. Oberlin, Kenyon, and Case Western Reserve—all private colleges in Ohio—are as, or more, selective. But we're thought to be in their company, and we certainly leave the other Ohio public institutions in the shadows. Why? Just mystique, I guess, and Miami's 'heritage of excellence.' Our graduates do well; we look and act like we're supposed to look and act, and the incredible loyalty of our college family is known and envied. Also, we're preppy as hell." Nods and giggles all around.

The admissions staff had no trouble listing Miami's pluses and minuses as perceived by high school kids and parents. On the plus side: the beautiful campus; the homogeneous student body; the strong liberal arts program and even stronger business program; the isolation of Oxford and Miami—true Ivory Tower; the no-car rule; the "straight" life—few drug problems, for example; the successful sports record and image; the presence, but not dominance, of the Greeks; the ability to house over half its student body on campus, including all freshmen; the strong regional prestige; and the moderate cost compared to good private colleges.

The admissions family differed a bit, oh so politely, on Miami's "perceived drawbacks." But a short list emerged nonetheless, ironically duplicating several items from their plus list: the no-car rule, the absence of a full engineering program, the "super-straight" image. As one young woman summarized it: "We are considered the country club of this area's public schools. That has a very prestigious, and surprisingly somber, connotation. On the whole, the Midwest loves the concept."

Down a well-manicured walkway, past tons of brick, sits the tailored and tan dean of the College of Arts and Sciences, also a professor of microbiology, who came to Miami over a quarter of a century ago. Despite longevity of service, he had a refreshing view of the place.

"The best colleges and universities, in my view, have a liberal focus for *all* of their students, not just those in so-called liberal arts. And so it is at Miami." This man delivered like a dean: articulate, authoritarian, stern but with feeling . . .

"Our problem is not academic tone, really. Our problem is homogeneity. It's everywhere—in the student body, even in the campus buildings. Do we attract it, or do we develop it? Actually, we do the best job we can with the students we get. And the students we get are okay. They don't have sharp edges, though. They expect a 'caring relationship' here, a college family, and they get it. Our reputation seems to bring the 'right' kids to us—somehow it just happens. Don't get me wrong: it's a *good* reputation—All-American."

The good dean had obviously done a lot of pep talks at prospective-student gatherings. He had that Voice-of-Miami touch.

"Yes, we're conservative. And that includes the academic program. We never reduced requirements, like many of our colleague institutions, in the sixties and seventies. For example, there was great pressure to drop the foreign language requirement, but we didn't do it. Thank goodness! Now there is renewed demand for foreign languages; I guess America has finally realized it's tongue-tied. We're not static, we keep improving and strengthening our program. In arts and sciences, for instance, every department chair has changed in a decade. In each case, there is a more scholarly presence. Remember: a department is only as good as its head. But the balance at a place like this is hard to keep because 'more scholarly' often means 'less good teaching.' Rigor is key. In all honesty, we've been slowly improving in that zone." He smiled, nodded, ushered a student in, and me out. Very deanlike.

A group of "representative" faculty, over lunch, gave the same impression as the trees and shrubs, walkways and building exteriors: manicured, cautious, tasteful . . . and a bit lifeless. The professors were like the admissions staff: nice folks, affable, lacking strong individual idiosyncrasies. But they conveyed a consistent message of a slightly uneasy comfortableness.

" 'Mother Miami' is the key phrase around here. And that's okay—warm and caring, and all that. But maybe there's a little *too* much 'mother' here. For example, do we need all these basic requirements? Everything we do is 'safe.' I rather like it, but at the same time, I know it's not the real world. And our kids show the signs of that: isn't it curious that when the town voted for McGovern some years back, the Miami students voted for Nixon?"

A potpourri of comments flew from this friendly group.

"I'm officially happy here—but unofficially, not yet. Quite frankly, it is tiring as hell to keep handing out all the right images."

"Eccentric teachers are not tolerated by the students at Miami. The closest thing we've had to excitement recently was a teacher who grew so upset with lawnmowers passing by his classroom that he threw a chair out the window. Strong personalities seem to emerge here as departments, not individual professors. One of them, incidentally, is the athletic department."

History and Tradition

Local guidebooks are full of Miami history. Founded in 1809, the second oldest college west of the Alleghenies, Miami nominated itself "mother of fraternities," the "birthplace of the McGuffey Readers," and the "cradle of coaches."

"The Miami triad" was a popular phrase well before 1900, denoting the founding at Miami of three well-known national fraternities: Beta Theta Pi, Phi Delta Theta, and Sigma Chi. An even more familiar household phrase was "the McGuffey Reader"; first published in the 1830s, it was a series that educated five generations of Americans. Named for Miami's Professor William Holmes McGuffey, the books sold 125 million copies, a record still unequaled in the history of education. The unique reputation as "cradle of coaches" is well documented: over two hundred Miami graduates are coaching teams at the professional or collegiate or scholastic level today.

Miami's "firsts" are a curious conglomeration: it claims one of the first audiovisual services; the university developed the first major in paper technology, one of only eight in the United States today; the degree program in systems analysis was probably the first of its kind anywhere; Miami was the first public university to organize an alumni association; and *The Miami Student* claims to be the oldest college newspaper in America.

A meeting with professor Walter Havighurst, the unofficial chronicler of Miami University history, provided a superb preface to a tour of the campus. He is a dignified old gent, thin and tall, who settled into the Miami tradition soon after marrying the daughter of the president of Western College, one of two women's colleges (Oxford was the other) incorporated into Miami along history's path.

"What's the essence of this place?" asked Havighurst rather officially of himself. "A good deal of quality, some class, and powerful regional mystique. With growth has come strength. We owe a great deal to the women's colleges we absorbed, for example. Many of our alumni have become eminent—U.S. President Benjamin Harrison, New York *Tribune* editor and publisher Whitelaw Reid, railroad magnate Calvin Brice, Pittsburgh's and NYU's President Henry Mitchell MacCracken, to name a few. And it didn't hurt us to start early.

"We're made stronger by an inseparable town/gown relationship. Oxford is probably one of the few college communities where the settlement was attracted to the academy, not the reverse. The campus has always been tidy and beautiful as a complement to our town. And we know our tradition as well as many southern colleges do. You'll pass by Elliott Hall (1829) and Stoddard Hall (1835), once known as 'North' and 'South,' where early Miami students lived spartan lives. And, of course, we're famous for the William Holmes McGuffey era. Through it all, we've maintained a sense of *decorum* as well as purpose. That is typified in modern times by President Phillip R. Shriver, who recently resigned to teach. In his annual opening talk, the president would always give the freshmen the charge not only to study and produce, but to stay off the grass."

Other tidbits of history and tradition are tucked into Miami's promotional publications. Named a university from the start, Miami was to all intents a liberal arts college—as distinguished from the then-current "normal" college for training teachers and school administrators—until 1830, when the master of arts degree was first awarded. (Since 1967 Miami has been conferring the Ph.D. in ten fields.)

When Miami began instruction in 1824, President Robert Hamilton Bishop summoned classes by blowing a trumpet, thinking the purchase of a bell an extravagance. The early offerings were rigidly classical: freshmen had to take Greek and Latin, reading six books of Homer's *Iliad* and some works by the Roman historian Sallust. Other required courses were algebra, modern geography, English grammar, and Bible recitation. Students cooked meals in their rooms on wood-burning stoves. Once a year, in June, the university swept the dorms, removing twigs and bark, apple cores and potato peels, and other remnants of student life.

At the start of the Civil War, companies representing both the North and the South were organized from the Miami student body. They marched down High Street together and boarded the same train for Hamilton where they separated, one group heading south, the other north. In 1888, the daughter of a trustee became Miami's first coed. That was the same year football came to the university, with President Ethelburt Dudley Warfield on the team; a knee injury kept him off the field for Miami's first intercollegiate game, against the University of Cincinnati. In 1920, Miami invented the artist-in-residence concept. Their first was poet Percy MacKaye. (MacKaye suggested that his friend Robert Frost try the same; the University of Michigan invited Frost as their first artist-in-residence.)

The Campus

Miami's 1,100-acre campus is spacious, well organized, and functional. But endless modified Georgian structures, although attractive, create confusion by their very sameness throughout the college grounds. Miami's vitality is evidenced by recent buildings: of the 100 major structures on campus, 40 have been built since 1955. And there are personality stamps throughout: alumni loyalty symbolized by the gift of the impressive Sesquicentennial Chapel; the fraternity/sorority tradition symbolized by the Beta Bells and the Tri Delt sundial in central campus locations and the Delta Zeta bells in the chapel; a National Historic Landmark plaque on the McGuffey Museum which houses the Schoolmaster of the Nation's famous Readers and memorabilia.

One jarring and most welcome departure from the Georgian is Miami's new art museum, opened in 1978. A handsome jumble of limestone angles and soaring glass, the museum houses lecture and concert halls alongside exhibits. But Miami cannot resist traditional architectural fare: administrators proudly say that the new, lush, large Marcum Conference Center is a near-perfect replica of the Wren Building at the College of William and Mary in Williamsburg . . . Georgian, of course.

The Center for Performing Arts is imposing, as is Millett Assembly Hall, seating 11,000 for Linda Ronstadt-type concerts. King Library, the central facility for Miami's one-million-plus catalogued volumes (growing at a rate of approximately 30,000 per year), can seat 2,000 students and has shelving for 700,000 books. The remainder of Miami's collection is housed in four branch libraries on campus: the Science Library, the Wertz Art and Architecture Library, Hoyt Library (on the nearby Western campus), and the Amos Music Library in the Center for Performing Arts. The libraries are especially strong in nineteenth-century American literature, history, and periodicals. There are first editions of George Orwell, Mark Twain, and James T. Farrell. Special collections include early American and British children's books, prerevolutionary Russian history and art, the history of the Ohio Valley, and, of course, the McGuffey Readers.

A special atmosphere is created by the tree-filled Western College campus, an adjacent ex-women's college incorporated into Miami as a multidisciplinary "alternative" program, a memorial to American's educational tone of the early seventies. Western has, aside from embarrassingly ugly modern dormitories, stone bridges over streams and gullies, a replica of a 400 A.D. Norman chapel, beveled glass doors to Civil War–era structures, and a magnificent tower of chimes given by an Oxford family.

Academic Programs and Staff

The last several State of the University speeches delivered to the faculty senate by Miami's recent president, Phillip Shriver, provide good insight into the Miami of today. During his sixteen-year tenure Miami experienced considerable growth: in student body size, in campus buildings, in the formation of a study center in Europe, in the acquisition of the former Western College for Women, and in the broadening of graduate and professional programs. But his commitment to liberal arts remained a constant theme. In 1979 he told the senate:

> Liberal education in these United States in recent years has been in a state of serious disrepair. Buffeted by excessive careerism, the disruptions and demands of war, the cry for "relevance," the intrusions of government, the strangulating constraints of budgets, and the fragmentation of the curriculum, liberal education has all but disappeared from many campuses and has been in a beleaguered state of siege on many others. . . . In looking ahead to the decade of the 80s, then, I would stress as our first commitment the reaffirmation of the fundamental validity of liberal learning in the education of our students. Every student, before leaving Miami, regardless of major, ought to have a firm foundation of liberal education on which the specialized course work of the major field can build. It is time to become earnest about our General Education discussions, about the increasing tendency of majors to specify particular requirements to the exclusion of elective possibilities, and about the implementation of Miami University's historic commitment to the liberal arts.

Dr. Paul G. Pearson, Miami's current (and eighteenth) president, moved from Rutgers where he was executive vice-president and a full professor of zoology who conducted research on the impact of pesticides and other pollutants on ecosystem function. He is earnest, plain, and midwestern. There were red, white, and blue themes in his tie *and* his office decor. The president is not animated, but his thoughts are clear and on target.

"Our student body is high calibre, but not the highest. We do well with the 1100 SAT crowd. Our undergraduates are conservative, religious, upper middle class. And they want a place now and later that is comfortable. They're good, clean-cut American kids. So, let's say we've become selective within a life-style group. Both students and parents love what they see here: we look like a college is supposed to look, and the tranquillity is obvious."

The president paused, clasped his hands, and spoke again, gently. "Miami is not on the frontiers of knowledge. But I can't imagine a better place for undergraduate classroom excellence—we're tops in the classroom. The liberal arts tradition is strong and will probably never fade. Yes, we talk a lot of strengthening arts and sciences by way of the practical—

education, business, applied science, etcetera. But the themes remain broad here.

"We're not a rich institution, but we're resourceful. I received dozens of letters from our alumni when my appointment as president was announced. Our alumni feel strongly about Miami. We're state-assisted, but the private help from them and others will mean more and more to us. Thank goodness for our strong tradition of family loyalty."

President Pearson discussed his goals of office without pause: "One, I want to increase the visibility of the presidency. My predecessor was reluctant to ask for money. *I'm* going after private money. Two, our physical plant is enviable. We must keep it up. Three, we must strengthen admissions, in light of demographic changes. That means we must heighten our external relations, our recruitment, seek new ideas of how to get the best students—perhaps increase our merit scholarships. Four, we must be more selective in our academic programs; some will have to be phased out as others increase. Five, finally, we must raise our standards for faculty tenure and tighten the administrative structure."

Down the hall was a lively executive vice-president for academic affairs and provost, a Princeton type who has been at Miami fifteen years. His office was more rumpled than those of the other administrators and his spirit more contagious.

Referring often to the major study he had chaired for Miami's reaccreditation, this striped-tie academic self-confidently described Miami's "heritage of excellence." Like the president, he highlighted the classroom integrity. "Not only does this faculty teach well—they help *others* teach well. We have a heavy concentration of textbook authors here. Just as the McGuffey readers carried Miami's impact across much of the world in the 1800s, some of today's most widely used university textbooks are by Miami authors: Nieswonger and Yeager in accountancy, Gloss in business, Snider in political science, and the nearly three dozen works of regional literature by Walter Havighurst."

The provost was animated, twisting in his chair, gesturing, smiling.

"We take great pride in the fact that *no* one is here to teach graduate students only. Most well-known professors are found with the freshmen as well as with grad students. An undergraduate research fund has enabled some of our best students to work closely with faculty on professional-level projects."

The provost vice-president lost no time in naming Miami's "best" academic departments. "They're the ones with doctoral programs attached, I guess: botany, zoology, chemistry, educational, administration, geology, psychology, English, history, political science, microbiology. I'd add on programs in the business school, particularly accounting. And paper science from our applied science division.

"But how do you rate departments? By faculty research and publication or by powerful teaching? Physics here, for example, ignites young people by effective teaching. That makes it a top department, right? And then there is our Western College School of Interdisciplinary Studies, with, in essence, its own faculty. Although enrollments are slipping in this alternative program, there is true academic rigor. Something special happens. Western's students have a high profile at concerts and lectures and often lead us in social action: women's rights, the nuclear power issue, the environment, wildlife preservation." The provost paused. "So there you have it: a rambling dissertation on what we do best—different responses to different definitions of what 'best' is all about."

Academically, Miami is organized into one college and six schools: the College of Arts and Science, the School of Education and Allied Professions, the School of Business Administration, the School of Fine Arts, the School of Applied Science (with programs such as manufacturing engineering, office administration, systems analysis, paper science), the School of Interdisciplinary Studies (at Western College), and the Graduate School.

There is some flexibility in academic programming. In the College of Arts and Science, for example, students can substitute the first year of professional school work for their senior year in business administration, dentistry, engineering, forestry, law, medicine, nursing, public health, or theology. Some undergraduate majors require a second admissions process: in the popular School of Business Administration, a prospective major is screened after completing thirty Miami semester hours, including calculus, and needs at least a 2.25 grade point average; to gain admission to the School of Fine Arts in music, a performance audition and theory examination are required.

The most popular majors, judging from what a recent graduating class elected, are management and accounting, economics, biology, English, government, history, philosophy, elementary education, mathematics, fine arts, sociology, chemistry, computer science, anthropology, and physical education. Some of the least elected majors (where a student can find some of the smallest classes) are Spanish, classics, German, religion, French, and secondary education.

The student response to Miami's serious side is uneven. On one hand, honors classes are available and popular. A 2.5 overall GPA is a prerequisite for admission, and a B must be earned in the course to get honors credit. To graduate with honors, a student must complete twenty-four or more hours of honors credit with a grade point average of 3.0 or higher. The honors classes are less crowded, less formal, with greater student exchange. And students seek these out.

On the other hand, there are clear signals that not everyone at Miami is interested in honors-level academic pursuits. Take the library situation, for example. All official records indicate that King Library is packed, very popular. But as President Shriver remarked in his 1980 State of the University speech, the library's popularity needs examining. He urged student cooperation to reduce the noise level at the library and indicated that "the atmosphere in some parts of our libraries has more closely resembled a social rather than a learning environment." In the year that the long-awaited science library opened, the president suggested that "the time has come for the establishment of new habits."

Miami's yearbook recently featured the same theme:

> The libe-nut liked the social scene. Depending on his mood, he went to one of three places in King. To study, he descended below where all the other book fiends dwell . . . When the libe-nut felt lonely, and wanted to make new friends of the opposite sex, he wandered to the first and second floors where there were many other lonely people . . . here, people usually spent the entire evening on one page alone. When the libe-nut felt a cultural urge, he visited the third floor where the Greeks converged . . . On this floor, studies reached the memorization level because most books stayed closed throughout the night. The pseudo-libe-nut went to Hughes Library (in the Chemistry Building) where he sat at tables arranged to prohibit public viewing. Persons seeking knowledge and seclusion generally went to Hughes.

Another possible crack in the scholarly dike at Miami is the growing popularity of art-of-living courses. Geography of wine, personal finance, and social dance are all crowded. Geography of wine is a three-hour credit course, offered both semesters. There is a long waiting list. As the yearbook reports, "During the semester the student tasted 29 different wines . . . More practical courses will hopefully be added in the future. Miami is trying to prepare its students for more than a career after college."

It would be wrong to imply that Miami is all fun and games, for that just isn't so. Yes, there is "country club" here. But there is also the desire to get the job done seriously and well. Miami is not "the frontier of knowledge," as the president pointed out, but a genuine learning center with a tilt toward preparing students for the professions and for leadership roles. Miami is All-American, wrapped up in academic gowns.

Students are serious enough about education at Miami to complain that professors are often not available for personal consultation and that papers are too frequently handed back with terse grades rather than with constructive criticism. There does not seem to be loud complaining about an overdose of homework; business, math, and political science majors reportedly are assigned the heaviest loads.

There *is* complaining about "pressure to get the grade," imposed by the times and the job-hungry students themselves, and classes that are too large. In documentation from the registrar's office, however, it would appear that A's and B's are not that difficult to come by, nor are small classes. The grade distribution in a typical semester is approximately 28 percent A, 38 percent B, 24 percent C, 5 percent D, 5 percent F. Of 2,766 courses offered in a recent term, 24 percent enrolled fewer than 10 students, 22 percent had 11 to 20 students, 40 percent had 21 to 40 students, 9 percent had 41 to 70 students, and the remaining 5 percent enrolled up to 376 students.

Student Life

So that students might express their views spontaneously and in a relaxed setting, the director of admissions assembled a group of undergraduates in his home (a tidy, large-lawned ranch house with a patent leather driveway) for dinner.

There was a dietetics major who was Chi Omega; the president of the Associated Student Government who was Lambda Chi Alpha and just back from an internship in Washington; a prelaw senior from little Bellefontaine, Ohio; a premed and zoology lab assistant who was in everything on campus, including Omicron Delta Kappa and Mortar Board; a hometown Oxfordian who was also premed and loved the place; and others. The students were casual, neatly dressed, restrained at first and then open and honest, enormously supportive of each other, and very positive. Again, individuals did not stand out but the group impression was consistent and strong.

After a few beers and general chit-chat, the subject of Miami Greeks struck a responsive chord.

"They're a little group with big influence. Most of our honor societies end up full of Greeks. And we have, of course, 'typed' houses: the jock types are TKEs and Delts, for example. But coaches discourage the *real* jocks from being in fraternities. Too distracting, I guess," said one talkative but plain-looking young man.

The undergraduates were high on Miami and indicated that most of their friends were too. (There is an overall two-thirds graduation rate, strong for any college, but particularly for a public one.) They lauded the "general importance placed by college authorities on learning" and the informal atmosphere of many classrooms. They thought Miami was noteworthy in bringing speakers (as well as rock concerts) to campus: Bill

Buckley, Bella Abzug, Jane Fonda, Shirley Chisholm, Ed Bradley, and Leonard Bernstein had appeared in recent months. They indicated "a lot is going on for a middle-sized place"—over 300 different student organizations, for example, and teams good enough to win the Mid-America Conference's all-round athletic excellence cup for ten of the last eleven years. "Academic hermits," those oblivious to all that was happening in student life, were also acceptable. The students felt that the faculty was approachable, that the town had "ambiance," and that everyone—town and gown—was "proud to be part of Miami." There was respect more than envy accorded the Western School of Interdisciplinary Studies. "They're really into things intellectual over there. And their 'norm' is a little higher than ours on the main campus. In a way, they're feared by the mainstream—too intense, searching, and often just too bright."

There was a long pause after I asked what might make Miami University a better place. More lasagna, garlic bread, and beer were required to pull any criticism of Mother Miami out of this crowd.

"Well," started one brave young lady, "we really should have more minority students and greater diversity in the student body." Agreement all around, but little was said. "And more really has to be done for women here—in athletics, in support groups." This theme was not particularly appealing to the majority.

"Money—the place needs more money!" one robust fellow blurted out. "But who knows how to get *that?* I do know that Miami alums are loyal as hell, so that's one good source."

"Town/gown relations probably need some tending to," offered another as the ice cream came out. "Oxford is getting a little shabby around the edges now because a few stores have moved out to the shopping mall. As the town goes downhill a bit, students are less respectful of the homes and apartments they live in, and that's causing a few problems." Agreement all around.

"Maybe we *are* a bit too conservative," risked one young woman, preppy from head to toe. "Pinning and lavaliering and serenades with candles are still popular at Miami, just like when my parents went here. And we still find plenty of women wanting to compete in the Miss Miami contest. You probably heard that a recent Miss Miami became Miss America. The fun part of that was the number of fraternities that hung out sheets the next day announcing: 'She slept here.' "

Most wanted to change the subject quickly. One lively premed jumped in. "Somehow, if I were president, I'd try to relieve the academic pressure. There is too much grade-grubbing, too much competing. After a while, you develop a kind of war strategy. As a result, we have too much plagiarism, too much cheating. Even if you're honest, though, you learn strategy.

You *have* to." Again, nodding agreement all around, but the consensus was that grade-grubbing was considerably more prevalent in some departments than in others.

Despite the mild and somewhat forced criticism, this group adored Miami. As did the relaxed, smiling director of admissions. As does almost everyone on campus or in the town.

College yearbooks often provide good insight into the tone of an institution, and Miami's *Recensio* does just that. A number of recent excerpts:

> Finally, the moment came that everyone had been waiting for—the announcement of the Homecoming King and Queen. Amid happiness, cheers and tears, Ernie Davis, an Evans Scholar, was declared King and Sue West, a Zeta Tau Alpha, Queen. After that announcement, many enjoyed a Miami tradition, the toasted roll served with hot cider.

> What are the rules governing alcohol and pot? According to Officer Dennis Barter, "Your room is your castle." In other words, the police were not allowed to come into any student's room without a search warrant.

> Were weekends dead in Oxford? Hardly . . . Many believed that uptown was just the place to be Thursday night. Going bar hopping or window shopping, getting an ice cream cone from Baskin Robbins, a warm bagel, or better yet, just watching people were some of the activities uptown . . . For juniors and seniors, especially those who had illegal cars, nothing against Oxford but . . . Cincinnati or Dayton was the place to go.

> On Friday, April 18th, at approximately 5:00 P.M., almost thirty buses rolled into Oxford carrying enthusiastic brothers, sisters, friends and sweethearts. It was Sibs Weekend!

> Because of an additional member ruling by SAC, the cheerleaders were caught in inflationary pressure. The cheerleaders had to add two slots to the squad to insure minority representation, but 12 cheerleaders could not operate on the same budget as 10.

> The legend behind the "Hub" was that if a student was unfortunate enough to step on the seal, that student would flunk his next test. Conscientious students avoided trodding upon the seal at all cost . . . Upham Arch has one of Miami's more romantic legends. If a couple kisses under the arch, they are destined to be married. Many couples avoid the sacred arch . . . The Sun-

dial, located in South Quad, was constructed on a marble slab that was placed on top of six turtles' backs. It was rumored that when a virgin walked by the Sundial, the turtles would chirp.

Admissions

Who are these students at Miami? Who gets in? The nice-guy director of admissions says the system is fairly cut and dried. First, a high school graduate must present seventeen units of preparatory study, including ten of any combination of English, speech, mathematics, science, history and social studies, and foreign language.

It's easy to gain admission if a student can commute. In Ohio, any graduate of a chartered high school who can commute to campus from the home of parents or spouse must be accommodated by the local division of the state university system. Miami has a solution: the two branch campuses, in Hamilton and Middletown, take most of the commuters. On the Oxford campus, the commuting group represents only 7 percent of the student body.

For the majority of freshman spots awarded Ohioans, Miami has a high standard. Admission does not come from numbers alone. The Viewbook says, "Admission is based upon high school performance (class rank, grade point average, and curriculum), test scores (SAT and/or ACT), recommendation by the high school, and special ability, talent, or achievement."

Successful applicants are informed of admission December through April, transfers later. Out-of-staters generally compose 20 to 25 percent of the entering class; they're judged by the same criteria but must meet a somewhat higher standard.

Miami seems to have become highly selective by an unusual, well-calculated route: placing severe limitations on housing. Since the university decided that all freshmen must live in dorms, Miami can accommodate only the number it can house in the first-year class; and it picks that number, using its own criteria, from a sizable applicant pool. Whereas the state system of Ohio normally supports open admissions, the housing gimmick has clearly worked in Miami's favor in accomplishing admissions selectivity.

When the class of '85 was matriculating, President Shriver bragged about Miami's admissions posture to his faculty and alumni body. "Like the oak, Miami's growth has been slow, steady, strong, and sure . . . Virtually alone among all of Ohio's state-assisted universities, we have had to say 'no' to thousands of applicants, a circumstance which in turn has made the University, if anything, more attractive in the eyes of prospective applicants." The president documented the new class's excellence by advanced placement exam activity: Miami's freshmen had taken more AP examinations that year than those of any college or university in Ohio, and they ranked twenty-seventh in the nation.

The president commended his institution's admissions stature only to sound an internal warning, a word of caution too infrequently voiced by today's top college leaders. He cited television and newspaper campaigns by some institutions to lure a full freshman class in a "buyers' market." His observations regarding the changed scenario were right on target. "The ending of the post-war baby boom, the falling birth rate of the past eighteen years, the out-migration from the frost belt to the sun belt, the increasing number of young people who are turning their backs on higher education as too costly or too chancy in terms of useful training, or who have too many other choices—all this has combined to create the prospective demographic depression and to stimulate the recruiting zeal of college admissions officers."

To dramatize Miami's challenge in this context, Shriver not only cited the declining number of high school graduates in Ohio—including a 50 percent anticipated decline within a decade in Cleveland's Cuyahoga County—but, paradoxically, the incredible recent proliferation of colleges within the state. "When I became Miami's president in 1965, there were only 6 state-assisted campuses in Ohio. Today there are 65, as the state has fulfilled its promise to put a campus within thirty miles of every citizen. In total, there are now 125 public and private campuses in Ohio."

Miami now has, as one might expect, an increased fascination with transfer students and older students to fill the possible shortfall of freshmen. And the college knows it must increase its minority representation, which is currently only 3 percent of the student body (and 5 percent of the faculty).

If Miami's enrollment should suffer during the demographic squeeze, although that is difficult to imagine given their strong position today, are there resources to bridge the gap of missing tuitions?

Resources

President Pearson has already put a high priority on raising private monies to augment Miami's public support.

His predecessor indicated that the university had "accumulated modest educational and general reserves, although not as large as we would wish." Miami's endowment was little over $10 million as the university entered the eighties. But their "Goals for Enrichment" campaign aimed to at least double that amount in short course. With a book value on the Oxford campus of over $175 million, Miami could not be considered poor.

But with public aid eroding due to a lagging state income, private resources become key to maintaining institutional integrity.

Miami's Goals for Enrichment financial campaign brochures were large and lavish. And informative. One learns that state appropriations account for only 36 percent of Miami's total operating income, with the remainder coming from student fees and other sources. The state provides 52 percent of instructional and basic costs—faculty and staff salaries, libraries, maintenance of academic buildings. Capital construction of academic buildings is funded by state appropriations, but residence halls must be funded by the university, repaid directly by room and board charges. Funds for construction of buildings not directly related to academic or residence programs must come from other sources, such as bond issues, students' fees, or private gifts.

As Ohio, like a majority of states, strains to keep pace with accelerating demands for basic public services, higher education comes under increasingly severe scrutiny. Miami will attempt to meet needs by raising student charges, although they already have one of the highest public university fee structures in the nation, and by more aggressive appeals to the private sector, particularly their own alumni. Miami alums have one of the highest giving ratios in the nation. But even that must improve now.

When the political mood of the nation and the campuses is conservative, giving by Miami alumni is most generous indeed. Maybe the nation is now returning to the mood that makes Miami supporters smile. Although their university is significant academically, and successful in keeping an eye on future leadership potential, the time for the "family" to demonstrate its unique brand of loyalty is now.

To the Midwest, Miami has been for some time and remains not *just* family but a down-home version of royal family.

University of Michigan

Ann Arbor

A University of Michigan promotional brochure describes what locals call the "Athens of the West" as ". . . potentially bewildering. Do all 40,000 students cross the Diag at the same time?" U-M's size is, at first glance, overwhelming. It is not so much the huge campus, which is disjointed and often difficult to distinguish from the average-USA-Main-Street town of Ann Arbor, as it is the maze of programs, schools, and divisions and the masses of people, 70 percent of whom are undergraduates. Before even visiting Michigan, one is bewildered by briefing the candid admissions materials:

> *Bulletins.* (Catalogs of the schools and colleges)—A complete set of catalogs, usually 13 volumes, is available in a special boxed edition for $12.00 . . . [but] the University's catalogs contain very little information that is normally of interest to prospective students.

Despite the immensity and the decentralization of it all, the University of Michigan has a strange and wonderful way of pulling the parts together, of creating order out of a seeming jumble, of satisfying its able students, and of offering its state and nation a symbol of excellence which, to many, is *the* prototype Public Ivy.

Michigan's symbolism seems to be a national presupposition. Even the *New York Times,* lamenting the nation's lack of respect for the State University of New York, did not have to qualify the statement:

> Nevertheless, none of its [SUNY's] units have the prestige of a University of California at Berkeley or the University of Mich-

University of Michigan at Ann Arbor

1) Size of Student Body

   Undergraduate __21,970__ Graduate __12,319__ Total __34,289__

2) 1983 Freshman Class Profile

   Class Size __4,280__ % Men __53__ % Women __47__
   Percent of Applicants Admitted __62__
   Average SATs: Verbal __550__ Math __620__
   High School Class Rank: Top Tenth __58__ % Top Quarter __91__ %
      Geographical Distribution (% of class):
   In-State __66__% Middle Atlantic __13__% New England __3__ %
   West __3__ % Middle West __80__ % South __1__ %
   Minority Students __5__ % of Class
   Financial Aid __60__ % of Class

3) Retention of Students

   __68__ % of freshmen graduate in four years
   __76__ % of freshmen graduate in five years

4) Ten Most Popular Majors of Graduating Seniors, 1983

   1. Biology
   2. Business
   3. Chemistry
   4. Computer Science
   5. Economics
   6. Engineering
   7. English
   8. History
   9. Mathematics
   10. Political Science

5) The Financial Picture (1982–83)

Annual Campus Budget	$ 758,000,000
1983–84 Tuition and Fees for State Residents	$ 2,218
1983–84 Tuition and Fees for Out-of-State Residents	$ 6,346

Revenues

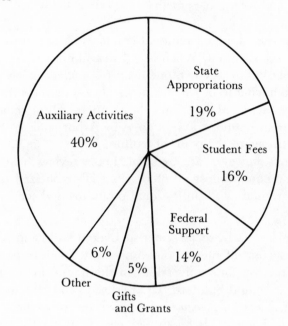

Expenditures

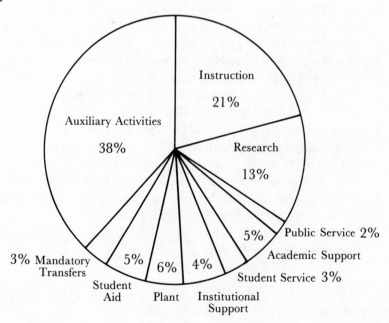

igan at Ann Arbor—with giant libraries and a wide range of scholars and researchers at the top of their fields.

Such taken-for-granted national eminence is not lost on Michigan's on-campus administration. When asked to summarize Michigan's qualifications for the Public Ivy list, one dean responded tersely: "We are not accustomed to having to prove our importance." Perhaps. But once someone else proves it, U-M loves to talk about it. Throughout Michigan's literature, and throughout a visit to Ann Arbor, talk of "our ratings" becomes repetitious to the point of tedium.

The ratings, however, are awesome. Let us review them early on, with one cautionary note: almost all of U-M's well-publicized ratings are assessments of graduate and professional programs and schools.

- In a 1977 survey by social scientists Everett Ladd and Seymour Lipset, a cross-section of the nation's university faculties named Michigan among the top four universities in the nation in the nineteen fields surveyed, behind Stanford, UC Berkeley, and Harvard.
- In 1974, *Change Magazine* reported a survey of professional school deans which found Michigan, Berkeley, Chicago, Columbia, and Harvard "the five universities with outstanding reputations which have the greatest number of top-ranking professional schools." It was also reported that fifty universities accounted for 63 percent of all academic memberships in advisory committees of federal departments and agencies. Among the fifty, Harvard was first, Michigan second.
- In a 1979 survey conducted by Korn Ferry International and the UCLA Graduate School of Management, Harvard, New York University, and the University of Michigan were the three universities most frequently mentioned by high-level executives in major companies when asked where they took graduate work.
- According to U-M sources, Michigan had more graduates listed in *Who's Who in America* during the decade of the seventies than any other college or university in the country. Among them were President Gerald R. Ford, playwright Arthur Miller, newsman Mike Wallace, Drs. Lee and Jonas Salk, actor James Earl Jones, several astronauts, and baseball's Branch Rickey.

As the high rankings of the University of Michigan kept surfacing during the seventies, the *Detroit News* fielded its own four-part investigation under the headline: "The U. of M.—just how good is it?" After reciting the list of recent accolades, the *News* said:

While the various ballots testify to the top quality of the U. of M. graduate and professional schools, the most persistent criticism is that undergraduate education at the university fails to measure up . . . "Nothing we do would match in importance in the public's eye the insertion of more professors into the undergraduate program," President Fleming said in his state-of-the-university speech . . . "Heavy reliance of assistants in our undergraduate program (1600 graduate students working on their Ph.D.'s employed as teachers) draws criticism in runaway proportions . . . but because Michigan is one of the few centers in the nation which does not have an outstanding private university, we have a particular mission to maintain this institution as a world-class comprehensive university . . . The only way we can afford to offer that diversity is with teaching fellows."

Perhaps U-M is a good example of what UCLA's Alexander Austin labels the halo effect—such exceptional graduate and professional programs that everyone believes the undergraduate training is also superb. Be that as it may, there is no question that undergraduates have a wealth of opportunity at Michigan. Quality is definitely to be found amidst the impressive quantity of programs and professors, if one walks through the maze judiciously.

The people of Michigan certainly believe that. A young Yale admissions officer, recruiting in the Midwest for Eli, reports that he met with an enthusiastic response in Minnesota, Illinois, Ohio, and Indiana. But Yale decided to essentially give up on Michigan because returns from the recruiting campaigns there were so paltry. At every turn, parents and kids would say, "Why Yale when we can go to Michigan, which is just as good for half the price?"

U-M's magnetic draw and enviable reputation have been alive for decades, and they are not based on mere appearances or first impressions.

Atmosphere

The approach to Ann Arbor is flat, very flat. There are acres of Queen Anne's lace, highway-side cattails in damp places, grain silos, patchy stretches of green farmland with red barns. Although the area is pastoral it is hardly picturesque, but it is a welcome relief from nearby Detroit (forty-five miles away) with its steamy inner city and bold but tentative attempts at "renaissance." After one passes dozens of franchise motels and eateries at the freeway exit, Ann Arbor emerges, a small river city of 100,000 people.

You can forget Detroit and its massive problems here. Ann Arbor is upbeat, self-contained. One senses purpose on every corner, most often related to the university, which dominates. The town is undergoing moderate rehabilitation and is tidy, without obvious sections of poverty, although it is rumored that "cheap labor" is employed at the university's hospital. There seem to be tennis courts on every other corner in the outskirts, and downtown has more than its share of shoe stores, video game centers, ice creameries, and small bookstores sprinkled along cracked but clean sidewalks and tired but clean streets.

Although the university is easily the town's largest employer, Ann Arbor is big enough to support a smattering of small companies and light industry plus ninety or so industrial research firms and government laboratories.

There is a cosmopolitan atmosphere. A visitor often does not hear English spoken on street corners and is confronted by foreign dialects in service areas: at the libraries, in the restaurants. The delightful international flavor comes as a considerable surprise after the approach miles of silos and the Queen Anne's lace. Ann Arbor's university area is something like Cambridge, Massachusetts: no stereotypical dress, people with distinctive behavior and appearance, a handful of obvious druggies, a handful of preppies, some bizarre town characters who have probably been campus adjuncts for years, and intent-looking, well-dressed professionals walking much faster from coffee shop to library to offices to nearby apartments than one would surely see in most Michigan towns or, for that matter, in most American college towns.

The mix and fast pace obviously create spicy town politics. The Republicans and Democrats continually vie for power, with results often hard to predict and sometimes contested. In 1977, the Democratic candidate for mayor beat his Republican opponent by one vote out of the more than 21,000 cast. In the election rerun, with 28,000 voting, the Republican won by a mere 282 votes. But Ann Arbor is, on balance, a liberal stronghold. The town drew national publicity for instituting a five dollar fine for possession of marijuana. Most progressive movements find heavy support here. It was natural for John F. Kennedy to choose to propose America's Peace Corps on the steps of U-M's student union.

The Campus

Thank God for the service people at the university who obviously take pride in colorfully decorating tiny plots of turf with flowering plants, shrubs, and shredded bark, particularly in the congested central "Diag" area. The few posies and patches of sod, complemented by Michigan's student tradition of keep-on-the-sidewalks-and-off-the-lawn, provide relief to U-M's generally undistinguished collection of buildings, so congested and so varied that the campus is a drab clutter of the new and the old, sporting all colors of the rainbow, only faded.

The central Literature, Science and Art Building is a massive orange brick fortress resembling a salmon loaf (red bricks were unavailable during World War II, they say). The "new" administration building looks like a 3-D IBM card with no holes at the bottom, as this building was designed during the era of student demonstrations. And curses on the architects of the fifties, whose contributions are much in evidence on the nation's campuses, since that was a time of considerable expansion. Michigan jumped right in. Smack in the middle of campus, next to the handsome graduate library, is their huge undergraduate library, opened in 1956. It is the most lamentable salute to that era imaginable, wearing turquoise blocks interlaced with glass and steel and brick. It is appropriately nicknamed "UGLi," pronounced "ugly," derived from the *U*ndergraduate *Li*brary. Still another salute to the fifties, made even less appealing by an interior decorator of the eighties, is the admissions office, with enough orange plastic in the waiting room to redo the lobby of the largest Budget Rent-a-Car, relieved by walls of white cement block with racing stripes of brown and orange (but U-M's colors are maize and azure blue!).

There are some unique and satisfying points of interest on the Michigan campus, to be sure, squeezed among the brick and granite or sometimes a good walk away from the center.

In the central area, an imposing cube sculpture in Regents Plaza weighs 1.5 tons but spins on its axis with the touch of a finger; it is said the president spins the cube each morning "to start the university." A campus symbol, the Burton Bell Tower, is 212 feet tall; with fifty-three bells ranging in weight from twelve pounds to twelve tons, it is the third heaviest musical instrument in the world.

The curious William L. Clements Library of Americana was designed in 1923 by Albert Kahn to reflect the architecture at the time of Columbus's voyage. The library contains an intriguing collection of treasures from America's founding to 1850. (Kahn, by the way, designed many of the U-M buildings.) Next door is the president's residence, built in 1840 and the only original U-M building still standing. Its second claim to fame is that the home was the first in Ann Arbor to have indoor plumbing (in 1871). Another "first" on the central campus is now called the Economics Building (1856); it is the oldest classroom building on campus and "the first building in the world to be devoted entirely to chemistry instruction."

Tucked away in the main campus congestion are striking Gothic buildings with rich interiors: the huge Law Quadrangle, built in 1933 with the largest single gift the university has ever received, and the Martha

Cook Residence (1915) with its formal gardens. Two other elegant buildings, the Betsey Barbour (1920) and the Helen Newberry (1915), were gifts
of Levi Barbour who was reacting to the "decidedly inferior" living conditions in the town. Several museums are as impressive as they are busy:
the Museum of Art (1910), known particularly for its Oriental collection
covering 1,200 years, and the Ruthven Museums (1928) with displays of
anthropology, paleontology, and zoology, complete with planetarium, di-
nosaur skeletons, and gift shops. On the outskirts of the central campus is
a building that is well named: the Power Center for the Performing Arts
(1971). With its spacious, manicured grounds, a mirrored facade reflecting
a park, and soaring design, it is a powerful statement indeed and a welcome
complement to old Hill Auditorium (1913), the worn but "acoustically
perfect" home of U-M's arts.

The "other" campuses at the University of Michigan at Ann Arbor
serve serious purposes but are aesthetically weak. The Medical Center, an
eighty-two-acre complex near the central campus, looks like a medical
center. But the adjacent large arboretum is lovely and contains every species
of tree native to Michigan. The "stadium area," which one reaches by
walking or biking through blocks of shabby private student housing, is an
assortment of large structures intercepted by an even larger railroad yard
complete with box cars. But clearly, the Michigan stadium is not to be
missed. It is the largest collegiate-owned stadium in America, seating over
107,000 on a good day, when Rose Bowl Fever hits full tilt.

At the other end of the geographical spectrum is the relatively new
(early fifties) North Campus, feeling and looking remote but green and
spacious. It houses science and technology buildings, drab student apartment complexes, a potpourri of campus service buildings, and, more recently, the Gerald R. Ford Presidential Library, a handsome brick structure.
Next door is the Bentley Historical Library, known for its Michigana
collection and resources regarding the Phillipine Islands and the American
temperance and prohibition movement.

All told, the campus covers 2,581 scattered acres, with 202 major and
mostly forgettable buildings.

History and Tradition

Appearances may disappoint and Michigan may not have the instant
Ivy aura of the University of Virginia or William and Mary. But its history,
tradition, and noteworthy accomplishment through the decades caused
Clark Kerr, former president of the University of California and chairman
of the Carnegie Commission of Higher Education, to say: "The University
of Michigan has fully earned its credit as 'mother of state universities.' "
Kerr told a Michigan commencement audience that Michigan

first demonstrated that a *state* university could achieve high academic quality. A Select Committee in Michigan in 1840 noted: "No state institution in America has prospered as well as independent colleges with equal, and often, less means." The record of Michigan subsequently made that observation no longer true. Michigan also pioneered in getting autonomy from the state. Your early constitutional provision (1850), giving to the Regents "general supervision" of the University, later became one model for California, and the two state universities with the greatest constitutional autonomy became the two great academic leaders among state universities.

What became the University of Michigan was initially founded in the town of Detroit as the "Catholepistemiad" or "University of Michigania" in 1812. The president of the university was a Presbyterian, the vice-president a Catholic priest. In the early years the university was a coordinating agency for secondary schools and did not actually offer college level instruction until 1821. When Michigan gained statehood in 1837, the "true university" became a reality and was reorganized; it moved to Ann Arbor (probably named for the wives of the two founders and a natural arbor of massive burr oaks in the area). After construction in Ann Arbor, the University of Michigan as we now know it opened its doors in 1841.

Michigan's pride regarding roots and ratings can be better understood in a review of the university's recorded firsts, only a sampling of which are included here.

The University of Michigan was the first

- large state institution to be governed directly by the people of the state (1817).
- to de-emphasize the classical college curriculum and sponsor such "new" studies as the sciences and modern languages (1842).
- to have a fraternity building designated for use as a meeting place— Chi Psi (1843).
- in the West to provide instruction in modern languages (1846).
- in the West to offer a program in engineering leading to a degree (1854).
- "real" university (having multiple schools) in the West, with the founding of the Law School (1859).
- to entirely own and operate a hospital (1869).
- of the large institutions to admit women (1870).
- to use the seminar method of teaching (1871).
- state institution to establish a Department of Dentistry (1875).
- to have a Speech Department (1884).

- to offer instruction in journalism (1890).
- to send a visiting football team to play in the Rose Bowl (1902).
- to provide instruction in aeronautical engineering (1913).
- to provide buildings with athletic facilities for the whole student body (1929).
- to offer a program in nuclear engineering (1957).
- public university to stage a major capital gifts campaign (1948).
- university to have an alumni association chapter on the moon (formed by Dave Scott, Al Worden, and Jim Irwin, three U-M alumni who landed in Apollo 15 in 1971).

Student Life

Where does one contact, in this decentralized academic and urban montage, a group of students who will help a visitor get a handle on what the "typical" undergraduate's life is all about? A random assortment of undergrads in one of many near-campus eateries—in this case an open-air Italian restaurant with a big-city-abrupt waitress but superb food and oversize pitchers of cheap beer—were very helpful. The students were majoring in a variety of disciplines and dressed in a variety of styles, from jeans-with-stringy-hair to madras-jacket-with-tie.

The students were open, easy to talk with. But they most resembled the Berkeley crowd; they were not quite so abrupt and cynical, but they were ready to disagree with each other if someone seemed the least bit off the mark.

"To me, a university should be judged by its success in placing students in the job market and graduate school," one articulate prelaw lad said firmly.

"Are you kidding?" responded the one in tattered jeans, a Residential College dweller. "Any school can zero in on practical skills and place students in the marketplace. I picture Michigan's purpose a cut above that: to expand the horizons of those who will ultimately *do* the hiring and lead in any number of ways. To find just the right job after college is a cheap goal."

"Well, Michigan *does* have more preprofessional students than any university in the country," asserted one casual fellow who was obviously more interested in the beer than the discussion.

The jeans responded sternly. "That sounds like one of those fraternity-front-room myths to me. Where the hell did you dig that statistic up? God, we're good at concocting 'the most' and 'the best' stories about ourselves around here."

The discussion switched to Michigan's general strengths and weaknesses. On the "strengths" list, approved by consensus:

- "Our diversity. There is anything and everything here. It's not only interesting, it teaches us all to be tolerant. Every odd duck, I've learned, has something good going for him."
- "Football! Let's face it: it's the rallying point of this place, the one force that seems to draw us all together. We're not really depressed if we lose, but it means a lot to the whole community for us to win. The place gets wild near Rose Bowl countdown time."
- "The seriousness of people here, including the undergraduates. Michigan is full of achievers. That may be partly just midwestern, but it's particularly true of U-M. We all want to make our impression, both now and later."
- "Despite the fame, the diversity, and the brilliant researchers, I think it feels like home here. There is something very warm about Michigan. 'Home' is the best word I can think of to describe it."

The "negatives" list evolved through an easy consensus also:

- "Housing. It's a mess. Only one-third of us can live on campus, and the off-campus living is not only hard to find but rarely desirable once you find it. It's the biggest drawback to attending Michigan, although I know it's a problem on other campuses too."
- "Getting the runaround in Michigan's chaotic bureaucracy. God knows this place is big. That means it's complicated. If you persist, though, you can get what you want and what you deserve."
- "The weather. Yuk!"
- "The foreign teaching assistants. Not only are many of them not at all experienced in lecturing, but dozens of them cannot speak English intelligently. I'm glad we're the center for hundreds of international students—but should they be allowed to practice their English on me when I'm struggling to pass organic chemistry? It's hard enough to understand chemistry in *my* language."

These U-M students were fun and impressive: high-spirited, bright, courteous but independently assertive, with vision well beyond themselves. There was a sensitive discussion of the traditionally important role of women at Michigan, little interest in the campus Greeks ("just one more local difference"), and strong appreciation voiced for the attributes of Ann Arbor.

The students' votes for the toughest majors: all engineering fields, all sciences, music, art, and architecture. Their votes for "guts": phys. ed. and education and natural resources ("All the super-jocks are ordered into one of these majors so they'll survive").

The undergrads were also willing to vote for the best of Ann Arbor night life: Dudley's for freshmen, sophomores, and jocks; Charley's for Greeks and preppies; Second Chance for townies; and the Village Bell and Rick's American Cafe for everyone. Not to be forgotten, they emphasized, is all that happens at Michigan in the arts, much of it free. *And,* not to be forgotten, they underscored, is all that happens in athletics.

There are signals of sports frenzy at every turn at U-M. The garish four-color "football recruiting book" breaks tradition with the other somber, informational, understated publications of the university. But if one wants to find the Michigan records quickly, they're up front:

> The Wolverines have won more Big Ten football titles than any other Conference team. Michigan had the best record in the nation during the decade of the 1970's—96-10-3. Eleven of the last twelve Wolverine contingents finished the season ranked in the Top Ten of the Nation. . . .

Football may be king, but there are plenty of other star teams in court. Michigan has an enviable record of champions within the Big Ten, particularly in baseball, track and cross country, golf, and tennis.

Athletic fervor in Ann Arbor doesn't stop with the winning intercollegiate teams; 225 acres of campus land are devoted to sports. And the money seems always to be available for renovated and/or new athletic facilities. If a new building looms on the horizon of this campus, you can be assured it is a new professional school facility or, more likely, a new intermural recreation center. The U-M intermural and recreational programs are "standing room only." And here again, another first: Michigan had the first intermural building in the nation.

Downtown in Ann Arbor, jock fever is at an even higher pitch. An attractive little restaurant has a huge sign in the window: "25% OFF on Pizza and Beer (soups, sandwiches, salads, desserts, and dinners, too!) for ATHLETIC TEAMS, any day of the week. YOU MUST BE IN UNIFORM."

It seems always to have been so. Some flavorful Michigan athletic memorabilia: the first attempt to organize a varsity athletic program was when Michigan invited Cornell to play football on neutral territory in Cleveland; Cornell's President White promptly responded to U-M's President Angell, "I will not permit 30 men to travel 400 miles merely to agitate a bag of wind." Michigan first met Ohio State on the gridiron in 1897; the score was Michigan 36, Ohio State 0. Michigan played its first Rose Bowl game in 1902 against Stanford; by the middle of the second half the score favored Michigan 49–0, at which point the Stanford coach waved his team off the field and the game was never completed.

No one at Michigan seems to feel athletics has grown too big-time:

sports are just a fun diversion, appreciated by all. There appears to be a consistent seriousness and maturity among Michigan undergraduates. Diversions have their place but are secondary to the educational task at hand.

Academic Programs and Staff

As the students had stated forcefully, it's a task to find which education you want at Michigan, as the choices are so broad. This is a list of Michigan's conglomeration of seventeen schools and colleges, with recent total and undergraduate enrollments:

College of Architecture and Urban Planning
    Total: 502   Undergraduates: 236
School of Art
    Total: 489   Undergraduates: 461
School of Business Administration
    Total: 2,030   Undergraduates: 618
School of Dentistry
    Total: 874   Undergraduates: 178
School of Education
    Total: 2,362   Undergraduates: 754
College of Engineering
    Total: 5,065   Undergraduates: 4,066
Rachkham School of Graduate Studies
    Total: 6,859
Law School
    Total: 1,176
School of Library Science
    Total: 291
College of Literature, Science, and the Arts
    Total: 16,019   Undergraduates: 13,503
Medical School
    Total: 851
School of Music
    Total: 851   Undergraduates: 510
School of Natural Resources
    Total: 858   Undergraduates: 622
School of Nursing
    Total: 959   Undergraduates: 801
College of Pharmacy
    Total: 375   Undergraduates: 308

School of Public Health
   Total: 656
School of Social Work
   Total: 750

The heart of the undergraduate program at Michigan, and indeed the heart of U-M's tradition, is the College of Literature, Science, and the Arts ("LSA" to most; "LS/Play" to the irreverent). Since 1841, when the college instructed seven students in Latin and Greek literatures and antiquities, rhetoric, grammar, algebra, surveying, science, and philosophy, LSA has been the most popular bachelor's degree program. Now the LSA faculty of 800 offer more than 3,100 courses, still emphasizing breadth of learning.

The major benefit of Michigan's size, of course, is the variety it offers. For example, within the LSA bachelor of arts and bachelor of science programs, a student can major in two disciplines simultaneously, can obtain joint liberal arts and architecture, engineering, dentistry, or medicine degrees, can choose from a long list of interdepartmental or area programs, or can create his or her own "individual concentration program." There is something to suit everybody. In one special project called the "Pilot Program," 450 students live together for their first two years, all enrolled in "theme experience," a topic chosen for a year, complementing regular LSA courses with pilot seminars and living on corridors with students studying similar "themes." There is another residential program called the "Medieval and Renaissance Collegium" whose students share the obvious courses, meet in the Gothic Law Quadrangle, and roast a boar annually. And there are several language houses.

Three programs deserve special mention: Interflex, the Residential College, and the Honors Program.

First, "Interflex." Fifty students are admitted annually to this six-year program allowing students to receive the B.A. and M.D. degrees simultaneously by packing premedical and medical training into a single program requiring ten months of each year.

The office of the head of Interflex is located in the congested, sterile Medical complex. This professor is a no-nonsense, slow-to-smile man with confidence in this project, which began in 1972.

"There are so many advantages to this program," said the doctor in his space-age modern office. "It removes much of the pressure experienced by the normal premed student who is clawing his way toward medical school. In Interflex, you're assured medical school admission by just passing your courses. But 'medical school' is, to a large degree, experienced nearly from the start: clinical exposure comes after the freshman year, and med school–level courses begin after the second year. Still, a near-normal courseload in liberal arts can be taken. Interflex students don't have to load up on sciences alone . . ."

The doctor wasted few words and continued with the essentials of the program. "This is obviously a popular program, and admission is extremely selective. We admit about 10 percent of the applicants and take around 20 percent of the class from out of state. An interview is required but doesn't seem to tell us much. The students who enter average 1370 on the SATs, have a 3.8 high school grade point average, and rank in the top 5 percent of their class. Thirty-five to 40 percent of the entering class are women. We find that most of the students finish on time in six years, but some take longer. The ones who drop out almost always do so for personal reasons. There are similar six-year programs around the country: Boston University, Northwestern, Jefferson [in Philadelphia], Johns Hopkins, University of Missouri, University of California at Riverside. We're all enthusiastic about the program, what it has done for medical education, and what it has done for both good kids and the profession."

It was dramatic to move from Interflex's pristine white offices across campus to the cozy "Residential College," another specialty program within LSA. Interflex is a highly structured concentration leading to a specific professional goal; the Residential College is a relaxed but demanding interdisciplinary program born in the late sixties but strong today with 700 enrolled students. The Residential College literature explains that the program is committed to proficiency in languages, the freshman seminar (dealing with subjects such as "values in knowledge and social life," "communities and institutions," and "the fifties: beyond nostalgia"), and visual and performing arts.

The extraordinarily enthusiastic, animated director of the Residential College described RC as "a child of the sixties. The University of Michigan is very decentralized among schools and colleges. This tends to detach people. The Residential College exists to reunite them, to make them feel part of a whole. We have integrated studies and living."

This man could not sit still. He blustered and smiled and continued. "Our super program could not have happened without a sensitive and supportive administration. President Fleming was so responsive to the unique problems and challenges of the sixties that the ACLU picked him as 'Libertarian of the Year.' Harold Shapiro, our new president from econometrics, strikes me as an enlightened insider. Both have supported the difference we offer kids at U-M, partly because of our results: we win more than our share of prizes in the Hopwood Competition for creative writing, for example. Our kids just stand for demanding intellectual inquiry. They have even *voted* to introduce more rigor—in required foreign language, for example."

Wandering the East Quadrangle grounds, RC's home, the director gestured widely. He rushed through offices, lounges, a library, dining halls, a theater, art studios, music practice rooms, and seminar rooms—a self-sufficient little campus-within-a-campus.

"It's curious whom we draw to this program: a lot of out-of-staters . . . a lot of Jewish kids, a lot of students determined to enter some form of social service—and our students are fairly affluent. For many, the Residential College replaces something like a fraternity or sorority in the social realm—it becomes the full Michigan experience. How *great* that a big place like Michigan can offer an intimate, demanding program like this."

Another demanding program that has brought U-M considerable notice is the Honors Program, which Michigan started for its most outstanding undergraduates in the early fifties, well ahead of most other campuses. Entry to Honors is open to about 15 percent of the LSA freshmen, who enroll by invitation only. Other students who achieve at a high level during their first, second, and third Michigan terms can apply later. For the first two years it is departmentally based, or in U-M's language, "concentration-based."

Many regular LSA courses have Honors sections—smaller, more accelerated. Honors students are also exposed to special team-taught courses, tutorials, independent study projects, junior and senior seminars. The Honors students can live together, if they choose, in designated sections of two dorms, "to continue the educational process outside the classroom." The program culminates in the student's Senior Honors Thesis. Some recent titles:

"The Effects of Allografts on the Immunity of Mice to RPC-20 Myeloma" (Zoology)

"The Coup D'Etat of 1926 in Lithuania" (Political Science)

"The Decline of the Victorian Gentlemanly Code: Conrad and Ford" (English)

"The Distribution of Personal Income in the US: Some Arguments for and Against Equality" (Economics)

"Plant-Insect Interactions: Selective Forces Underlying the Evolution of Phytoecdysoids" (Botany)

"Roman Freedmen and the Cena Trimalchionis of Petronius" (Classical Studies)

"Thermal Biofeedback and Progressive Relaxation Training as Treatment for Insomnia" (Psychology)

"Burgundy Wine Growers and the Crisis of 1907" (History)
"Aspects of Bilingualism in Greek Vase Painting" (Classical Archaeology)

A dour professor of chemistry explained selection to the Honors Program to me. Proudly. In a recent year, Honors freshmen had SAT averages of 650 verbal and 710 math. In fact, 54 percent of the Honors freshmen had verbal scores over 650 (compared to 11 percent of the entire U-M freshman class), and 85 percent had math scores over 650 (compared to 27 percent of the entire class).

"Why go to a highly selective, elitist little private college when the University of Michigan can provide the same competitive atmosphere among Honors students, plus our huge wealth of programs and faculty, for a fraction of the cost?"

It was a fair question.

The "huge wealth of programs" cannot, of course, be fully explored in this space. Within the School of Engineering, within the School of Music, within the School of Natural Resources—within *all* schools and colleges—there seem to be options and opportunities as varied as those that the majority of undergraduates are exposed to in the College of Literature, Science, and the Arts.

Class size at Michigan varies considerably. Residential College and Honors Program students enjoy a smattering of seminars. But for the majority of undergraduates at Michigan, classes are surprisingly small, according to figures released by the Office of Academic Planning. Fifty-five percent of the classes enroll 21 or fewer students; 21 percent have 22 to 30 students; and 19 percent of the classes enroll 31 or more students. In a recent term, 106 LSA courses listed enrollments of over 100 students; 180 seminars or tutorials were listed with enrollments of 1 to 3 students!

Grade point average charts from the registrar's office confirm the national trend: a C is no longer "average." For a recent term, the freshman average grade for all U-M schools and colleges was 2.89; sophomores, 2.91; juniors, 2.95; and seniors, 3.09. Across the board at the University of Michigan, women earn higher grades than men.

Admissions

Publications from the admissions office are direct, honest, with no frills. Michigan earns high marks for its informative, comprehensive but succinct publications for prospective students. In fact, the entire admissions operation seems enlightened, fair, fast, and up-front.

One reason for Michigan's stature in admissions is the leadership.

Their director has been in office for over a decade now and is a visible national force. He's "Mr. Midwest"—the friendliest fellow in town, portly, bald, with several ballpoint pens sticking out of his shirt pocket, certainly knowledgeable, and with a down-home approach.

"We're really not in the business of generating applications. We're in the business of telling students what Michigan is all about, so they can see if it seems right for them or not. And we're lucky: far more good kids want to come than we can accommodate. But it's not that we don't have competition. Michigan State, with its aggressive National Merit Scholarship program, competes strongly with us now for in-staters. And private Northwestern is our strongest competition for out-of-staters. We visit schools actively—that's new for us since the sixties. And our staff telephones to encourage 'blue-chippers' and minority students to apply and visit. But despite all the new circumstances, we remain the most selective public university of the Big Ten."

He continued in a straight, matter-of-fact manner: "Informing students of Michigan, of course, is only part of the process. The more difficult part of it here is admitting the class. Each of the nine schools and colleges that admit freshmen, you see, decide what their own criteria will be. It differs from school to school—largely related, of course, to the popularity of that school and how selective they can afford to be. Fortunately, I'm given the authority to admit—to apply *their* theory to *our* admissions practice, to decide on individual cases. We'd have bedlam if I couldn't do that."

The members of the large U-M admissions staff have individual assignments: "publications," "computer," "minority recruitment and processing," "secondary schools liaison," "overall recruitment coordinator." Members of the staff discussed why Michigan has such a strong reputation.

- "We're old: we were on the frontier of America for a long time. 'The Champions of the West,' says the school song. We're now enrolling the sixth generation of some old Michigan families."
- "Our reputation regarding job placement is one of our long-standing assets. It's justified. And 'getting the job' seems to mean everything to these kids today."
- "Just the fact that we're so big, and offer nearly everything. I don't mean just in courses and special programs—I mean people, too. We've always been strong on foreign students, for example. Any individual or group can find a comfortable circle here."
- "I think student contentment is our largest attraction. The fact that about 60 percent graduate in four years and nearly 75 percent graduate in five years speaks to how much undergraduates are satisfied with Michigan, once they're here. That's almost a Yale-Harvard level of

retention. The word passes that students like it here, and others follow. The alumni enthusiasm, of course, helps us enormously."

- "It's funny, on the road. We don't point to our importance—we don't have to. But we do have to be a little defensive about 'too big' and 'too costly.' They still want to come, though."

The admissions officers' list of U-M's strongest and weakest undergraduate departments didn't exactly mesh with the student group's. Strong: computer science, all social sciences, engineering, music. Weak: education, nursing, and some natural sciences.

Michigan's admissions director is frequently interviewed and quoted and is always most candid regarding U-M's admissions picture. He considers Michigan to be among the two or three most selective public institutions in America. On the other hand, he attributes the decline of nonresident applicants since the mid-1960s to escalating costs, limited financial aid for out-of-staters, and limited recruitment efforts outside the home state. He worries about rising costs at U-M. New evidence clearly suggests that price has had an adverse affect on Michigan's ability to attract the unusually well-qualified applicant. Still, Michigan turns away hundreds of qualified students because of space limitations.

Another issue the director has addressed forthrightly is that of student writing. In a letter to Michigan school superintendents and principals, the director says: "Faculty members at the University of Michigan find far too many of their students unable to organize and write clear prose, term papers, reports, and answers to essay questions. The causes of the current deplorable state of student writing are unquestionably multiple, complex, and deeply imbedded in broader cultural trends. But one cause is easily identified, if not so easily eradicated: students are not given sufficient opportunity to practice writing before they come to the University. . . . In the main, our students at Michigan are as bright and as engaged as their predecessors; but in the skills of literacy, they are clearly less practiced."

In discussing credentials for admission to Michigan, one must first analyze U-M's quite specific suggested curriculum for high school (see page 80).

Admission to the University of Michigan is not determined by specific formulae. U-M gathers as much information as possible on a candidate before the readers make judgments. The high school record is by far the most significant predictor of academic performance at the university, studies indicate, so rank, grade point average, selection of courses in high school, and the record of the high school's previous graduates at the university weigh most heavily in the review of an applicant. Generally, if Michigan residents have undertaken a rigorous college preparatory program and

Suggested 9th–12th Grade Subject Patterns for Students Who Plan to Enter the University
(One unit equals one year of study)
Note: This plan is advisory only.

Subject Group

School, College, or Program	English	Foreign Language	Mathematics	Science	Social Studies	Other	Total Units
Lit., Sci., and Arts	4	2	3	3	3	5	20
Engineering	4	2	4	4	2	4	20
Nursing	4	2	4	4	2	4	20
Natural Resources	4	2	4	4	2	4	20
Music	4	2	3	3	3	5	20
Education	4	2	3	3	3	5	20
Art	4	2	3	3	3	5	20
Dental Hyg. (2 yr.)	4	2	3	4	2	5	20

have achieved at least a 3.2 grade point average, they will be admitted. GPA standards are higher for nonresidents. College Board scores are also reviewed with keen interest at Michigan, but a student's grades in school are always more important. Alumni families are favored, particularly among out-of-staters. Minority students and students with disabilities are given special consideration, not to mention, of course, strong athletes.

"The worst part of my job is getting football and basketball teams," the director said. "I want to win as much as anyone, but wow, there is *terrific* pressure to admit some athletes who just don't belong here. I do like to think we don't have 'open admissions' for jocks as some Big Ten schools have. But still, we go a long way. Almost all the varsity athletes here, male and female, are on full athletic scholarships. It's big business, all right. Clearly, we dip lower academically for athletes than for other special groups—minorities or legacies, for example."

Regarding the actual process of admitting the class, the director said: "Regional travelers in our office read folders from their areas first. We like to say that no one is rejected on personal grounds if academically acceptable. There are, of course, borderline cases, and they come to committee. At that point there are some severe disagreements. I personally decide on the supersensitive ones. But everyone is involved: staff, faculty, school counselors. We have general guidelines but no hard-and-fast rules. I guess our class profile over a period of years is the best statement of what we've had and what we're looking for. A major theme is that out-of-staters will normally make up 25 to 30 percent of the new class, but those spots in the class are more difficult to land than the majority of places held for kids from Michigan."

The director made this massive admissions operation sound easy. Perhaps it is just that he and his long-term staff have learned to *make* it easy. And it works.

Resources

U-M can claim the nation's respect for diverse academic and extra-curricular offerings, far more qualified applicants than can be accommodated, and enviable freshman class statistics. But what about money?

Once again, Michigan is up-front with details. Their financial picture—some would say "plight"—is openly discussed. It has to be. The media has been full of the state of Michigan's financial problems recently, largely due to the sporadic auto industry. Although the university seems to get a similar cut of the state budget each year, the dollar value goes down. Faculty, administrators, and students at U-M form a chorus of lament regarding the thrust of further cutbacks. Two of the university's financial gurus, hidden away in a lavishly decorated office, were willing to share their views.

"During the last few years, Michigan has suffered notorious economic problems. So we're going to have to live with less money in more expensive times. It probably won't be noticed at first. We'll cut back maintenance and overlook long-overdue renovations. And, regrettably, we'll have to lay off some human luxuries—we had to fire the university carillonneur, for example."

When one striped-tie financier stopped speaking, the other began. They were both earnest, concerned, and absolutely committed to keeping the University of Michigan strong. "Fees will have to go up. We're already high in the national context, but we'll have to see what the market can bear. Look what the Stanfords and Northwesterns charge—we compete with them for top students, so maybe we can afford to come closer to them in price. We *will* remain the best of the Big Ten."

With the University of Michigan in a state that appears to be wilting economically—or is at least beyond full flower, even when auto sales surge— private funding has to look more enticing. With a private endowment of over $120 million, the university is not poor. But dwindling public resources are creating enormous financial pressures.

Enter the alumni. And they are strong. Although the University of

Michigan has been seventh in student body size in the Big Ten for some years, it claims the largest number of degree holders—not just in the Big Ten but in the entire nation: over 280,000, and U-M confers over 10,000 new degrees per year.

The influence of U-M alums seems as strong as their numbers. From a long list of living and deceased alumni celebrities (not included earlier) in *Who's Who:* Dr. Robert Warner, director of the National Archives; Bill Flemming, ABC "Wide World of Sports"; Joseph Livingston, Pulitzer Prize-winning economics columnist; Gilda Radner of television and movies; Roger Smith, chairman of General Motors; Betty Smith, author of *A Tree Grows in Brooklyn;* Janet Guthrie, first woman in the Indianapolis 500; Tom Hayden, politician; Nancy Kassebaum, U.S. Senator from Kansas; Bob McGrath of "Sesame Street"; William Kerby, publisher of *The Wall Street Journal;* John Rich, director of *All in the Family;* William Shawn, editor of *The New Yorker;* Clarence Darrow; Thomas E. Dewey; Jerome Weisner, president of MIT; Lynn Townsend, chairman of the board of Chrysler Corporation; Marshall Nirenberg, Nobel Prize-winning biochemist; Michael Dann, president of CBS and NBC; Jack Vaughn, director of the Peace Corps; Mennen (Soapy) Williams, governor of Michigan; William Schiller, chairman of the board of Hershey Foods.

The Michigan alumni represent a phenomenal resource. Their power of leadership is well documented. Their loyalty to alma mater has yet to be fully tested.

On a nostalgic last walk through the Michigan Diag, an activities bulletin board came into full view. It was crowded, a testimony to the vibrancy of this campus. A sampling of the organizations (there are more than 500 on campus) with announcements: the Stilyagi Air Corps, Students for Progressive Government, PIRGIM (Public Interest Research Group in Michigan), the Gilbert and Sullivan Society, the Mad Hatters' Tea Party, and the Earplug Opera Company. Next door at the UGLi library there were brochures reminding the visitor that U-M has thirty-five separate libraries with holdings of over 5.5 million volumes. At the suggestion box near the front entrance, posted memos provided further insight into what students call "home" in this massive university:

Student: *Please* attend the plants by the copy machine. They're nearly dead.

Answer: The people who used to water plants here have been eliminated due to budget cuts. The plants near the copy machine are none too healthy and will be sent to Property Control soon. What happens to them there, God only knows. The *healthy* plants in the lobby have been adopted by a graduate student.

Student: Would it be possible to have paper towels in the women's room? The handblowers are just too hot. Also, could we have small wastebaskets?

Answer: The decision was made by the Plant Department to use blowers, and I doubt this will change. Small wastebaskets were requested in 1979 and the request was refused. But I'll ask again.

If there is a "microcosm of it all" in Academe, Michigan is probably it. Granted, the graduate and professional schools pull up the ratings and were judged in better economic times. But the undergraduates today don't feel one bit overlooked and busily thrive on their riches of variety. They're smart, serious, ambitious, diverse in background and in goals. This place is big and complex. But the spirit is quite contagious—the quality must be, too.

University of North Carolina

Chapel Hill
Atmosphere and Student Life

The University of North Carolina is not known as "Chapel Hill" by accident—North Carolina may have the best college town in America. Chapel Hill's size, atmosphere, appearance, location, resources, and spirit are difficult to surpass. Yes, Williamsburg, Virginia, makes the more perfect postcard; Boston is more cosmopolitan; Palo Alto has ideal weather; Austin, Texas, is ascending . . . but Chapel Hill is *the* College Town. *Time* magazine pegged it one of the dozen best places to live in America. And one newspaperman said, "The spell of Chapel Hill captivates." All the good people at nearby Duke know that—they abandon their Durham at the smallest excuse to travel an eager twelve miles to Chapel Hill. No one seems to know how or why it happened, or what ingredients the perfect college town must have, but it all somehow came together here.

Chapel Hill feels like a remote village. But approximately 33,000 people live among its gentle slopes, lush greenery, and the university, the only "industry" in town. The beach and mountains are three hours away. The climate is fine, with mild temperatures much of the year, one annual snow, and a somewhat muggy summer.

The half-hour proximity of Raleigh and Durham is meaning more to Chapel Hill these days: student and faculty exchanges are growing quickly among North Carolina State (Raleigh), Duke (Durham), and UNC. More important, the three have converged in becoming closely associated with the Research Triangle, located more or less in the middle. A national think tank has developed: among the one hundred largest metropolitan areas in the country, North Carolina's three-county Research Triangle ranks first in number of Ph.D. scientists and engineers per 100,000 population (Wilmington, Delaware, ranks second and Washington, D.C., third).

University of North Carolina at Chapel Hill

1) Size of Student Body

   Undergraduate __14,558__   Graduate __7,199__   Total __21,757__

2) 1983 Freshman Class Profile

   Class Size __3,207__   % Men __41__   % Women __59__
   Percent of Applicants Admitted __43__
   Average SATs: Verbal __505__   Math __549__
   High School Class Rank: Top Tenth __67__ % Top Quarter __91__ %
      Geographical Distribution (% of class):
   In-State __85__ % Middle Atlantic __5__ % New England __1__ %
   West _____ % Middle West __1__ % South __93__ %
   Minority Students __16__ % of Class
   Financial Aid __30__ % of Class

3) Retention of Students

   __52__ % of freshmen graduate in four years
   __72__ % of freshmen graduate in five years

4) Ten Most Popular Majors of Graduating Seniors, 1983

   1. Business Administration
   2. Industrial Relations
   3. Nursing
   4. Journalism
   5. Economics
   6. Psychology
   7. Political Science
   8. Pharmacy
   9. Chemistry
   10. English

5) The Financial Picture (1982–83)

Annual Campus Budget	$ 357,800,674
1983–84 Tuition and Fees for State Residents	$ 765
1983–84 Tuition and Fees for Out-of-State Residents	$ 3,127

Revenues

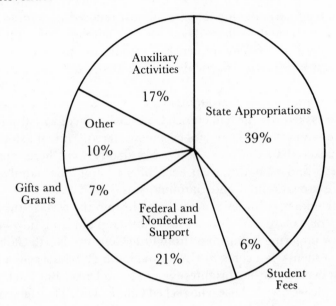

Expenditures

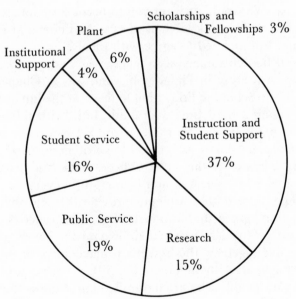

Although technology and research abound next door, one hardly senses it in lively, protected Chapel Hill with its Bluegrass night spots, preppy clothiers, and wholesome-looking, almost tailored undergraduates smiling their way through college days. All the hallmarks of traditional college life are here: the Greek influence is strong, the party quotient is high, and interest in athletics, particularly basketball and football, nearly off the scale.

A student waiter at the Carolina Inn, a lovely old hotel adjacent to the campus, was asked why he had chosen Carolina. "There was absolutely no other choice—no other college was even considered," he said slowly in a drawl far thicker than the roast beef. "My daddy went here, and his daddy went here, and *his* daddy went here, plus a lot of other family folks in between. We are Carolina, and Carolina is us."

Two other undergraduates provided insight into the ecstasy they call "Chapel Hill" or "Carolina." One was a rather plain and tidy young woman, a senior majoring in business, from little Concord, North Carolina. She said eight students had come to UNC from her high school senior class alone. "Almost every year our brightest would go to Duke. But the faculty always seemed pleased with those who picked Chapel Hill. They felt college life was more well-rounded here, the 'complete college experience.' As one of my teachers said just before I left for college: 'Oh, I'm so glad you're going to Carolina. We wouldn't want you to become *too* intellectual.' The people in Concord really think UNC is mecca. And now that I have three years behind me, I'm inclined to agree with them."

Another satisfied customer was a fellow who had already earned his B.A. at Temple University in Philadelphia and was at Chapel Hill completing credits in the School of Education to teach at the junior high school level. He was having a hard time with math, but "with three tutors and a lot of beer the night before the exam, I think I can make it." He was wild about the place. "There is incredible spirit here, partly related to athletics, partly because of the super college town, and partly because everyone sort of goes his own way and is tolerant of everyone else."

The students agreed that athletics provide the "tie that binds" at Carolina. They also agreed that although there is tolerance of "many lifestyles," students tend to stick close to their own mirror-image groups. "The football players live together, the basketball players live together, the sorority girls live together. Although there is a little crossover among groups, we all just live with people who are naturally akin. I guess that means we don't expand our horizons too much . . . Actually, though, it's because of the housing situation. Once you're off campus—and fewer than half of the students are *on*—you stick with those you know well," said the Concord coed, fully satisfied with her own experience.

History and Tradition

The University of North Carolina was the first American state university to open its doors. In 1776, the state constitution provided "that all useful Learning shall be encouraged in one or more universities."* In 1789, the North Carolina General Assembly made it official: "It is the indispensable duty of every Legislature to consult the happiness of the rising generation, and endeavor to fit them for an honorable discharge of the social duties of life by paying strictest attention to their education . . . A University supported by permanent funds and well-endowed would have the most direct tendency to answer the above purposes."

In 1795, 41 students arrived at UNC to study under a faculty of two. During the Reconstruction period following the Civil War, Carolina closed for five years, until 1875. In 1897, the first women students were admitted. By the turn of the century, UNC had 512 students, thirty-five faculty. During the early twentieth century, there was quick growth, both in student body and in programs. In 1931, North Carolina's Consolidation Act joined the university with Women's College in Greensboro and North Carolina State in Raleigh. At that time, engineering programs were moved to State, elementary education programs to Women's College. In 1947, the now huge Division of Health Affairs was initiated by the legislature, with schools opening quickly thereafter; North Carolina Memorial Hospital opened in 1952. Increases in the entire student body, undergraduate and graduate, were dramatic until 1972; since then, growth has been controlled at approximately 1 percent per year.

In 1971, the general assembly substantially modified the organization of higher education in North Carolina. The Consolidated University of North Carolina (which had grown to include six campuses: Chapel Hill, Raleigh, Greensboro, Asheville, Charlotte, and Wilmington) was joined with nine other state institutions under the State Board of Higher Education. Each campus in the system now has its own chancellor. But, to relieve the anxieties of the Chapel Hill faithful, the assembly stated:

> The Board of Governors declares as one of its planning objectives the continued development of the University of North Carolina at Chapel Hill as a major research university. This objective means continued responsibility for that institution to serve as the principal center of graduate education at the doctoral level (except in those scientific and technological areas which are offered at North Carolina State University at Raleigh), and for

*Historical notes and quotations from *Record of the University of North Carolina at Chapel Hill.*

first professional education. It has further special responsibilities at all degree levels in the health professions.

Thus, Chapel Hill was assured continuation of its flagship status. Tradition would have it no other way.

Carolina's list of accomplished alumni has always been impressive: James K. Polk, eleventh United States president; author Thomas Wolfe; actors Andy Griffith and Louise Fletcher; playwright Paul Green; bandleader Kay Kyser; Senator Sam Ervin; newsmen Charles Kuralt and David Brinkley; pollster Louis Harris; and cartoonist Jeff MacNelly. And Chapel Hill's roster of firsts is lengthy, including the first astronomical observatory connected with an American university (1831) and the first university to open a summer school (1877).

The First State University, by Professor William S. Powell (North Carolina Press), provides delightful insights into Carolina's pride in history. A few vignettes of early Carolina college life follow.

Robert Chapman, a Presbyterian minister, a native of New Jersey and graduate of Princeton, was chosen president of the University in 1813 in the midst of the War of 1812 with Great Britain. Chapman was a passivist, "a Peace Federalist" he was called, while the students at the University favored the war. Groups of students committed several outrages on campus; buildings and trees were damaged and many of the large trees died, apparently from injury caused by the students. Some of them cut the hair from the tail of President Chapman's horse, took away a cart, took the gate off the hinges, and turned over a house, undoubtedly one of the "necessary houses" constructed for the President's House. A threat of tar and feathers for the "Torian" president frightened him still further. At the meeting of the trustees on 23 November, 1816, it was reported that President Chapman had "in solemn form resigned his office."

On Friday night, 26 January 1855, friends of the candidates for the posts of marshal and managers of the coming commencement ball were discovered to be holding "rebels" in South Building. After the young men were dispersed by the faculty, the faculty called on them in their rooms where they were found "to be more or less intoxicated." At a faculty meeting the following morning, four students who admitted to being drunk were suspended for three weeks. One reveler, David Settle Patrick, was found by the faculty "to be too much intoxicated this morning to come and answer the charge of being intoxicated last night." Yet the same Patrick, in 1869, became a member of the University faculty as a professor of Latin language and literature and bursar.

When the Union's General Atkins called upon President Swain on 19 April 1865, he met Swain's daughter, Eleanor. There occurred one of the legendary cases of "love at first sight" and in Chapel Hill on August 23, the daughter of the president of the University was married to the Union general whose forces occupied the town and campus. During the ceremony and for a total of three hours, University students tolled the South Building bell and afterwards they hanged President Swain and General Atkins in effigy. The University almost over night lost many of its old friends and gained a host of powerful enemies. There were some who denounced the University as a stronghold of "unreconstructed Rebels" who abhorred the idea of a return to the Union, and they applauded the apparent destruction of the University because it had been a "pestilential hotbed of slavocracy." On the other hand, to the "unreconstructed Rebels," the marriage of the president's daughter to a Union general indicated that the University was a center of Unionism and disloyalty, or at the very least of people guilty of fraternizing with the enemy.

The man with the top job at Carolina, Chancellor Christopher C. Fordham, III, is consumed by the Carolina tradition. He has been in office since 1980, coming from a two-tiered UNC position: vice-chancellor of health affairs and dean of the medical school. His installation address as chancellor was structured around Carolina traditions.

> It was not until well into this century that the University emerged as an important national citadel of scholarship. By then several important traditions had become its heritage. I shall mention only five . . . First, the University has deep roots in the soil and in the people of North Carolina . . . A second established tradition is the University's commitment to freedom—freedom of expression, freedom to dissent, freedom to be wrong . . . A third deeply ingrained tradition which we today celebrate is the University's steadfast commitment to scholarship, to excellence and achievement . . . A fourth tradition which we inherit is that of societal leadership and the tradition of important contributions from among our former students . . . The fifth great tradition of

the University is to be found in the special human spirit which exists here. The warmth of the human environment and the easy collegiality among faculty, students and townspeople have been noted and recorded through generations. . . .

In times past, this institution was for the education of white male youth. Today our student body is over 50% women and almost 8% black. And our potential for fuller service to society and greater productivity in the future has thereby been immeasurably enhanced . . . Can these great traditions of this institution and its service to North Carolina and the nation be sustained and advanced? The answer surely must be "yes," but the challenges are formidable. . . .

The man who gave this southernly, gentlemanly speech is just that. And he wears a white suit.

"What legitimizes us as a Public Ivy? Well, a number of things. First of all, our selectivity in admissions. The legislature complains that 90 percent of our students come from the top 10 percent of their high school graduating classes. But if we're a superb institution, and are selective, only the best can compete, right? Actually, our admissions staff knows the better high schools and will go down a bit further in class rank if the case is justified. In some cases, depth can count for more than breadth—take an outstanding football player, for example. But let me tell you, this college cannot be bought or bartered. No one interferes with admissions here. The youngsters must qualify. I like to think we follow the state motto: 'To be rather than to seem.' "

Chancellor Fordham is graceful. Although the suit is right, the acerbic Mark Twain is not there. One knows the strength and the commitment are there, but the delivery is gentle.

"Some other traditional strengths of ours would be the library, Number One in the Southeast, with its marvelous North Carolina Collection; our rankings in national faculty polls and our success in getting funding for research; the Ackland Art Museum which was established in 1958 but has already become a national force; the unique 330-acre Botanical Gardens; the University of North Carolina Press which has published about 2,000 scholarly books with more than 100 awards for excellence; and the Carolina Playmakers, prominent in their field since 1920. Summarizing it all, I would have to say that our distinguished faculty, our freedom of expression, and our soft human spirit capture the quality of Chapel Hill."

This man delivered more like a pastor than a chancellor. Carolina's leader walked around his formal but hardly elegant office and continued.

"Coming to Chapel Hill is an obsession with some people, you know.

And we certainly don't mind that. On leaving, almost all carry away a warm, sweet feeling. What alumni care more about a place than ours? Perhaps that says it all."

Several days after this discussion, the author received a letter from the chancellor. He wanted to underscore UNC's very good showing in recent rankings of graduate programs and also Carolina's high standing in faculty salaries "even in comparison with the Private Ivies." But he particularly wanted to emphasize that, contrary to what others might say, athletics are not allowed to overshadow other important elements of the university. He wrote:

> Although it is true that the athletic programs are generally excellent, it is also true that they are of very high character and quality, not only as to win/loss records but as to the character building factors as well. Our coaches are high type people who tend to put academics first and who generally feel a sense of security in their jobs without extraordinary emphasis on winning. The quality and character of our coaching staffs and our teams are reflected also in the general good nature and good sportsmanship of the students in their behavior as crowds. Although these things may be deemed of relatively little value by some, I hold them in high regard, as does the faculty. I believe that, in sum, the athletic programs contribute far more than simply a source of pride in winning. They are commensurate with the general thesis that we seek to achieve excellence in all our programs.

The Campus

Time has not favored the University of North Carolina's campus. Gone are the days when Carolina had well-ordered design, great expanses of flowering trees and lawn. The campus once drew high praise for its southern charm, the first university building constructed in America ("Old East," 1795), the botanical gardens, uniform Colonial and Georgian architecture, visible landmarks like the Old Well and Davie Poplar, and meticulous care of the grounds. Now, as a result of tripled size in three decades, Carolina has become a hodge-podge, a montage of architectural styles, many of the buildings significant, perhaps, if left to stand alone, but hardly so when cluttered together with few consolidating transitions. There are exceptions, such as the impressive, spaciously lawned Paul Green Theater. On 729 acres, there are 127 buildings, quite unequally spaced. And construction continues at a fast pace. For example, Carolina's library has just moved from an imposing old central campus structure to a new 400,000-square-foot granite-and-glass facility. With 2.6 million volumes, making it the largest library in the Southeast and the fifteenth largest in North America, that move was essential. Its Southern Historical Collection and North Carolina Collection are particularly significant.

The saddest aspect of the UNC campus is that the whole place looks a bit tattered, despite spanking new structures. Someone cut the maintenance budget, and it shows.

Academic Programs and Staff

The dean of the College of Arts and Sciences lives in a pine forest off campus in a house with a traditional front and a glassy-modern rear that can't be seen from the road. The dean is as crafty in speech as in house design.

"There are distractions so severe around Carolina that intellectualism often isn't allowed to emerge. The final blow was eliminating Saturday morning classes. Realistically, we're now in session from Monday morning through Thursday noon except on football weekends."

The dean, who stopped at Tulane, Harvard, and West Point en route to UNC, teaches history. Sitting in the traditional half of his house, he was enthusiastic, but balanced, in his comments.

"Yes, we have some large classes—very large—and it is normal for a freshman to experience only one 'real' professor in the first year. But if a student picks and chooses cleverly here, I don't know a university in America where an undergraduate could fare better. And believe me, we have students who are capable of picking and choosing cleverly. Our top 20 percent could compete effectively against anyone. And the best are rewarded. Good teaching is a function of research, and nearly all faculty teach both graduates *and* undergraduates and do research as well. The spin-off from one level to another is clear."

A little iced tea relieved the early summer afternoon heat. But the dean kept right on talking.

"The only major flaws I see at Carolina are that we depend too heavily on our state for funding, and in terms of student life, the social and living situations are too vertical—people just don't mix. Athletes with athletes, Greeks with Greeks, and so it goes. I don't quite know how we can correct that."

The dean was obviously excited about the "new curriculum," which had roots in a faculty study in the late seventies and is now in place.

"This is not a 'back to basics' program but 'back to fundamentals.' We all read and heard about Harvard's new general education requirements a few years back. UNC followed the Harvard example of a full curriculum review. The result is that new students must now satisfy requirements in one literature course, two history courses—one pre-1700—two natural science courses, one fine arts course, three semesters of a foreign language, and one year of math. There are, of course, broad choices to be made within these areas. I think we now have 'programmed flexibility.' "

The administrator/professor was forthright in what he called "one man's appraisal" of undergraduate departments:

Chemistry: we have the largest number of undergraduate majors in the country, and the department ranks in the top dozen in the nation.
Sociology: top 10 in the country.
Classics: top 5 in the country.
History: top 10 in the country. (By the way, history and chemistry have fought for years for domination of the intellectual life at the university.)
Political science: superb.
English: the department thinks it's top 10, but that's doubtful . . .
Foreign languages: there is not a great department in the country, including ours.
Religion: very interesting.
Philosophy: competent.
Psychology: top 20.
Computer science: basically a graduate division. The Research Triangle, you know, is about to make us the "Silicon Valley of the east."
Statistics: top 10.
Economics: mediocre.
Mathematics: top 20.
Physics and astronomy: re-grouping.
Zoology: lots of money.
Botany: strong.

The pitcher of iced tea was drained and so was the dean after his candid review.

The office of another top administrator, the dean of the School of Business Administration, is buried in the middle of campus. This dean is that always-a-collegian sort of fellow, nice looking, warm and fun, smart and accommodating. There seem to be a handful of this type on each campus, called upon mercilessly for committee assignments and up-front assistance to the administration. And so it has been with this man: once assistant to the chancellor, a member of the undergraduate admissions committee, and so on. His current office is swank, coldly redecorated to *look* like a successful businessman resides there—considerably more big city than the dogwood-and-magnolia campus. But the man himself could not be more cordial. Thanks to broad experience and the knack of articulating it, the dean provided a good overview of UNC.

"The atmosphere and quality of life here are captivating. It's hard to explain . . . Extraordinary personal attachments develop to Carolina. Part of it is just history. We are the oldest state-supported university in the country, you know. Our state has always had a tradition of strong support to higher education in general, but to Chapel Hill in particular. And, to some degree, that is explained by personal attachments—a sizable number of the North Carolina legislators who vote to fund this place are alumni of UNC.

"Although life here is somewhat segmented, the single rallying point is the sports program. Granted, we'd be a more intellectual community without it. Games have a way of pushing lectures, plays, and concerts aside. On the other hand, the people involved in sports are top-flight, particularly the coaches. They add quality to the community.

The dean swiveled in his silver chair. "But athletics are not the only rallying point. One example: During the sixties, it was the 'speaker ban controversy,' a unified reaction to Jesse Helms's attempt to muffle free speech on campus during explosive times.

"It was during that era, by the way, that 'business administration' was a very dirty phrase. My, how times change: it is not unusual today to have one in five undergrads wanting a major in business. 'Pragmatism' is the key word now and business obviously fits.

"In the early seventies, the changing mood at the faculty level meant a tough look at the intellectual content of our liberalized curriculum. Significant changes have since evolved, particularly in general education. The curriculum had become diffused. We're returning now to minimal common standards.

"But the standards, after a student's first two years, are uneven. It takes only a 1.75 to graduate from our General College, the two-year program every underclassman enters. But the more popular and demanding the major, the higher the grade point average for entry at the junior level. We in business require at least a 2.5. Even so, I wouldn't call our major intense. For one thing, classes are too large: 250 to 300, three times a week. That's the result of the incredibly sudden growth of interest in business after the Vietnam era. Our current provost wants to keep the so-called professional majors—journalism, education, business—in the broader liberal arts context. This means a professional rather than a vocational emphasis, and a more academic approach.

"But we're not the only strong undergraduate program here, by a long shot. Others that seem to me of real national significance are history, chemistry, math, sociology, and English. Across the academic spectrum we're strong. The honors-level student can have a field day here."

When top-flight students arrive at Chapel Hill, as the dean indicated, they need not sit idle. There is a Freshman Honors Program, a Sophomore Honors Program, and departmental honors programs. The Freshman Honors Program is by invitation only, to about 10 percent of the incoming class; other students with high grades at the end of each semester may be invited in. This program is thirty years old now, and features seminars for Chapel Hill's brightest and most motivated on topics such as medical ethics, the media, nineteenth-century American literature, anthropology of religion, current economic problems, dissent and free speech.

The coordinator of the Freshman Honors Program is a dynamic woman whose cramped, jammed office does not suffocate her enthusiasm for the honors project or for the university. She is a woman of tremendous accomplishment, having been named a full professor of English in creative writing *without* having earned a B.A. degree herself, not to mention graduate degrees. She is now also chair of the faculty.

"Honors students are easy. They're motivated, inventive. They never complain about homework, extra reading, or deadlines. They are better read than most and want to read more. We have spirited discussions in these groups because the students themselves are so good and so eager. The only real problem is getting some of the best freshmen to enter the program—they're afraid it will be difficult to get high grades in the seminars. Grades today mean everything, you know. But those who enter, stay. They find rewards quite beyond the grade."

On UNC matters beyond honors courses, the sharp-featured, animated professor was talkative.

"UNC is the state's intellectual mecca. We have been and will remain the classic introduction for North Carolina's young people to the world of ideas. And as important, we have made a liberal impact on a potentially conservative state. Chapel Hill has let in the fresh air. Look at the career of Frank Graham as president, the importance of Howard Ackerman to blacks in the South, of Paul Green to theater. The liberal spark is quiet, but it is certainly here."

The professor kept a lively pace. She leaned forward and talked intently.

"Although the honors program and a good many other programs here are strenuous and imaginative, I sometimes wonder if Carolina doesn't scare off the real intellectuals. All the trappings are here, including important social movements: the black movement is alive at Carolina now, and the women are actively testing some obviously sexist departments. But things get in the way . . . for example, athletics, and the 'Jesus' movement, which is very strong. We seem to have more closet-cases in religion than in sex."

In another cramped office with books on boxes, boxes on books, sits a math professor who has been at Chapel Hill fifteen years. He administers the general education program. The professor's purple shirt was some relief from the constant diet of light blue in Chapel Hill (bumper sticker: "If God is not a Tarheel, why is the sky Carolina blue?"). And his tennis racquet was ready—on top of the books, not under.

"Carolina is a curious dichotomy. Because we're a liberal center, we're both loved and hated. This is an agrarian state, remember. Chapel Hill has always been a high class place for a poor man's state. And that presents problems. But basically, there is a widespread feeling of pride in the university. Actually, we've always had a component of the far right here, but the left has a larger group of sympathizers. UNC is increasing its black population—that is because we want to, not because we have to."

The trim professor eyed his tennis racquet.

"Athletics are *really* important here—and so is tradition. But UVa is probably the last outpost of the true 'gentleman's university,' not Carolina. We're open, tolerant. Our biggest problem is just contending with size—keeping classes down. In math, we try to have no class over 35 *except* for requirement-filling introductory courses; they can run 100 to 125. After the first two years, students can really dig into this place."

All new students enroll in General College for the first two years. Following that, life grows complicated. As the admissions booklet indicates:

> When you enroll at UNC–Chapel Hill as a freshman, you enter the General College. You take five academic courses per semester (normally, five 3- or 4-hour courses), for a total of twenty academic courses during the freshman and sophomore years. Some of these courses may be exempted by Advanced Placement.
>
> Once you have completed General College requirements, you choose a major. Many departments (such as Nursing, Physical Therapy, Music) have limited enrollments and cannot permit all interested students as majors. *Admission to the General College, therefore, does not guarantee you a place in one of these areas.*

Here is the rather complicated maze students at UNC must walk through, with the assistance of a superb guide given all freshmen, "An Academic Self-Advising Manual" (100–101).

Chapel Hill takes considerable pride in its growth as a research center.

The campus recently ranked twenty-third among all United States universities, public and private, in federal obligations for research and development. And, according to a recent chancellor's annual report, UNC ranks nineteenth in the nation in the number of faculty serving on federal committees and commissions. That report also indicated that a recent poll of over 4,000 faculty members throughout the country put UNC in good favor. The group was asked to "name the five departments nationally in your discipline that have the most distinguished faculties." Chapel Hill was ranked among the top five by at least 10 percent of the respondents in four disciplines: English, foreign languages, mathematics and statistics, and sociology. Only thirteen universities (including six state universities) had a larger number of distinguished departments. Chapel Hill finished first in the Southeast.

But Carolina also takes pride in the fact that those who do the research almost always teach. The chancellor's report cites a professor of political science, as being typical.

" 'My salaries and promotions have been based on teaching and service to the University rather than strictly on research and publications. If I were at a comparable university, I probably wouldn't be where I am today. I'm the kind of person who thrives on personal contact and interaction, and for me, teaching is the most satisfying occupation I can think of. Research is important, but it's just not the favorite part of my occupational role. No matter how big the classes are, I never had a grader or graduate student for final exams. Through finals, I can judge how well the students are receiving, digesting and integrating what I'm trying to get across,' said the professor. 'Graduate students are in a more professional, occupational frame of mind. School is like an apprenticeship for them. But undergraduates have different objectives. They're here for growth and liberating ideas and ideals. The teacher is here to help them widen their horizons.' "

For the student who cares deeply about academics, Chapel Hill is ready, winning basketball teams or not. A southern brand of intellectualism and liberalism is there, just beneath the surface. One must dig a bit, but it is there.

Admissions

One member of the faculty admissions committee said, "The Carolina admissions office has a brown-bag approach to marketing—no matter how you hide it, its quality will become known if it's really good." He was right. Hard sell does not exist here. But a highly selective admissions situation does.

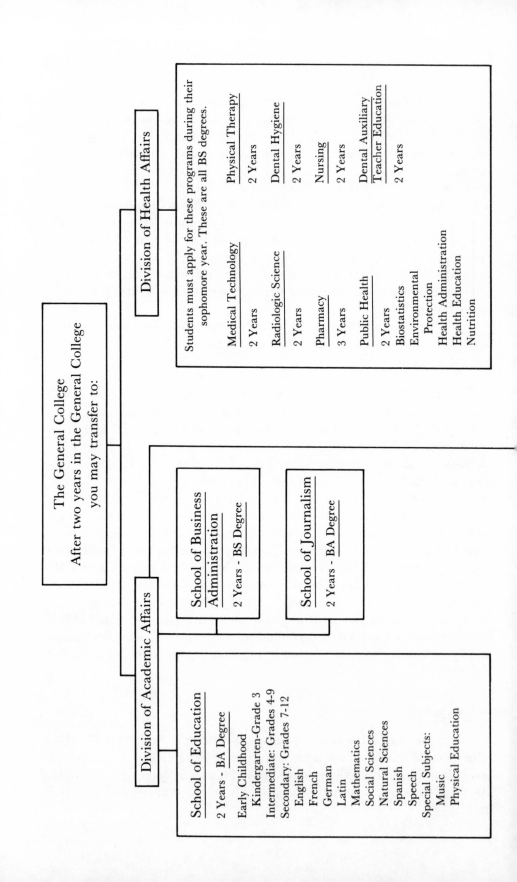

The General College
After two years in the General College
you may transfer to:

Division of Academic Affairs

School of Business Administration
2 Years - BS Degree

School of Journalism
2 Years - BA Degree

School of Education
2 Years - BA Degree

Early Childhood
Kindergarten-Grade 3
Intermediate: Grades 4-9
Secondary: Grades 7-12
English
French
German
Latin
Mathematics
Social Sciences
Natural Sciences
Spanish
Speech
Special Subjects:
Music
Physical Education

Division of Health Affairs

Students must apply for these programs during their
sophomore year. These are all BS degrees.

Medical Technology

2 Years

Radiologic Science

2 Years

Pharmacy

3 Years

Public Health

2 Years
Biostatistics
Environmental
Protection
Health Administration
Health Education
Nutrition

Physical Therapy

2 Years

Dental Hygiene

2 Years

Nursing

2 Years

Dental Auxiliary
Teacher Education

2 Years

College of Arts and Sciences
2 years

Humanities & Fine Arts

BA Degree

Art (History)
Art (Studio)
Classics
  Classical Archeology
  Classical Civilization
  Greek
  Latin
Comparative Literature
Dramatic Art
English
German
Linguistics
Music
Philosophy
Radio, Television &
  Motion Pictures
Religion
Romance Languages
  French
  Italian
  Portuguese
  Spanish

Slavic Lan-
  guages
  (Russian)
Speech Com-
  munication

BFA Degree

Art (Studio)

BM Degree

Music

Social Sciences

BA Degree

Anthropology
Economics
Geography
History

Physical
  Education
Political
  Science

Psychology
Recreation Ad-
  ministration
Sociology

Special Curricula

BA Degree

African Studies
Afro-American
  Studies
American Studies
Arts and Law
East Asian Studies
Interdisciplinary
  Studies

International Studies
Latin-American
  Studies
Peace, War & Defense
Public Policy Analysis
Russian & East Euro-
  pean Studies
Urban Studies

BS Degree

Administration of
  Criminal Justice
Industrial Relations

Natural Sciences

BA Degree

Astronomy
Biology
Botany
Chemistry
Geology

Mathematics
Physics
Psychology
Zoology

BS Degree

Biology
Botany
Chemistry
Geology
Mathematics
Mathematical Sciences
  Actuarial Sciences
  Applied Mathematics
  Computer Science
  Operations Research
  Statistics
Physics
Zoology

The admissions office at Carolina is slightly off the beaten track, in a beautiful wooded area, with space surrounding it. The building, called the Monogram Club, has a curious history: it was first a World War I U.S. Navy center, once a faculty club, once a training table hall for athletic lettermen, and now the admissions office. It has an inviting, warm atmosphere . . . except for the room where admissions staff members talk with candidates and parents. This hot-yellow-walled, crowded seminar room is under the main entry, more or less exposed to the outside, and is very dank.

A small group of eager students and parents awaited the middle-aged lady's pep talk on Chapel Hill. (Kids and parents *expect* college pep talks these days, as declining enrollments nationally force even the most selective schools to put their best foot forward.) But there was no pep talk. Instead, the pleasant lady asked if there were any questions regarding the university that she might answer. After an embarrassing silence, there were a few: "What's the notification date?" ("If you apply in the fall, one month from completed application; if you apply in the spring, you wait six to eight weeks"). "How many students can be housed on campus?" ("About half, with a lottery for rooms after the freshman year"). "What percentage are in fraternities and sororities?" ("About one quarter, but this is such a marvelous college town that you really don't need a fraternity or sorority for social life"). "How do students get around here?" ("Freshmen can't have cars, but you don't need one because our bus system is so good"). "Are there many rules and regulations in the dorms?" ("None—you are on your own"). "How tough is it to be admitted?" ("If you're from North Carolina, you have an 80 percent chance of getting in if you rank in the top 5 percent of your class with 800 or higher combined SATs; if you're lower in the class, even with 1000 SATs, your chances are only about 50 percent; if you're from out of state, you should have 1300 SATs and top 5 percent rank unless you are a superb athlete, musician, or actor"). "What is the toughest department here?" ("Probably chemistry, but there are others"). "Are classes large?" ("Yes, some are *very* large—it's according to the department and course level; our average class size is forty to sixty"). "Is there a special program for exceptional students?" ("Yes, our freshman honors program for one hundred and fifty students is absolutely superb; also, each department has an honors section for outstanding majors").

No more questions. Session ends. No rah-rah here, ex-letterman's club or not.

Carolina's prospectus or "viewbook" for admission candidates is definitely a brown-bagger. Small, featuring a few hackneyed student-on-bike-in-front-of-historic-building photos, the booklet does little to "sell" but does a good job of "tell," particularly regarding admissions specifics.

Students are advised to take as tough a courseload as possible in secondary school and are warned that analysis of courseload is extremely important to the committee on admissions. Minimum requirements for admission are listed as four years of English, three years of mathematics, (two algebra, one geometry), two years of one foreign language, one year of science, one year of social science, and at least five additional courses in languages, literature, mathematics, natural sciences, or social sciences. The booklet includes a helpful time chart of when applicants should do what, and the warning that UNC has a subjective approach to admissions decisions, so numbers do not tell all.

Although College Board achievement test scores are not required of candidates as they are at most selective universities, UNC pulls a clever trick to lure class rank out of hesitant secondary school counselors (who feel some applicants, particularly in small competitive high schools, can be hurt by divulging rank). If the secondary school will not provide rank, UNC requires that the student must take three achievement tests: English, foreign language, and one other.

Carolina's admissions booklet also contains two charts, unique among the selective colleges, to help applicants predict their chances of admission based on SATs and class rank.

UNC's director of admissions is an ex-Marine. One senses that rather quickly. His modern, functional office has no frills. Nor does he, in appearance or speech. This is a direct, no-nonsense fellow with a short-haired approach to admissions. Having been at Carolina for nineteen years, he has developed a system. The system functions well under his watchful eye and probably will remain the same for some time to come, changing times in the nation or not. And the system works, judging from Carolina's admissions health.

UNC's staff does not travel outside North Carolina. Instead, they concentrate on three hundred high schools within the state, visiting top feeder schools several times a year.

"We're fat, dumb, and happy," says the director with a wry smile. Carolina *is* fat with applications that roll in without a heavy recruitment effort. In deciding who gets in, the admissions staff has two processes—one for in-staters, one for out-of-staters.

On the first round of folder-reading, the staff instinctively finds about 3,000 who are irresistible and about 3,000 who are out of the running—all this based on the past few years' experience. The remainder of the folders go to second readers, the really tough cases to even more. Although numerical evaluations (1–5) are given for leadership, extracurricular activities, recommendations, and work experience, as well as the academic components, there is no pat formula for admission or rejection. Top-10-

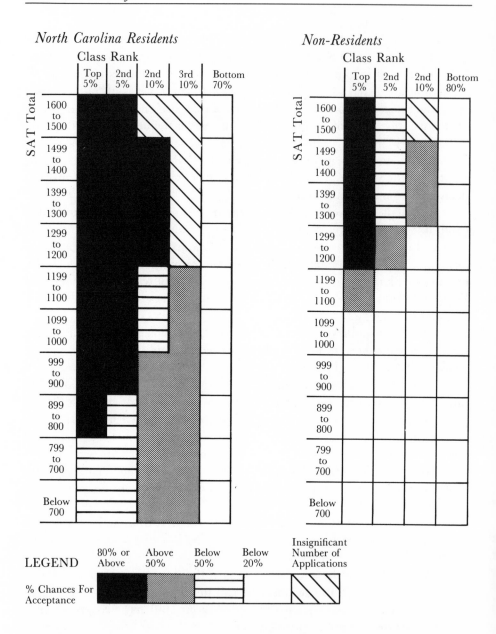

North Carolina Residents

Non-Residents

LEGEND

% Chances For Acceptance

| 80% or Above | Above 50% | Below 50% | Below 20% | Insignificant Number of Applications |

percent class ranking and 1100 SATs become the mean, with North Carolinians forgiven if they're slightly below the mark, out-of-staters rarely. Football players come in with the lowest profile, says the director, although minority students are considered "imaginatively" also. Anyone with below 400 on the SAT verbal is required to take a composition course at matriculation.

"Our applicant pool is hurt somewhat by the fact that we don't offer engineering or architecture—they're offered at State—but we're doing just fine. We really have to search only for blacks. The faculty complains very rarely about the student body, and the trustees complain only that we have too many women and should take more 'gentleman C' students," the director of admissions mused. "But let's face it: admissions is in good shape here."

Resources

North Carolina, as a state, is generous in support of higher education. It usually ranks among the top ten. For 1983–1984, North Carolina ranked ninth in the nation in overall appropriations for higher education, and seventh on the basis of per capita appropriation. UNC just raised $80 million privately and is en route to a $100 million goal (a separate $30 million has been raised for a recreational sports facility). Chapel Hill has a strong tradition of "the big giver."

One reason admissions is in good shape at Carolina is the presence and power of the Morehead Scholarship Foundation, a fabulous endowment from an alumnus with the goal of luring young scholars/leaders to Chapel Hill. The Morehead Scholarships were the first generous no-need grants in America for nonathletes, since copied by a wealth of millionaires at a wealth of alma maters. But none of the followers has become quite as prestigious as the original. Some call the Morehead the "Rhodes of the undergraduate world."

That is just what John Motley Morehead and others of his family intended. Motley graduated from Carolina in 1891 and became a chemical engineer. He was an expert on the manufacture of calcium carbide and/ or acetylene gas, inventor of an apparatus to analyze gasses (still used in schools today), cofounder of Union Carbide, an author, mayor of Rye, New York, and minister to Sweden under Herbert Hoover. "It is my ardent desire to perpetrate as far as possible the great service which The University of North Carolina has rendered to the State of North Carolina, the South and the Nation, and I can think of no better way of extending its influence and increasing its prestige than by attracting youth of superior character and ability to become students thereat," said he. And it works. The Morehead Scholarship provides full expenses at UNC, plus spending money. Now a fully financed summer intern program has been added. Prior to the freshman year, the internship is in outdoor leadership; prior to the sophomore year, public safety, including training with police departments in major United States cities; prior to the junior year, private enterprise; prior to the senior year, government; and following graduation, foreign study/

travel projects designed independently by each Morehead scholar. And it's all free!

The Morehead is so significant because the endowment has provided for so many. There have been over 1,600 scholars thus far; there are usually 240 Moreheads on campus at one time, plus 45 graduate "Morehead fellows." In a recent UNC graduating class, one-third of the Morehead scholars were Phi Beta Kappa. Other Moreheads in that class were the university's senior class president, "Jason of the Golden Fleece," chairman and vice-chairman of the Men's Honor Court, president of the student union, chairman of the student supreme court, president of the Old Well, President of the Campus Y, and five winners of special chancellor's awards for outstanding service to the university. What's more, nearly all of the Rhodes scholars at UNC have been Moreheads, including America's first black woman Rhodes, named in 1979.

Competition for the Morehead Scholarship is, of course, severe. The initial provision of who could compete brought instant national prestige to the program. Not only could all North Carolina schools nominate candidates but so could twenty-six of the nation's blue-blood Eastern independent schools, where college prestige labels are often invented. So Andover and Exeter and St. Paul's and Groton and Woodberry Forest and the others started scrambling for Moreheads along with all the little rural North Carolina high schools. The free ride in North Carolina often tempted starry prep school seniors, even though admitted to Yale. The Morehead Scholarship, perhaps more than any other one element, made "Carolina" a household word among the savvy regarding selective college admissions.

Mr. Morehead did not leave his family name on scholarships alone. A magnificent building on campus combines his planetarium, where United States astronauts are trained, with the Genevieve Morehead Art Collection and the Scholarship Foundation. And the famous Bell Tower at UNC, providing the logo of the university, was given by Mr. Morehead and his cousin Rufus Patterson.

There are other rich scholarship foundations at UNC. More than four hundred top students are on James M. Johnston Scholarships, and the Joseph E. Payne Scholarships lure outstanding black students from North Carolina.

Like other state universities, however, UNC will have to find more Moreheads, Pattersons, Johnstons, and Paynes to build the private coffers as public monies decline. But Chapel Hill clearly has a head start, one more aspect of its "tradition of excellence."

A student tour guide at Carolina suggested that all visitors, before leaving the area, should walk through the old graveyard, now surrounded by the jumbled campus. One inscription captured the contagious spirit of Chapel Hill:

> I was a Tar Heel born
> And a Tar Heel bred
> And here I lie
> A Tar Heel dead.
>   Born June 2, 1896
>   And Still Here, 1980.

University of Texas

Austin

Remember when "Made in Japan" meant "cheap," "just-a-copy-of-the-real-thing," "buyer beware"? No longer: Sony, Toyota, Nikon and their quality-conscious colleagues changed all that. But images die hard in America. Consider "Texan," for example. "Big," "brash," "nouveau riche," "prime-time soap-opera," "fashion boots," and "serious football" come to mind, connotations that have been around for years.

It's not fair. Although images stick, realities change. Down in the Southwest, the University of Texas at Austin has quietly been building the forces to become Ivyer than Ivy. If this kind of institutional happening were based in Massachusetts or Pennsylvania or even in California, America would nod with approval. But in *Texas?*

The question at this point is not whether the University of Texas is first class. The question is whether the nation will notice and accept it.

True, there is ammunition for the old-image diehards: ads in the UT alumni magazine for leather-bound "Cook 'em Horns" cookbooks at $100 each, baguette-diamond UT rings for $795, and buy-a-condominium-in-Austin-for-your-child-at-college ($40,000–250,000) advertisements. And one traditional Texas legacy does "hang true" in this story: UT's climb to the top can be unabashedly attributed to money, big money. But "nouveau riche" just no longer fits. The University of Texas has been wealthy for some time now. It has been spending on a vision that seems to have come of age.

"Whenever a distinguished scholar came here to lecture or teach, we used to put out our best linen and get all a-twitter, like a young socialite," confesses the dynamic director of UT's progressive Plan II curriculum, an honors program for outstanding undergraduates. "Not so anymore. Today it's *expected* that the best will come here."

University of Texas at Austin

1) Size of Student Body

Undergraduate __36,676__ Graduate __10,955__ Total __47,631__

2) 1983 Freshman Class Profile

Class Size __5,493__ % Men __51__ % Women __49__
Percent of Applicants Admitted __72__
Average SATs: Verbal __520__ Math __515__
High School Class Rank: Top Tenth __46__ % Top Quarter __90__ %
   Geographical Distribution (% of class):
In-State __88__% Middle Atlantic __2__ % New England __1__ %
West __2__ % Middle West __2__ % South __91__ %
Foreign __2__ %
Minority Students __18__ % of Class
Financial Aid __57__ % of Class

3) Retention of Students

__38__ % of freshmen graduate in four years
__55__ % of freshmen graduate in five years

4) Ten Most Popular Majors of Graduating Seniors, 1983

1. Accounting
2. Finance
3. Marketing
4. Journalism
5. Electrical Engineering
6. Advertising
7. Radio-TV-Film
8. Government
9. Nursing
10. Management

5) The Financial Picture (1982–83)

Annual Campus Budget	$ 386,518,462
1983–84 Tuition and Fees for State Residents	$ 420
1983–84 Tuition and Fees for Out-of-State Residents	$ 1,506

Revenues

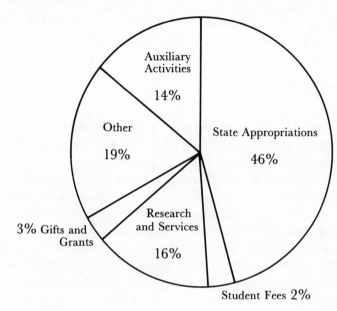

Expenditures

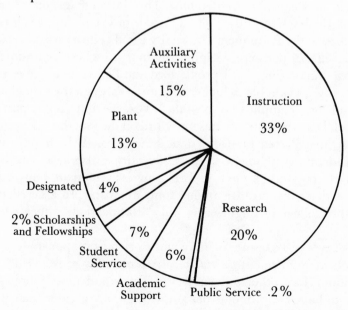

The best are going there, and many to stay. Nobels. Harvard and Princeton faculty. "They're recruiting physicists like football players!" a faculty member at MIT complained. The response, from UT's vice-president: "It is quite true. If MIT learned the technique, they'd have a better football team."

Resources

The wealth, quite simply, comes largely from oil. At UT's founding in 1881, the state donated 2.1 million acres of not-very-promising land in nineteen counties of barren West Texas to provide the new school some revenue. Little was gained from the land in grazing leases. But in 1923 the "Santa Rita One" oil rig in Reagan County blew. The oil from that land has gushed Texas to the top of the nation's endowment ladder. The *Alcalde*, UT's alumni magazine, reports: "Aside from getting bigger, the University is also getting richer. Barron's financial weekly has called the Permanent University Fund, which UT shares with Texas A&M, the nation's largest endowment fund in higher education. On the books, Harvard's is bigger at $1.7 billion, but the Permanent University Fund, now at $1.5 billion, includes only oil and gas royalties and *not* a realistic market value of 2.1 million acres of land."

UT takes its oil wealth for granted now. The alumni magazine carried a small notice in the back recently: "The 71st sale of UT oil and gas leases added $17,842,000 to the Permanent University Fund. The leases on 72,887 acres averaged $224.79 per acre, yielding the fourth highest figure in the 46 years of lease auctioning." Oil profits feed the Permanent University Fund. Interest only is available to higher education through the "Available University Fund" via complicated formulae. Texas A&M (not a part of the University of Texas system) creams one-third off the top; the UT system collects the rest, distributed first for "debt service" on PUF bonds, and second for "academic enrichment at the University of Texas at Austin."

Surprisingly, the public envy of UT's huge Permanent University Fund prompts a defensive posture among some at Austin. In a newsletter published by the College of Engineering, this "clarification" appeared:

> The University of Texas at Austin is not as rich as it appears to be. In fact, in endowment *per student,* the University ranks 24th in the nation. Two other universities in Texas and three more in the South have endowments per student that are greater than UT Austin's. The Permanent University Fund is quite large, but its proceeds are widely spread . . . Certainly a university with a $100 million endowment and 2000 students is much better off

than another with a $200 million endowment and 20,000 students. The UT and Texas A&M endowment, composed primarily of the PUF, is the second largest university endowment in the U.S. . . . and amounts to an endowment per student of $16,379 to earn the rank of 24. Yale, whose endowment is less than half of the amount of the Texas endowment, ranks fifth, with $68,637 per student . . . other institutions which have greater endowments per student than UT/Texas A&M include the California Institute of Technology (No. 1 with $109,791 per student); Rice University of Texas (No. 2 with $94,442 per student); and Harvard University (No. 1 in total endowment but No. 3 in endowment per student).

Whether UT has the first or second largest university endowment in America, and regardless of method of ranking, the institution is rich. Oil is not the only resource. Texas, as a state, ranks third in the nation in percentage of tax revenues allocated for higher education. UT shares heavily in that largesse but complains loudly that the legislature will not approve a long overdue increase in tuition which would provide even greater revenues. Also, UT alumni aren't poor. Their gifts, together with private gifts from foundations and corporations, are the basis of hope for the Centennial Endowment Program which plans to create 300 new endowments: 100 endowed faculty positions, 100 endowed student scholarships and fellowships, and 100 endowment funds for "a variety of other academic purposes."

Money speaks, and no one in Austin is shy about talking. A consolidated sampling of what UT brags about:

Faculty: The UT faculty includes the winner of the 1977 Nobel Prize in chemistry, the winner of the 1979 Nobel Prize in physics, the winner of the 1967 Pulitzer Prize in history, fourteen members of the National Academy of Sciences, and fourteen members of the National Academy of Engineering.

Quality of Academic Programs: The University of Texas at Austin is the only southwestern member of the Association of American Universities, often called the fifty most distinguished universities in the United States and Canada. UT leads all institutions in the South in the number of doctoral degrees awarded. A recent assessment of doctoral education ranked four UT Austin programs (linguistics, German, Spanish, and botany) among the top five in the United States. Four other programs (population biology, civil engineering, classics, and geology) were among the top ten. Graduate professional programs in education, business, and law also rank in the top ten among United States public institutions.

Library Resources: The University of Texas at Austin has the eighth largest academic library in the United States, with almost five million volumes. The Benson Latin American Collection is one of the most important libraries on Latin America in the world. UT's law library is the fifth largest academic law library in the nation. The university owns one of only five complete copies of the Gutenberg Bible in the United States. The Lyndon B. Johnson Library, operated by the federal government, was the first presidential library placed on a university campus.

Computer Resources: UT Austin is No. 1 in the nation among 107 institutions cited as exemplary for their use of computers in teaching and learning.

Graduates: Rhodes scholarships have been awarded to twenty-one UT Austin graduating seniors. UT Austin has produced more than half the world's Ph.D.'s in petroleum engineering. The College of Education at UT Austin has graduated more community college presidents and deans than any other university program in the nation. UT Austin's alumni are chief executive officers at seventeen of the nation's major corporations. Six Texas governors graduated from UT Austin, as did the president of Peru.

Size is another strong resource at Texas. UT Austin has the third largest student body in America, following Ohio State at Columbus and

Enrollment by Colleges

College	Undergraduate	Graduate	Total
Architecture & Planning	428	225	653
Business Administration	9,930	1,283	11,213
Communication	3,517	462	3,979
Education	2,157	1,331	3,488
Fine Arts	6,096	1,182	7,278
Law		1,561	1,561
Liberal Arts	6,937	1,460	8,397
Library & Information Science		166	166
Natural Sciences	5,921	1,320	7,241
Nursing	860	218	1,078
Pharmacy	677	88	765
Public Affairs		177	177
Social Work	169	162	331
Total UT Austin	38,111	10,034	48,145

the University of Minnesota at Minneapolis. In two decades, UT Austin's student body has grown 116 percent to over 48,000 combined undergraduates and graduates. (In the same period of time, university employees doubled. The entire university community of students, faculty, staff, and families now has a population of over 90,000, larger than the city of Galveston.)

During the last twenty years, UT has expanded its physical plant enormously to accommodate the dramatic growth in population: it completed 101 building projects at a total cost of $313,173,000, increasing the gross area of campus buildings by 133 percent.

But even in Texas, bigger is not always considered better. With bulging classrooms, inadequate housing, and a reluctance to expand the teaching faculty of approximately 4,000, UT has finally decided to cut back the student body to between 45,000 and 46,000, with a goal of 35,000 to 36,000 undergrads, 5,000 new freshmen, and 13,000 new transfers. The deceleration will be accomplished largely through tightening admissions standards for undergraduates.

Admissions

This is UT's weakest area. Rather than tamper with the populist notion of full access to higher education, the flagship campus of the UT system has just grown and grown. But as the provincial has given way to the cosmopolitan in faculty and research and world-class facilities, so it must in student body if UT is to reach its goal of "first class" and to win its self-proclaimed "war on mediocrity."

For the past ten years, UT has been moderately selective for out-of-state students, barely selective for in-staters. Newly established admissions standards will still not bring the undergraduate student body in line with the quality of Texas's faculty and facilities, but the tightening represents a major step forward and all that is politically possible at this time. The up-dated admissions requirements:

> *Texas Residents:* Acceptance of all students in the top 25 percent of their high school graduating class. Those in the lower three-quarters of the graduating class must score 1000 or higher on the SAT or score 27 or higher on the American College Testing examination.

> *Non-Texas Residents:* Acceptance of students in the top one-quarter of the graduating class, with an SAT score of 1000 or higher or ACT score of 27 or higher. Those in the lower three-quarters of their class are not eligible for admission.

UT has traditionally been kind to even the Texas residents who do *not* qualify minimally, offering them "provisional admission" with the stipulation that the students enter summer session immediately as a "bridge" to freshman year. Whether that generosity can continue in the face of growing demand and stiffened entry requirements is yet to be seen. Meanwhile, popular divisions and colleges within UT Austin—architecture and business, to name two—are so impatient with overdue admissions reform that they have taken matters into their own hands, upping requirements for entry to the major in the junior year, or in the case of architecture, to the freshman class.

Another important dimension of UT undergraduate admissions reform is strengthening requirements for courses taken in high school. The faculty has recommended the following prerequisites: four years of language arts, two years of foreign language, three years of mathematics, three years of social studies, two years of science, one-half year of fine arts, and one and a half years of electives.

UT has launched an aggressive campaign to lure the brightest students—"the *best*," as they say at Texas. And once again, wealth helps. Some say the game plan "to become first class" is now reaching its final stages: with faculty and physical development well advanced, it is time to work on the student body. So, here come the bucks . . .

First, there has been an attempt to get to the top of the nation's charts in National Merit Scholarships. (To many admissions professionals, this goal is of dubious distinction. National Merit scholars are picked with a near-total emphasis on standardized test scores [SATs], not on accomplishments in the classroom or in the extracurricular zone, nor on motivation or other personal strengths. Also, the selection formula applies different cutoffs to different states to assure geographical representation; thus, a winner in low-cutoff Mississippi might not have had a chance if that student had been from high-cutoff New York.)

In 1982, UT Austin enrolled 361 National Merit scholars. That placed them ninth nationally in total number of Merits, a considerable accomplishment. In the South, they placed third, surpassed only by Rice (505) and Georgia Tech (404). But there are two types of Merits. There are the prestigious Merits sponsored by corporations, whose winners can attend *any* institution in America; and there are Merits sponsored by institutions themselves, whose winners *must* attend the sponsoring college. The most selective private colleges sponsor no Merits themselves. Even without that built-in assurance of a good showing, Harvard, Yale, and Princeton annually rank at the top of the nation in total National Merit enrollees. A few of the other highest ranking colleges and universities have sponsored a majority of their own Merits. Texas is one, with 76 percent of their Merit scholars financed by UT money—a little gamy, but Texas has made the honor list, nonetheless.

There is more to UT's campaign to lure "the best." The almost nine hundred high school juniors in Texas who score high enough on the Preliminary SATs to become probable National Merit semifinalists all get a warm letter from President Flawn saying "Because we believe that academic talent deserves to be recognized and because we want you to think seriously of us as you make your academic plans, we are awarding you a University Scholarship in the amount of $1000 for your freshman year at the University of Texas at Austin. Over the coming months, you will be made aware of other scholarship opportunities for which you may be eligible . . . for instance, if you are in the top 5 percent of your high school graduating class, you may be nominated by your high school for one of the Ex-Students Association awards of $10,000 over the four undergraduate years." This is sent to a student before he or she even *applies*, not to mention is admitted or committed to matriculate there!

Also, a splashy "Honors Colloquium" has been launched for this same crowd, held in the summer before the students' high school senior year. The three-day event displays some of UT's academic stars for full and personal viewing, career counseling, discussion of timely events, and social unforgettables which travel from one new UT superhall to the next. And, of course, each student gets an orange Izod shirt, orange being UT's school color.

Money to improve the admissions picture is not limited to no-need scholarship campaigns. The director of admissions, a motherly, soft-spoken administrator who trained in financial aid at an assortment of institutions, has been making the most of a $300,000 grant to create a "Model Admissions Project," a consumer-acceptable name for a fully computerized admissions office. The system, designed to speed the processing of a candidate's credentials ("The $300,000 has made it possible to reduce response time from weeks and months to days and hours," says one vice-president) is also intended to make the process "seem less bureaucratic." In a chatty newsletter to high schools that is issued quarterly, the director of admissions tells counselors to "throw out all of the old UT application forms. When a student applies by the *application* method, it bogs down our new computerized processing and slows response time to the student." With the new method, the formal receipt of College Board scores starts the "application" process moving, even though there is no application at all. The high school transcript with the student's birthdate, middle initial, and Social Security number completes the data needed to pump into the big machine. The computer does the letters to candidates, emitting the appropriate "admit" or "no admit" response.

The admissions office is under the tower, on the ground floor of UT's vast administration building. The director's desk and chair sit atop a Texas orange rug. The director has the manner of the financial aid officer she has been—a technician, wanting to improve the way the numbers flow in the system. "Our goals at this point are to (1) control growth, (2) enhance the academic quality of entering students, and (3) increase the minority population." The director enthusiastically approves of the upgrading of admissions standards, speaking to goals 1 and 2; work is underway, with appropriate funding, to move on goal 3. Of the total UT population, approximately 12 percent are minorities, with Hispanics the largest group. And UT ranks thirteenth among universities in America in the percentage of foreign students enrolled.

Several of the admissions office recruiters are Mexican-Americans. They agreed perceptions of UT throughout the state were extremely mixed. "It's a state school, so anyone can go there—right?" is a common response in rural areas; "Bubba went there, so I will too" among the old-boy crowd. To most people in the state, rich means good, so UT qualifies. But to many minority students there is real fear of racism at the university because of the wealth—will the nontraditional, minority, poor student be welcome? "Some kids don't fear racism only because they don't know what it is—until they enter UT," said one Latino recruiter. But no one was quite willing to say whether UT's "racism" was perception or reality.

Actually, Mexican-Americans (the term "Chicano" is not popular here) have been attending UT for years, although housing was segregated until the sixties. Blacks made no impact on UT until the early seventies, when top-rated black football players were successfully recruited for the Longhorns. Although all the world seemed to know the 1977 Heisman Trophy winner, Earl Campbell, and associated this great black athlete with the University of Texas, the fact is that UT Austin has a miserably low black student representation of 2 to 3 percent.

All that may change soon, if a mandate from the Regents takes hold. An ambitiously funded Educational Opportunity Assessment Project is underway, surveying parents, counselors, community leaders, and students on questions such as "Why don't minority students come to UT?" "If they get there, what are the primary reasons for leaving before graduation?" The project is research-oriented, but the Regents expect its findings to pave the way for the enrollment of 450 to 500 more blacks, and considerable increases in Mexican-Americans, within several years. Although the project directors feel a "critical mass" of Mexican-Americans has been achieved on campus, combining students, faculty, and staff, the challenge is achieving the same for blacks. The commitment, the personnel, and the money seem to be there. Special scholarships for minority students through the

National Achievement Program and the Texas Achievement Award Program (the latter has grown from a 1975 commitment of $240,000 to $1.9 million in 1982, affording 350 new awards each year) are expected to increase minority enrollment, and probably will. UT is backing talk with movement in this key area, unlike many other leading colleges and universities who have the will but not the way.

The Campus

A Mexican-American senior man and a white sophomore woman proved to be superb tour guides. She was eighteen going on thirty-two—giving balanced, restrained comments on issues—a blonde, articulate, native Texan, somehow more Vassar than UT. He was the extroverted enthusiast, a Longhorn through and through, a top scholar, and convincing in his assurance that being Mexican-American had not meant being second-class *anything* for him during his college years—"Well, maybe it kept me out of the fraternity system, but who needs that in a place this vibrant?" Their tour was extensive and satisfying. Both were wild about the place but eager nonetheless to hear what was happening elsewhere. These two Texans could not be labeled "provincial."

The UT main campus is reassuring. Forty-eight thousand students in one place suggests "city" more than "campus." But in slightly more than 300 acres, UT has built a compact compound of 125 buildings that, although architecturally bland, create a welcoming atmosphere, a good feeling."Spanish Renaissance" is the prevailing architectural style, they say. Surely a Neiman-Marcus designer told them that congestion would look better if the color remained constant. It is: nearly everything is adobe tan or white with designer "earth accents" of browns, grays, and, of course, orange. Everything blends. And there is grass—surprising stretches of it (one central plot was just replanted at a cost of $2 million)—and tree-lined streets, and magnificent fountains that work! The whole thing somehow comes together into a cohesive unit, not overpowering despite the volume of buildings. The best tribute to the cohesion is that students are given only ten minutes between classes.

Scattered about the grounds are a few structures that are memorable, more often because of size rather than aesthetics. The famous 307-foot Tower, symbol of UT, is floodlit in orange from top to bottom whenever the Longhorns win a football game, when any other local team wins a championship, or for a big happening: winning a Nobel or a Heisman, or to celebrate a significant occasion or anniversary. Almost next door to the Tower (atop Main) is the Academic Center, an impressive undergraduate library with the latest in audiovisuals and closed-circuit television, and some curious special collections including a full-scale replica of Erle Stanley Gardner's entire study, bursting with bizarre memorabilia and his incoherent ramblings on tape of what it's all about. *The* library, the Perry-Castaneda, shaped like the state of Texas (!) and opened in 1977, is named for the first black on the faculty and the professor who developed UT's prominent Latin American collection. The Perry-Castaneda Library, which cost $21.7 million, can hold 3.2 million volumes and is dazzling in Indiana limestone. The Frank C. Erwin, Jr., Special Events Center, better known as "the Drum," is billed as the best multipurpose arena in the nation. It throbs with basketball much of the time, but it can also accommodate from 2,000 to 18,000 people, depending on the configuration, for concerts, ice shows, circuses, Broadway shows, and symphonies. The Erwin Center is named for the powerful Texas politician who was key to UT's dramatic physical expansion and who, some say, "still runs UT from the grave."

The Texas Memorial Stadium, a World War I memorial and home of the Longhorns, is overwhelming. It was completed in 1924 and has been expanded again and again; it now holds 80,000. Its decks go straight up, rather than out. It is an awesome structure, housing awesome scores. Another symbol of little UT restraint is the mammoth and totally impressive Swimming Center, opened in 1977; it holds 800,000 gallons of water, facilities for every imaginable water sport, underwater viewing windows, and generous spectator seating. The LBJ Library is big too, sitting somewhat by itself with spacious grounds around it; it has nine floors, an exact replica of the White House Oval Office, a roof heliport, extensive libraries, and, of course, political celebrity Barbara Jordan. (Lady Bird Johnson is an Austin citizen and maintains keen interest in the library.)

But *the* powerhouse new facility is the Performing Arts Center, adjacent to the new College of Fine Arts. The center is a five-building complex which includes a 700-seat Recital Hall, a 400-seat Opera Lab Theater, and a Drama Workshop Building. The concert hall seats 3,000 and is magnificent. This facility alone, built at a cost of $43 million and often compared to Washington's Kennedy Center, has convinced more than a few that Texas means business in becoming a cultural hub.

The most fun building on campus—and yes, educational too—is the Harry Ransom Center. It houses a substantial art collection, but it also contains Mr. Ransom's personal collection, which started with British manuscripts but evolved toward the obscure: John Foster Dulles's living room furniture; Harry Houdini's manacles; Greta Garbo posters; several hundred "important" Bibles, 2,500 pieces of unusual antique equipment including detectives' cameras hidden in watches and canes; four million photographs; the original handwritten manuscript of Evelyn Waugh's *Brideshead Revisited;* a self-portrait of e. e. cummings; art works by authors Henry Miller, Dylan

Thomas, T. H. White, D. H. Lawrence, and Tennessee Williams; English silver; original scores by the Gershwins, Chopin, and Cole Porter; and letters from Verdi, Wagner, Schubert, and Beethoven. The Ransom Collection curators have the reputation of being a bit casual in keeping track of their riches: recently several Rembrandt sketches were reported missing, but they were soon located on faculty office walls, having been "temporarily loaned out" but not recorded.

Within the approximately half-mile-square confines of the campus, more buildings are going up: a $25 million Engineering Center ("Teaching Center II"), two Architecture School renovations tagged at $16 million, a law school addition, a major redoing of the multisport Freshman Field and Intramural Field, and an $8 million Pharmacy Building addition. And that's not all: not yet in the air but planned are a $20-million classroom facility; a "front door" to the campus that will include parking lots, street rearrangements, and the renovation of an old Custer family home (at $3 million); plus a Fine Arts Museum "to unify the University's major art holdings."

One wonderful historic tidbit: when the Confederate Army's Major George Littlefield donated the first acreage in Austin for the university, there were stipulations: no statue ever erected on campus could face north, the main entrance to the campus could not face north, and no building could have the word "north" in its name. Littlefield's conditions have not been abused.

It is easy to forget Texas's maligned image while wandering the UT campus, seeing firsthand the superb libraries and collections and the obvious commitment to research and the arts, and realizing that in Texas there is history beyond the Alamo.

History and Tradition

UT has been busy reminding itself of history via a three-year Centennial Celebration, including a blue-ribbon Centennial Commission's comprehensive review through eight committees of what the university still must do to become first class.

That the University of Texas has come this far is surprising, given the struggle one hundred years ago to get the school off the ground. The Civil War and the immediate post-war political conflicts and poverty deferred public ambition to develop higher education in Texas. It was the Constitution adopted in 1876 that enshrined the words "provide for . . . a university of the first class," proving that Mirabeau B. Lamar, president of the Republic of Texas, was not alone in his vision. That constitution provided for a Permanent University Fund.

But prior to that, some legislators had registered considerable objections to the founding of the university. They deserve a smiling encore:

> I protest against the whole thing as wrong, as monstrous. . . . What, half a million dollars for one or two universities, before we have built two school houses! . . . If put on foot before the people call for it, a university, not being wanted by the public, or properly constituted, will be sure to set itself up as a secret, malignant enemy of the people.
>
> Senator Samuel Augustus Maverick, Bexar County, 1855

> I am no advocate of the University system. . . . Universities are the ovens to heat up and hatch all manner of vice, immorality and crime.
>
> Senator James Armstrong, Jefferson County, 1856

President Mirabeau Lamar, at the Third Congress of the Republic of Texas in 1838, had predicted this fury:

> I pity, from my innermost soul, the few carping place-hunters who periodically ride to the halls of legislation on the necks of little children, promising the paradise of elementary education for mediocrity, and yet sneering at the great work of university education by the state for those whether many or few, whom God hath marked for leadership.

Other legislators were more favorably inclined toward the university, provided UT would accommodate the many, not the few.

> But to the question—who, sir, is to be benefitted by this outlay? A privileged few, in the enjoyment of wealth and prosperity? Or the hard-working, barefooted, wool-hatted, coperas breeches, one gallowsed, double-fisted, road working and tax-paying masses. Are these the beneficiaries? If so, I will support the bill.
>
> Representative Burnett, 1858

And there were the proud, voicing the Texas of popular image:

> Yes, sir, when these limbs of mine shall totter from the infirmities of age, I want to lean upon my boys, and be enabled, in the

fullness of a joyous heart to say, these are Texas made, Texas reared and *Texas educated*.

> Representative Williams Kittress of
> Grimes, Walker and Madison Counties, 1857

Finally, it was done. The 1876 constitutional imperative resulted in an "Act to Establish the University of Texas":

That there shall be established in this State, at such locality as may be determined by a vote of the people, an institution of learning, which shall be called and known as the University of Texas. The buildings shall be substantial and handsome but not loaded with useless and expensive ornamentation.

In 1881, Governor Oran Roberts gave the official Populist charge:

Nor will the benefits of the University and its branches be confined to the sons of the wealthy few. By no means will that be so. Place the facilities of a higher education before the people of the State, make it a reality, make it complete and cheap by a splendid endowment, and youths all over this broad land who catch the inspiration of high native talent in our common schools, will, if necessary, struggle up through poverty and through adversity by labor and by perseverance, until they will stand in the front ranks of the most gifted and favored in the halls of learning, and afterwards will adorn every sphere of life with their brilliant accomplishments and practical usefulness. So it has been in other countries, and so it will be here.

No problem here. The founding fathers would be proud of the broad representation today. Although the public relations people at UT fret about kids from "the better families" still wanting to "go East" to college, the University of Texas at Austin is the goal for many of the students at the wealthiest, and perhaps the best, secondary schools in the state—Hockaday, St. John's, Highland Park High School, for example. More important, although some teenagers and their parents prefer that agricultural/mechanical, gritty country-folk image of A&M, and a few wonder if minorities can be happy at UT, socioeconomic differences abound in Austin. The primary reason: UT is the least expensive flagship state university in America to attend. A recent UT Austin freshman class self-reported family incomes as follows:

Income	All Freshmen Responding (In Percentages)
Under $6,000	2.3
$6,000–11,999	7.3
12,000–17,999	10.4
18,000–23,999	12.5
24,000–29,999	13.3
30,000–39,999	19.9
40,000–49,999	12.3
50,000 or over	22.1

Student Life

Students at UT are diverse—in background, in appearance, in point of view. At this huge place, it is easy to assemble a group of undergraduates who do not know each other. In doing just that, two themes kept emerging: without prompting, individual students often referred to the academic rather than the social component of the university; although positive about their UT experience, the students had pondered the weaknesses and were able to articulate them sensitively.

What few words, in their view, best summarize UT?

"Diversity!" a fellow from the town of Temple, a journalist, blond, wearing shorts and a T-shirt, stated firmly. "Well, now, wait a minute," urged a precise young man in coat and tie from Mississippi, who had attended prep school in Georgia, was a humanities major and a concert pianist, and had performed with the local Austin Symphony. "Wouldn't it be more on target to say that we have *segmented* diversity? We have people who are 'different' off in little corners by themselves, consoling and nurturing each other, while the majority in the mainstream are predominantly conservative and not particularly open-minded." The group, not quite comfortable with how this session would evolve with the assertive pianist present, conceded that he was probably on target.

"Powerful," piped up the pianist again. "God knows we have bidding power for faculty, for jocks, for whatever we choose to buy. Our problem is that sometimes we don't know how to exercise that power gracefully. But we do have 'power'—and don't you just love to say the word?"

A soft-spoken, blonde coed, elegantly dressed, mislabeled earlier as a certain Susie Sorority, said, "Much of the 'power' here is in the classroom. I remember my marvelous honors English course as a freshman. And in two years of business courses, I've only had *assistant* professors twice. The best professors here usually teach." Most agreed, although the liberal arts division students felt one had to "beat the system" to get the better teachers, smaller classes. "Register for more classes than you can take, just to have a choice after you know which ones you're in . . . There is a frustration of the masses here, but it's easy to cut through," said a seemingly shy (obviously *not* at registration, however) young woman from Houston in bright turquoise.

"We think we can apply our power to getting a top student body now," offered a Mexican-American woman who sometimes helped out in the admissions office. "*All* my friends are here on big scholarships . . . And this new Honors Colloquia—Well, I don't know if it will work in convincing the best students that they should be at UT."

"It *won't* work," snapped the pianist, "if it is purely manipulative. But we have to make more of the best students in the state and the nation aware of UT. Merit scholarships, offered for achievement rather than financial need, are OK. We've given them to athletes for years—why not to scholars? We're just trying to *grow* to respectability. The judges will have to forgive our clumsiness now and then."

"Stimulating," said the president of the marching band, a biology student from a small town in southeast Texas. "For example, the people who show up on the mall outside the Union each day to sell their wares, material or spiritual, are incredibly stimulating. And we have some real characters in the classroom, both students and teachers. Even the super facilities here make life, particularly the academic life, 'stimulating.' " The others nodded in agreement.

"Apathetic," said two students almost at once. "A small percentage of students—maybe one-sixth of the whole student body—run this place, from the Union on through. The rest are at class and the ball games, living their own lives somewhere off campus, trying to get a job or into grad school. A few are all wrapped up in the Greek system and we never see them anywhere else—yuk," said one.

"Yes," the pianist responded with a sweeping gesture, "but there is a certain youthfulness here, and *hunger*. It may not be directed just at obvious student activities, but it is present nonetheless."

"Opportunity," said the minority woman. All agreed. "Size may have its drawbacks, but opportunity abounds."

"Chauvinistic," said the elegant blonde. "The word still applies, but less so than a few years back. Still, the English teacher who spearheaded the local feminist movement has had her problems. And the gays had to defer to the Greeks who didn't like their float in the big Round-Up parade. The place is in transition, but there is plenty of old Texas left. Just go over to the Pi Phi, Phi Delt, or SAE houses—you'll see."

"Your list of adjectives comes as something of a surprise to me," said

I. "One comes to UT with the words 'Football, rich, and huge' in mind. Unfortunately, I may represent the masses."

"Oh, that definition of us is *bruising*," the pianist blurted. "We *demand* a different kind of notice because UT is such a fertile ground of growth now. We're just going to have to get out there and spread the word."

One can gain considerable student perspective by wandering to Jester Center, the university's newest, largest, and only coed dorm, named for Beauford Jester, once governor of Texas and once chairman of the UT Board of Regents. Jester is incredible: a fortress of brick with mammoth common space and miniature hallways, it houses 3,000 air-conditioned students and is so large it has its own zip code. Several entering freshmen were more than willing to share their expectations of UT.

The first raucous chap, from outside Dallas, had no doubts about his college choice or his chances for success there. "Rice's standards are higher than MIT's—I could have gone there but decided I didn't want to work that hard. Harvard put me on the waiting list, so here I am." He laughed, flexed what was inside the tight T-shirt, and continued. "Hell, I guess I've wanted UT all my life. My parents didn't go to college, and they've been drumming UT into my head since I was a kid. But *I* have to pay for it, all by myself. Dad says 'I'm a self-made man, so you'll have to be one too.' And I don't resent that. Well, maybe a little bit . . . But I'll go to med school and be a damn fine doctor, right here in Texas. I may have to stop along the way to make some more money, but it will all work out. Meanwhile, *Go You Longhorns!*"

Two freshmen girls sitting nearby giggled. One of them was Latino—lovely, articulate, with an accent, not a bit shy. "I'm from a little town in the south of Texas. But UT is our family college now. I have three brothers here and one at Harvard. Next year, six of us will be in college at once, all on scholarships. I fear the size of this place—some say to join a sorority to 'find a group,' but a sorority is not for me. My *real* fear, though, is whether I can make it academically. I just don't know, but we'll soon see. My brothers have done so well, but I'm the first girl of the family to enter college . . . I'll just die if it doesn't work out. What if I get *lost* in this huge place?" she said, glancing about vast Jester West.

One young man from Corpus Christi said he was at UT because his father made him come. "To my dad, there is no other place to go. I want to go into business, and Dad says all the contacts can be made here—'UT people *run* Texas after they're out,' he told me. Well, we'll see what happens. Some kids back home say this is really a party school—and I don't know if that's me. I've worked in a grocery store and a hospital for a long time now to get the money together to come here. I have $6,000 saved, and it will all go into this education. Dad will help out too. We're not country bumpkins. We know what's going on. I'll just quietly go about my life here and will probably do OK." He shook hands, and with an uncertain smile, walked off alone.

It is difficult to describe student life at UT because there is no tie that binds. One contributing element to this lack is the very limited on-campus housing. Jester holds the masses that UT can accommodate on campus, assisted by an assortment of small men's and women's dorms, some air-conditioned, some not (one pays accordingly). But in total, the university provides housing for less than 10 percent of its 48,000 students. Hundreds of others live in privately owned dorms adjacent to campus, high-rise structures with malls attached, looking very Hyatt or Marriott. Another option, buying a condominium, is catching on—it is estimated that over 800 condominiums in Austin are now owned by UT parents. And then there is "Riverside," a huge jungle of apartments twenty minutes from campus, served by a free shuttle bus. As student Rebecca Phyme said in *Cactus*, the yearbook:

> Above the expanse of concrete, multi-colored neon lights accent the community's prefab architecture reminiscent of "60s Waco." It is in this urban jungle that thousands of UT students do their best to work, play, study and live. As you travel down Riverside Drive, you are drawn into a kaleidoscope of images—gray asphalt parking lots, stacks of uniform apartment complexes that would make a sardine claustrophobic and the greatest conglomeration of fast-food joints this side of Coney Island . . .
>
> Some would say that Riverside leaves much to be desired. Still, even with overcrowded shuttles, seedy apartments and deaf landlords, the region is a veritable bastion of luxury when faced with the prospect of "doing time" in Jester.

Students at UT operate in different little worlds—some at Riverside, 14 percent with the Greeks (who, despite the balking of the sororities, were forced to sign a nondiscrimination clause in order to be pictured in the yearbook), some quite to themselves, some within the campus milieu.

On campus, the Union is the hub of life. The forty-eight-year-old Spanish Renaissance center has been renovated and expanded again and again, most recently for $5.7 million in 1978. It is a wonderful building—attractive, alive, clean, obviously enjoyed *and* respected by its huge clientele. An estimated 27,000 students pass through the Union daily, making use of assorted eateries, the Texas Tavern (which claims to have the longest bar in the state), copy machines, television rooms, the bowling alley, and the cinema, which offers nearly 1,000 classic, foreign, and Hollywood films a year. The Union, with a 150-member staff, also offers a constant roster of concerts, lectures, roasts, minicourses (tap dancing to calligraphy), and anything else that can be crammed into an annual budget of $8 million.

Another centerpiece of student life at UT is the *Daily Texan*, a superb student newspaper. The paper, which first appeared in 1900 as the only college daily in the South, now focuses largely on international and national events. No gossip columns here—the only UT news that creeps in is timely and serious. But the political upheavals related to the paper lend intrigue. The 1980–1981 editor was jailed briefly for refusing to give authorities all unpublished photos of students who had participated in a protest on the Iranian issue. In 1982, twenty staff members walked out to protest the student editor's "improper interference with newsroom operations and lowering the *Texan*'s professionalism and credibility."

The *Daily Texan* is not the only publication of importance to UT students. The ambitious, 700-page yearbook—traditionally a comprehensive, detailed presentation of the year (unlike the free form, impressionistic yearbooks found on many campuses today)—is a hot seller even at fifteen dollars. And *UTmost*, the quarterly student magazine that stumbles along from one budget crisis to the next, is, like the *Daily Texan*, one of the best of its kind in America: probing, ambitious, well written, funny, serious, balanced. *UTmost* will take on anybody on any issue, and it seems always to end up on its feet.

Although more than 400 student organizations are listed at UT, including the very obscure, centralized student government just can't get off the ground and stay afloat. In the "old days," prior to 1970, that is, the Student Association's accomplishments were noteworthy: SA was responsible for starting the Health Center, the University Co-op, the shuttle bus system. But when student fees started leaking into the support of sit-ins, protests, and even abortion, the Regents, and particularly Frank Erwin, started checking the distribution of the funds. That was the beginning of the end of the Student Association. When the SA president became too intimidated to actively protest the appointment of Lorene Rogers as president of the university, an appointment that met with unified campus opposition, there were further outcries. Then came an absurdist reaction— two fellows ran on the "Art and Sausages" ticket to head the government. As *UTmost* records:

> They ran on snappy patter and outrageous jokes a la Firesign Theatre, and they changed the face of student government by throwing a pie into it . . . A & S maintained, "It's time we got

these amateur clowns out of office and put some professional clowns in." . . . Some Art and Sausages campaign gems:

- We will change the inscription on the Main Building from "Ye Shall Know The Truth And The Truth Shall Make You Free" to "Money Talks," to symbolize the University's standing on the academic world.

- When my opponent says "issue," I say "gesundheit."

- Politics makes strange bedfellows, and we'll sleep with anyone.

- We of the Art and Sausages ticket are against mandatory busing. Every day thousands of University students are bussed great distances to campus. We propose that the students who live in the Riverside area attend St. Edward's University, that the students who live in the East Austin subdivision attend Concordia College. This will be done to preserve neighborhood integrity.

They won! And by a 2–1 margin, the largest student mandate in more than a decade.

As president and vice-president, A & S kept the campus entertained for a brief period but accomplished little. Other administrations less humorous but just as weak followed, and finally the seventy-five-year-old Student Association was abolished by student vote in 1978. After several attempts at resurrection and battles between rival groups, a puny 8.5 percent of the student body turned out in the spring of 1982 to give the nod to try once again. But centralized anything at UT, given the size and scattered residencies, doesn't seem to work.

One thing that works is athletics. Football is king, but the other sports are razzle-dazzle too, not to mention Texas-size programs in intramurals and recreational sports (500 football teams) and megafacilities to match. UT's championships:

MEN

Baseball	*Basketball*	*Football*
54 SWC	18 SWC	21 SWC
3 national	1 NIT	3 national
		Earl Campbell, 1977
		Heisman Trophy Winner

Golf
32 SWC (team)
 3 national (team)
 5 national (individual)

Swimming
23 SWC (team)
 7 national (individual)
 1 national (team)
 2 national (relay)
 2 Olympic Gold Medals

Tennis
15 SWC (team)
 5 national (team)
 3 national (singles)

Track
37 SWC (team)
16 national (individual)

(SWC = Southwest Conference)
(NIT = National Invitational Tournament)

WOMEN

The Texas Association of Intercollegiate Athletics for Women awards the Mildred (Babe) Didrikson Zaharias All-Sports Trophy each year to the Texas college or university with the most successful performance in TAIAW state championship competition. UT Austin has won the trophy for eight straight years. The 1981 women's swimming team won the AIAW national championship.

Atmosphere

In the fall, they say, all Austin turns orange when the Longhorns play at home. That is but one interesting component of this college town. Austin, the capital of Texas, is a surprising and delightful oasis. For starters, it is green, it has hills and lakes—this is Wisconsin!

Even the *Christian Science Monitor* has discovered prosperous Austin, a town of 345,000. In an article entitled "A Lone Star City Rises in Brilliance at Sensible Speed" (March 31, 1982), the *Monitor* records:

> A swatch of green in a state better known for tumbleweed and dust bowls, Austin is finding that word of its allure has been leaking out. Its population has been spiraling upward like a Texas twister, and businesses are snapping up pieces of its rolling real estate. . . . The city owes part of its charm to a freak of nature. Austin sits on a geological fault line, giving it a wrinkled surface in a state better known for table-flat plains. The Colorado River kinks its way through the city and has been dammed to

create a series of lakes, framed by miles of parks and jogging trails . . . Austin is home to the University of Texas, a pool of Sunbelt brainpower which has lured many companies, particularly high-technology ones, to the area, and has developed some new ones of its own. IBM, Motorola, Texas-Instruments, and Tracor, Inc., have plants here. A string of others are coming in, adding to Texas's rise as a "silicon prairie." What's more, the university is moving strongly into the technologies of the 1980s—robotics, energy, biotechnology, microelectronics, telecommunications—which should give the area an edge over some other communities.

Austin's unemployment rate has been running less than 3.5 percent, says the *Monitor,* despite the fastest population growth rate of any city in Texas. There is a go-slow movement in town now, particularly as the shortage of water threatens. But what a delight! One might expect to find only a-barbecue-pits-on-Main-Street town, but Austin is overflowing with variety and sophistication. The symphony does well as does the ballet, writers and poets find plenty of company, the restaurants are cosmopolitan, newly transformed Sixth Street is Bourbon Street sans filth, and it's a country music fan's paradise, hosting "Austin City Limits," Willie Nelson, and many others.

The university is next to all this bustle but remains somewhat apart, as so often happens in college towns. In fact, UT's own "city," lengthy Guadalupe Avenue, or "The Drag," is one of the least interesting strips in the area, greatly in need of a face-lift and an ordinance at least to hide the X-rated movie theaters. But Austin, in general, is one lively, vital discovery.

Academics and Staff

UT's new glow is multifaceted. Its town is coming into its own, a symbol of new technology, prosperity, and "high quality of life." With a pleasant environment, first-class facilities, a program for everyone, an improving student profile, and the resources to plug holes or continue expansion, one essential element remains to be reviewed: the faculty. Building the faculty is what has prompted most of UT's recent widespread publicity in such publications as *Time, Forbes, The Wall Street Journal,* and *The New York Times Magazine.*

Most of the excitement was sparked when UT Austin succeeded in luring Nobel winner Steven Weinberg, a physicist, away from Harvard in 1982. Weinberg had an endowed chair in Cambridge but was attracted to

Texas by a salary of reportedly more than $100,000 and promises that UT would develop a top-flight cadre of specialists in elemental-particle theory. UT had already snagged John Wheeler, a nuclear-fission physicist renowned as the expert on black holes, from Princeton in 1976. To add insult to the Tigers' injury, Marshall Rosenbluth, Princeton's highly regarded fusion specialist, came to UT Austin also. Part of the attraction for Rosenbluth was UT's winning a $5 million federal fusion grant over the stiff competition of MIT, the Ivies, and the University of California.

So much for a few of the stars, who infrequently mix with undergraduates but certainly add lustre to UT's crown as a research center that now rivals the traditional elitist institutions. What about the college-level *teaching* faculty?

In January 1982 the UT alumni magazine ran a feature on fascinating campus intellectuals who *also* are prominent in the classroom.

DR. ISABELLA CUNNINGHAM
Chairman, Department of Advertising
College of Communication

Born in Italy and reared in Brazil, she is a member of an illustrious family whose credentials include nobility, academic achievement, and business acumen. Her mother was a physicist-mathematician Ph.D., her father a physician who built up textile, cosmetics, and photographic businesses, and her sister is a nuclear physicist. One of five women to hold departmental chairs at UT, marketing expert Isabella Cunningham, thirty-nine, holds law and M.B.A. degrees from Brazilian universities, M.B.A. and Ph.D. from Michigan State. When she speaks (five languages) of her department, she uses the word "best": best department, hiring the best people, building the best graduate program . . . Widely published, she has written books, monographs and articles with numerous co-authors including George Kozmetsky, Robert T. Green, R. Moore—and her favorite, Dr. W. H. Cunningham, Associate Dean for Graduate Programs in UT's Graduate School of Business. The latter is the Michigan State sweetheart she married—and with whom she shares hectic careers, a four-year-old son, John, and a Mesa Drive home. Jumping to UT from a post at St. Edward's University, Dr. Cunningham teaches, supervises students, consults, makes frequent talks. She chairs the Women's Athletic Council, is a member of the University Co-op board and serves on the editorial board of three major reference journals.

DR. CECILE DEWITT-MORETTE
Professor,
Department of Astronomy

Businesslike and perfectionist, she keeps a photo of John Houseman (*Paper Chase*) on her office door as a warning. However, she smiles, "I'm really more like Laura Wilder in *Little House on the Prairie*." Paris-born and educated, child of brilliant parents, she works in the challenging field of mathematical physics. In 1981, she received the prestigious *Chevalier de l'ordre nationale du Merite* from the French government in recognition of Les Houches School of Theoretical Physics, which she founded in 1951 to fill a post-World War II void in physics-teaching in France, and with which she is still deeply involved. The revised edition of her co-authored book, *Analysis, Manifolds, and Physics,* soon comes out; December *Physics Reports* published her co-authored "New Stochastic Methods in Physics." Now fifty-nine, DeWitt-Morette came to America in 1948 on invitation of J. Robert Oppenheimer to join the Institute for Advanced Study at Princeton. Here she met her husband, Dr. Bryce S. DeWitt of the UT Physics Department. In addition to four daughters, they produced illustrious careers, coming to UT from stints at Berkeley and the University of North Carolina. Happily subscribing to "minimal" cooking and housekeeping, DeWitt-Morette is an outdoors person: she wind-surfs, skis, rides horseback, has the judo Brown Belt. She and Bryce have been known to parachute-jump and to backpack for miles in remotest Africa. Devoted both to teaching and to research, she nonetheless has a retirement-age career change in mind: she will go to medical school in France. After 65. And don't doubt it.

DR. ROLANDO R. HINOJOSA SMITH
Professor,
Department of English

He is one of fourteen included in *Chicano Authors—Inquiry by Interview,* written by Yale University's Bruce-Novoa and published by UT Press in 1981. He has most recently been Chair for Chicano Studies at the University of Minnesota, guest-teaching at UT in summers. Last fall, he joined the UT English faculty full-time. Hinojosa writes in English, in Spanish, and sometimes in both, as he produces novels, poetry, and essays about his people. Born and reared in Mercedes in the Texas Rio Grande Valley, his mother an Anglo teacher, his father a Mexican farmer, he had a tortuous road to college degrees (UT, New Mexico Highlands, and University of Illinois) and to authorship (Chicano literature "started" about 1965). In 1972, his book, *Estampas del Valley ostras obras,* won the Premio Quinto Sol Prize for best novel. His *Korean Love Songs* are well-known. *Mi querido Rafa* (1981) was published by Arte Publico Press of the University of Houston. Hinojosa teaches five courses a year, among them "Literature of the Southwest," once Dobie's domain. His barren basement office in Parlin Hall in no way reflects the humor and erudition of its occupant, but his Allandale home is filled with books and has a kitchen aromatic with his homemade tortillas, tacos, and rice. Hinojosa's Danish wife, Patricia Sorensen, has just passed the bar; daughters Clarissa and Karen Louise attend Anderson High and Burnet Junior High Schools. Ahead for the professor: two books in progress.

DR. PATRICIA STALLINGS KRUPPA
Professor, Western Civilization
Department of History

Dr. Patricia Stallings Kruppa's multi-media presentations on Western Civilization are so interesting that even students not enrolled in her courses come to watch, listen, and learn. That is one reason the College of Liberal Arts professor was given ESA's Jean Holloway Award for Teaching Excellence, which carries a $2,170 stipend. In addition to teaching Western Civilization, Kruppa taught, in 1972, the first course in women's history ever offered at UT. As a result, she has focused her research in that area. She also was instrumental in establishing the new Women's Studies concentration at UT. Kruppa says women's studies courses, always popular at UT, are now being taken seriously by scholars. A native Texan, Kruppa received a bachelor's degree from the University of Houston ('58) and Ph.D. ('68) from Columbia University. She says that even since childhood, she never really thought about becoming anything but a teacher. And the mark of a good teacher, at least in history, she says, "is one who makes history come alive, one who lifts a page out of the dead past and makes it pertinent today."

The vice-president for academic affairs and research oversees UT's academic program. His office is filled with orange rugs and white plastic furniture. "A Public Ivy? Well, maybe. Places like Berkeley have that built in: they're old, they can legally admit only students who are in the top 10 percent of their class, and they stumbled on fame by dramatic atomic research in the thirties and forties. In a way, UT doesn't fit that mold, largely because of the populist tradition within the state. But our 'big shine' seems to be emerging now. The foundation, however, was laid some time ago. Some of our graduate programs began to be acknowledged in the sixties, thanks to heavy and inspired recruitment of faculty in the fifties and early sixties. Logan Wilson, Harry Ransom, and Frank Erwin masterminded all of that, and it worked."

The vice-president, with massive eyebrows, flicked ashes from his third cigarette as often on his tie as in the ashtray and continued, animated and involved.

"UT now is certainly on a par with a place like UNC/Chapel Hill, but we haven't quite made it to Berkeley's level. Part of our handicap has been one of simple geographics. We're out of the way. Everyone finds it easy to fly between California and New York in a fairly straight line. But that is changing too. Some of us who did not used to be 'on line' are attracting more scholarly visitors, drawing more faculty conferences. That helps.

"I do favor tightening belts here. We just need logistical relief—fewer students, for starters. And would that our incoming students had more uniform preparation in secondary school. I don't mean to sound like a snob, but those with SATs under, say, 900, shouldn't be here—they *need* a smaller place, one with more individual guidance."

The vice-president started to walk around.

"We have two faculties here, you see—liberal arts and specialists. Each gets confused about the other and often about themselves. Give a business faculty member a drink or two and he'll wax eloquent about the merits of general education. But leave him sober and he'll shout, 'Goddammit, kid, get into statistics immediately!' The 'Vick Report' is out— recommendations on general education by a blue-ribbon committee. It will surely mean a return to more uniform early year requirements in English, math, science, and foreign languages. But not every faculty member can *be* a generalist, a good liberal arts teacher. I recognize that. Some physicists would be ruined if they were forced to teach at lower levels, in more general courses."

What about the typical undergraduate teacher at UT? Another cigarette, more twisting on the white plastic chair.

"Well, quite frankly, we do have some complaints, but kids today want to be patted on the head three times just for attending class. If anything is salty or truly different or too strong, they are easily affronted.

So they complain if anything is not ordinary: if a professor has an accent or if a professor has an obscure point of view. But in the big world out there, people have to take what there is, and then *invent*. If our students would do that here there would be less carping. This is not to say we will tolerate sloppy teaching. Nor will we provide a book of jokes so the classroom will be entertaining. In fact, we're quite proud of our Center for Teaching Effectiveness—young TAs or new teachers *have* to attend and are paid to do so. This is symbolic, by the way, of the president's enormous interest in the quality of undergraduate teaching."

The more this administrator talked, the more forthright he became.

"What are our crown jewels? Botany, physics, petroleum engineering, civil engineering, computer science, linguistics, Spanish and Germanic languages, the business school as a whole (but particularly accounting), chemistry, and in liberal arts, classics. But we can be uneven. We're supposed to have a hell of a physics department. Well, some in physics are super and some are poor—most of the latter were top-notch in their time. But we *do* have a fine faculty overall, and fine teaching, not to mention fine research. We need better faculty salaries and support systems, although I'm not certain that just means more sabbaticals—on that popular issue the faculty are calling for an old dog that just isn't around any more. We need a more diverse faculty *and* student body: the nothern governments will continue to beat hell out of us to pay for our sins in the war until we take more blacks and more women. We *will*, if we can lure the best ones. And again, we need more consistent quality among our undergraduates."

He leaned forward. "But what we need *most* is the recognition we deserve. It's like being old enough to drink—you just have to wait."

In conclusion, this resourceful, animated man commented on the current president's "legacy to UT": improvement in undergraduate education, including strengthened general education requirements; rewards for undergraduate teaching of excellence; upgraded admissions requirements; and perhaps most important, a dramatic increase in faculty endowed chairs.

TV's *Dallas* would surely like to film inside the UT system president's office. It is a penthouse in Main Building, with a lot of stained glass and pink marble leading to it. There are plenty of polished-wood-and-glass-enclosed-bookcases, of deep, burnt orange carpet and of space. Adjacent to it, a waiting room for visitors, is a gemlike Victorian library, ornately fixed with walnut and wrought iron, lovely paintings and sculpture, and 7,500 volumes "rich in nineteenth century English poets and novelists." Next to the little library, a perfectly maintained roof garden.

Peter Flawn, president of the university since 1979, is a professor of geology who attended Oberlin College in Ohio, studied for advanced degrees at Yale, then headed to UT as a research scientist in 1949. After a term as executive vice-president at UT, he was lured away to become the first president of the University of Texas at San Antonio until he was called "home" again to lead the flagship campus.

All the marble and fine wood and glass and thick burnt orange carpets don't feel quite right after meeting this man. He is restrained, gentle in speech, intense but casual—surely more at home at an alumni barbecue than in this elegant executive fortress. If one is patient, he is easy to talk with. Also, he has the reputation of being a fierce administrator. Flawn is given credit for being the basic ingredient in the swift movement and sensibility at UT these days.

"UT as Ivy? Well, I don't know. Time and again we are asked— 'What will it take to make UT into the Harvard of the Southwest?' But, you see, we don't *aspire* to be the Harvard of the Southwest. The mission of a superb public university is basically different from the mission of a great private university. We can compare our academic programs with Harvard's, and our research program with Harvard's, our faculty, our students, and our facilities, but we must make the comparison knowing our mission is different. We are accountable to the general public. In the final analysis, the test of 'first-classness' must be how well we do what we are *charged* to do. We are charged to do a lot for Texas. UT is very special to Texas. Nearly everyone feels a *right* to attend. And we've become the most prestigious university in the Southwest, so hundreds more than we can accommodate want to attend.

"That whole picture represents change. Prior to World War II, we were a rural, agricultural state with some oil patches. Higher education was not much in vogue. After the war, getting a college degree became a common aspiration. The next step was wanting a degree from a certain place. And that sophistication has grown, knowing the value in the marketplace of *certain* degrees. As a result, UT and A&M are swamped, while the other public institutions in Texas are hurting. So what should we do now? We don't want to become elitist; on the other hand, it is a perverse kind of egalitarianism to think we must take everyone who wants to come, while sacrificing quality. So we're tightening admissions requirements somewhat, and I'm strongly in favor of that. We must exercise intelligent enrollment planning and that means, at this point, cutting back on the student body by a couple of thousand and maintaining a steady state. While cutting back, however, we must simultaneously build in a mechanism for increasing the percentage of minority students. We're working on that, working hard."

Flawn compliments his listener by carefully thinking through questions, then responding with sharp, concise comments. There is little left between the lines when this man speaks. He forms a steeple with his long fingers and continues, swiveling in his overgrown chair.

"Our undergraduate program is very good now. It has a few weak spots, but we're tending to them. You see, the commission that studied us carefully on our seventy-fifth birthday, twenty-five years ago, recommended we make research development the new priority. We did, and we succeeded. And now it is the undergraduate program's turn. We have a *superb* undergraduate liberal arts honors program called Plan II, smaller honors programs in business and engineering. These accommodate our top-flight new students who we're enticing now with new scholarship programs. I've started a series of awards for excellence in undergraduate teaching. And we're excited about the Vick Report, recommending a strengthening of general education. All that will rest in the hands of the individual deans of programs and colleges, as we're fairly decentralized in authority here. But we *must* build a common education in the early years, maybe even develop a 'University College' for two years that all students will be part of before heading to specialized programs. I think each student must master *at UT* effective communication skills—both speaking and listening—good concepts of numbers and of our place in history, and foreign languages to understand other important cultures; and students must be able to develop individual creative talents and, of course, communicate with the scientific world. One problem we have is that most of the accrediting agencies seem to favor our becoming more technical, more professionally oriented. Our individual colleges, then, balk at general education. But it *must* happen.

"Class size is always an issue here. UT is big, and many classes are going to be big. But the challenge is to make them all interesting. A TA is never in front of a class, although we use them often in the lab or with discussion groups. We're very keen now on training teachers well before they perform.

"But we'll never achieve the perfect score. If we do, we probably won't hear about it. We're in an era of criticism. We hear so little praise of our significant accomplishments—as though everything *was* perfect and has somehow slipped. We can fall from grace quite easily, it seems, listening to our students. But they must realize that all learning can't be 'fun,' and some faculty members with beards grade as tough as those without. I'm grateful for the courses Oberlin forced me to take—I wasn't at the time, but I am now. We at UT have never thought that the students can tell us how to run our academic program—they're simply too young. The undergraduates are just beginning to think they may have to perspire here a little—maybe even sweat, like in my day. That might be a very good thing."

President Flawn, addressing the Centennial Commission, provided this low-key but compelling summary of UT:

> It is a university city built around teaching, learning, and scholarship. It has a well-qualified student body. It is not an elite

student body—some are brilliant; some are without academic talent; some are dogged and determined to succeed; some are "fooling around." About 30 percent fail to graduate within the traditional four years. But those that do, go forth to lead the state, the nation, and the nation's great corporations. Those that fail have had their opportunity. The University has an outstanding faculty. Some are distinguished; others are on their way to distinction; others are solid, respected teachers, investigators, and counselors. There are those who have not achieved their potential; there are those whose best years are behind them. In sum total—it has an outstanding faculty. The University is a center for the humanities, the sciences, the fine arts, and the professions. . . . Its physical plant is second to none and has recently been adorned by a magnificent performing arts complex. Its campus includes a great presidential library. . . . It has the financial resources to excel. . . . The University of Texas at Austin is the single most important asset that Texas has.

UT's viewbook for prospective students, a child in the mature world of college publications today, can sound a little hokey:

You may have heard that we have a lot of folks on our campus. You have heard right. . . . Yes, indeed, you will have your chance to blow off steam before getting back to that chemistry problem. . . . Isn't it rotten that just when you've gotten used to being the seasoned veteran in your school, you have to start all over again as the new kid? . . . As you see, you will be challenged at UT, but you also can turn the 'BIG U' into a bite-size 'u'.

Someone had best tell the folks in publications: UT has made it, UT *is* first class. The confidence must start at home.

University of Vermont

Burlington

Atmosphere

"OK, so Lake Champlain has the best sailing in America and Vermont living is idyllic, even in winter. But aren't you angry that you have the second-to-worst faculty salary scale in the Yankee Conference?"

The professor of philosophy—direct, articulate, and joyful—responded with a quick toss of his Nordic hair. "We *could* be obsessed with our poor salary situation, as faculty are at so many other universities." He leaned forward and looked intent. "But I feel I'm claiming more than my share of the world's resources. With that sense of comfort if not guilt, to complain about salary would be obscene." He smiled softly and leaned back, and the others of this earthy, tweedy group nodded in agreement.

Everyone seems compatible at the University of Vermont. Everyone: faculty with faculty, students with students, faculty with students, administrators with faculty. It's not that they're necessarily from the same mold and instinctively agree. But they smile and listen and nod at each other, whether agreeing on a topic or not. One leaves this campus after a few days feeling less complicated, more tolerant of differences, a bit more willing to smile in the midst of a traffic snarl back in Boston. UVM has a contagious, relaxing, and refreshing spirit.

Or maybe it's just Vermont. As a salty, down-home, elder statesman said at the Senior Class Day celebration on a very green green, "Vermont is an Idea, a Song. Vermont is a Fourth World—few places create more powerful images in people's minds. And what makes a real Vermonter? Born here? No. Moved here? No. Buried here? Yes. If a sense of *place* is more important to you than career, Seniors, you are Vermont. In Vermont, we all become Agriculturists of Time."

Even traditionally soulless segments of the university tilt the hat to

University of Vermont at Burlington

1) Size of Student Body

Undergraduate __7,500__   Graduate __1,500__   Total __9,000__

2) 1983 Freshman Class Profile

Class Size __1,895__   % Men __42__   % Women __58__
Percent of Applicants Admitted __57__
Average SATs: Verbal __510__   Math __570__
High School Class Rank: Top Tenth __34__ % Top Quarter __75__ %
   Geographical Distribution (% of class):
In-State __39__% Middle Atlantic __22__ % New England __71__ %
West __1__ % Middle West __4__ % South __1__ %
Foreign __1__ %
Minority Students __2__ % of Class
Financial Aid __47__ % of Class

3) Retention of Students

__55__ % of freshmen graduate in four years
__65__ % of freshmen graduate in five years

4) Ten Most Popular Majors of Graduating Seniors, 1983

1. Business Administration
2. Political Science
3. Economics
4. Psychology
5. Nursing
6. English
7. Mechanical Engineering
8. Zoology
9. Computer Science
10. Animal Science, Special & Elementary Education (tied)

5) The Financial Picture (1982–83)

Annual Campus Budget $ __121,000,000__
1983–84 Tuition and Fees for State Residents $ __2,613__
1983–84 Tuition and Fees for Out-of-State Residents $ __6,491__

Revenues

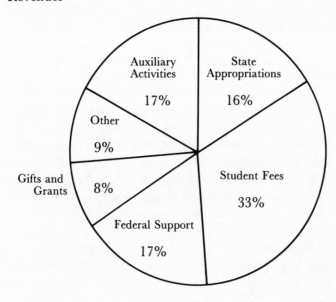

Expenditures

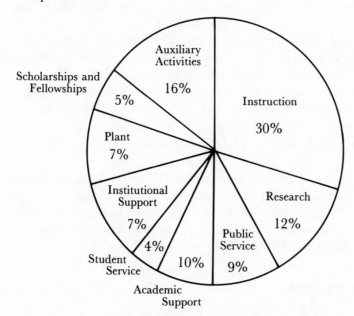

Vermont. From a recent Academic Affairs Committee report: "Vermont is rich in its commitment to a special quality of life and to an ethos which champions the individual and the opportunity for full personal growth and development."

Vermont *is* special. But so is what everyone refers to as "the college town," Burlington.

It's a long drive from Boston. Beautiful, but long—200 miles. One heads northwest through touristy, billboard-cluttered New Hampshire, with views of dramatic mountains and valleys, passing close to America's perfect picture-postcard campus, Dartmouth, then across the line into Vermont for the no-billboards-allowed, verdant roll toward the upper far corner of the state. "More cows than people," they say, and one grows to understand that on this picturesque journey. One learns also that this place is remote. But the remoteness is forgotten once in Burlington.

True Burlington, with approximately 50,000 people, is not large for a major university town. But this is a spunky, tidy, comprehensive, and cultural little city—and Vermont's largest! There is a surprising choice of good restaurants, some out-Californiaing California in rich natural decor and superb organic foods (try one called Deja Vu, for example), and an array of lively near-campus hangouts and bars (The Bone looked and smelled like the set of *Animal House* after the filming, but nearby Hunt's and Finbars were civil, fun, and unpretentious). New hotels, rather tasteful ones, are popping up near the lake and posters everywhere publicize concerts, lectures, campaigns—some gown, some town. There is an annual Mozart festival here, and a Shakespeare Festival too. Also, a wealth of nineteenth-century churches and homes. All this on the shores of a lake that appears to be clean and fresh, with the Adirondack Mountains to the west and Vermont's Green Mountains to the east and Canada close by. Although the "urban feel" is here, smiles on the street to friends and strangers persist.

The campus is the usual state university hodge-podge of architecture, saved at UVM by tidiness at every turn. One has the feeling in May that the winter snow was provided only to assure green lawns for commencement. Green is everywhere. As are well-manicured flowering shrubs with neat sawdust circles underneath.

History and Tradition

The place is old: the fifth college in New England, preceded only by Harvard, Yale, Brown, and Dartmouth. UVM ("Universitatis Viridis Montis" or University of the Green Mountains) was chartered in 1791, when just five of the young state's citizens were college-educated. Ira Allen (Ethan's brother), credited as founder, said on the original subscription:

> Having honorable views towards the Public and having a desire to make the Place I have chosen for my residence respectable by the Establishment of Liberal Arts and Sciences I therefore name Burlington for that purpose, being situated on the Lake Shore has a most pleasant Prospect together with the advantage of an inland navigation where the waters are clear & Beautiful, the soil dry & good for Building or Gardens, the best of Spring water may be brought in pipes to every part of the Plain. (From *Tradition Looks Forward* by Julian Ira Lindsay)

With the site selected, the legislature established a university, anticipating funding from rents "fixed at $.25 per acre as long as grass is green and water runs."

Although the wet and the green remained, the puny rents did not support the university, so a public institution developed funded largely by private donations. To this day that is true.

The citizens of Burlington paid for early construction. After fire destroyed the first structure, General Lafayette laid the cornerstone to its successor, "Old Mill," which stands proudly to this day. Actually, private monies paid for the entire "University Row" of five imposing structures. They are all dwarfed in atmosphere by "Billings," once the library and currently the Student Union, surely one of the great nineteenth-century college buildings ("Richardson Romanesque," they say): dark, with flying balconies, ornate gas lamps, rich woodwork—and kept spotless by the Vermonters.

UVM's catalog records other historic idiosyncrasies. For example: given the social and religious attitudes of eighteenth-century New England, it is surprising that Vermont was the first university in America to declare in its charter that "the rules, regulations, and by-laws shall not tend to give preference to any religious sect or denomination whatsoever." The egalitarianism of UVM was accompanied by a pioneering practical education, the model for the establishment of the land grant institutions. Vermont, for example, is believed to be the first nonmilitary institution to have offered engineering courses. A late-nineteenth-century alumnus of UVM, John Dewey, espoused ideas about practical education that, although often adopted, are still being debated.

UVM also pioneered in according women equal status in higher education. In 1871, two women were admitted; four years later, Vermont became the first university in the nation to induct women into Phi Beta Kappa.

The Campus

Tours of campus are conducted by student guides from the admissions office. Ours loved the place and desperately wanted us to. She had a big smile, was well scrubbed, wore no make-up, and spoke her opinions with grace. She was not scholarly but was always thinking.

The Main Campus is just that. University Row, with historic buildings and a magnificent chapel, provides an impressive centerpiece. What remains is a montage of the big and the little, the fairly ugly ranging to the quite attractive. A number of nineteenth-century homes scattered throughout the 425-acre campus have been converted to office use, lending considerable charm. The Green in front of University Row was mandated by Ira Allen to remain pastoral forever, as a bronze plaque explains. A tacky little shopping-mall fountain nearly ruins the vision, but the lush green compensates.

Huge Waterman Building, facing University Row, houses the administrative offices and the heart of the College of Arts and Sciences. Elsewhere throughout the Main Campus are scattered pods of the eight academic "colleges" or "divisions," interrupted by a handsome theater (a copy of the Guthrie in Minnesota and converted from the old heating plant), the archetypal bookstore, a rather shabby-looking fine arts museum ("the only one in Vermont," they say) with huge metal abstractions on the lawn looking somewhat like mistakes, a rather splendid library which was doubled in size recently ("the first and second floors are purely social," said the guide; "all the studying is on the third"), a dreary little triad of freshman dorms formally named "Ivy Lane" but more popularly known as "the shoeboxes," a subterranean security office where names and numbers are engraved on students' possessions (free!) to thwart thefts, and—a delightful surprise—a dairy bar with long lines in the Animal Science Building that sells tasty homemade ice cream to the public (try the maple walnut!).

A tunnel leads under the main street into town, connecting Main with East Campus, the newest of UVM's three campus divisions. East houses a near-college-unto-itself, the Living/Learning Center, a fascinating sixties remnant where 600 students not only live in interconnecting buildings, accompanied by everything from photo labs to computer terminals, but "create a learning environment" by designing independent programs with faculty members, some of whom live there also. This is a self-sufficient community—handsome structures, a progressive program, serious students. "No preppies here," said the guide. "This is more the granola set who are serious about alternative-styled education."

Further along, in a segment of campus obviously visited less frequently by the maintenance crews, is a row of 1950's dorms—brick, ugly, featuring orange plastic seats. But here, the guide said, is where the more scholarly, reserved, and "somewhat older" students reside. The bonus on East Campus is proximity to the indoor athletic facilities. And UVM has them. Hockey is the frenzied sport here, but the comprehensive facilities, including considerable new space, document popular recreational and intermural offerings not to mention the intercollegiate programs (twelve sports for men, twelve for women). Vermont did not skimp on bringing the outdoors in for athletics.

Close by is Redstone Campus, originally an estate, now hosting a mix of Georgian and Awful Fifties architecture plus a couple of gems tucked away—the new Music Building, for example, shaped like a grand piano, which deserves greater exposure. This is Preppyville for those who don't live in the fraternities and sororities. The loud dorms are here and the "younger" students, "in every sense of the word." (Freshmen are assured of on-campus housing; upperclassmen are thrown into a lottery system. In all, 55 percent of the undergrads live on campus.) There are specialty dorms in this area also—a nifty old estate for women only (most UVM dorms are coed by floor or area, with cohabitation "possible"), a somewhat isolated dorm for "the environmentalists," another for "multicultural" students.

There are two religious centers. The Protestant one doesn't show much spirit on the outside, but the Catholic gathering place looks interesting and is a favorite spot for quiet study. (It is particularly quiet now, since the popular Catholic chaplain was recalled recently by his bishop for stances too liberal, specifically for allowing a gay speaker. At that time the campus, including the Protestant center's leadership, spoke in outrage against the bishop's action, but to no avail.)

Student Life

The tour full-circled us back to the admissions office, one of those stately old converted homes where a group of "representative undergraduates" was assembled to chat about UVM over warm beer. Two of the young men were decked out in suits, two of the women in heels; most of the others wore the national campus costume of jeans and shirts and a sweater or two; there was the slightest hint of preppy green and pink, and gold earrings, particularly on the sorority girls.

This group, smiling all the way and ever so kind to each other, had little to say spontaneously about academics at the university. One had the feeling that UVM was a "good place to be," stimulating but hardly intense, an academic community with less emphasis on the "academic" than on the "community."

When asked what adjectives best described UVM, a thin, rather pale young woman responded immediately: "Cold!" All agreed. But they added that Cold is Good in Vermont: hockey, skiing, fireplaces, hot toddies.

"Diverse," responded a robust, freckled fellow, with certainty. "Surely no other state university has half the student body from in-state and half the student body from out-of-state, or from 'away,' as we say here. And we have socioeconomic diversity—the Vermonters, on the whole, aren't so well off, and the kids from 'away' are usually wealthy."

"Diversity" created considerable friendly discussion. "Doesn't nearly *everyone* here enjoy the outdoors?" said one of the pink-and-green ladies. "And even though the Vermonters may not be rich and as well prepared academically for college as the kids from Boston and Connecticut, it's those of us from 'away' who come wearing Bass Wejuns, doing our *damndest* to 'be Vermont.' " Still, the group thought "diverse" was fair.

"Friendly." No contest.

"Small," said a local Burlington sophomore. "This place has a lot to offer, considering its size." "That's the same as diverse," retorted the freckled one, but with a warm smile and accommodating gesture. The rest had trouble with "small," particularly in reference to class size during the first two years and the impersonal atmosphere created by some large dorms.

"Challenging!" said one with a tilt of the chin, as though it was the right thing to say. But the just-graduating senior who planned to move to Cornell or Harvard retorted: "Well, it could be considerably *more* challenging. But if you seek it out, it's here. I sought it out, after transferring to UVM from an easier place. There is little pressure to be scholarly here, but the resources and the faculty are ready for any comers. It *is* challenging, I guess, for the minority who want it that way."

"Fun." No contest. Until someone mentioned "the Greeks." Then, for the only moment of the evening, the discussion grew intense. A classy brunette from outside Boston with huge silver-platter earrings defended the Greeks, contending they "add another dimension" to the campus, have service projects, and aren't just social. Then there was a rather hushed and somewhat embarrassed reference to "our jock house" that was reputedly guilty of a recent sexual assault. Silence . . .

After a few more comments about the Greeks that were mildly negative, a suave young man who said proudly that he is "third-generation UVM" remarked, after picking up one more warm beer: "If we don't like the Greeks, it may be that we just don't know them well enough." The group let the subject die.

There was ready agreement on Vermont's strongest and weakest academic departments. Tough and good: engineering (particularly electrical), physical therapy, biology, chemistry, and nursing. The guts: education, psychology, sociology, and agriculture.

One engineer in the group—serious, with short hair for ROTC—complained about the "old faculty . . . *really* old" in engineering. Others responded that the state gives the university so little money that it can't compete with industry for young and vital authorities in technical fields. But there was universal praise around the room for the president, "Lattie" Coor, and his top administrative team for maintaining a first-class university despite a declining funding base.

Questions regarding the future—the tight job market, tight graduate school admissions—didn't excite this crowd. One had the sense they were working hard, partying hard, had a good feeling about themselves and others, and felt the future would somehow take care of itself.

When asked if any UVM student groups get so excited about their cause that they become a nuisance to others, a relaxed and friendly Joe College–type responded: "The gays are rumored to be the second largest organization on campus, next to the Outing Club (*"Really??"* fluttered the sorority girl), but they don't ruffle anyone's feathers. This is a tolerant place. And liberal. Hey, we have a socialist mayor in Burlington, put there largely by student vote!"

"I just wish the nation, rather than the state, knew all about us. We're really more than a ski lodge away from home, although we're that too." (Giggles all around.) "A big problem here is public relations. I don't know, but it doesn't seem our alumni are as gung-ho and as helpful as they are at some other schools, like Dartmouth. Maybe it's because we dropped football a few years ago. We're the only flagship public university in America without a football team, you know. *We* think that's okay, but it may sap our alumni spirit. The old boys have to have something to come up here and cheer about—and it's not exactly easy to make the trip during hockey season," he said, stretching for the pretzels.

A quiet fellow with the enviable Vermont name of Todd Yankee spoke up. "And we don't *rally* like some other schools. We go to Dartmouth's Winter Carnival because our Winterfest doesn't quite make it. And we're all irked that they let some traditions, some big ones, fade away here. The 'Cakewalk,' for instance. Sure, it was a minstrel with blackface and you can't do that any more, but it was the *big* event here. Nothing has replaced it—they even tried to revive it with greenface but that didn't work."

But the group had had enough of being critical. Suddenly they turned back to all the positives: the town, the weather (winter here is considered a big plus, not to mention the foliage-decked fall and the azalea-and-tuliped spring), the accessibility of faculty if one wants to seek them out, the tolerance of "those who are a little different," and the serious but not morose academic climate.

Academic Programs and Staff

The meeting with the faculty was similar. Instead of warm beer, the professors were enjoying colorful pastry surely influenced by UVM's proximity to French Quebec.

"Most people must think of us as Squeaky Clean University—and, quite frankly, that may be fair," said a talkative professor with sailboats on his tie and stripes on his belt. "Many of us came here originally for the *place*. This has to be the most cosmopolitan little city in America; the sailing is the best in the world; each season brings its differences and its tourists, forcing us out of isolation. No doubt about it: the 'place' brought us, but the inherent quality of almost everything here keeps us. It's an odd thing: UVM's image is overblown, given our minimal resources. But we are so positive and resource*ful* that we climb to greatness—we really 'make do' wonderfully with so little. That is thanks to a rather incredible administration. Our last president said: 'Austerity is not a reason to restrain progress,' and it has stuck. Perhaps too much so. To be financially responsible is to be cautious—we're too cautious. But we're doing just fine. There is tremendous job satisfaction here, despite low salaries. I've never been among so many who, despite differences, are so compatible."

Again, there was that nodding consent among faculty that I had noticed among students. The sailor continued. "Our biggest problem is that the legislature resents us. Our county, Chittenden, is perceived as Vermont's Sausalito. Much of the state's wealth—what little there is—is concentrated here; we have one-fifth of the state's population; our students are, on the whole, upper middle class; we're thought to be too well paid by Vermont's standards, too cosmopolitan, and in every way, 'on the hill.' "

The philosophy professor—the one who had said he was satisfied with his "share of the world's resources"—agreed. "Vermont can be used as an escape—by teachers, by students. And that probably happens among some. But certainly not among all. My students here are more animated and speak up more in class than the ones I taught at Wellesley. Yes, it's pleasant here. But that doesn't dim the vitality. And, quite frankly, we're pleasantly smug about having such a good, simple package to attract others."

What would the professors do to improve UVM if each of them could succeed the current president? They seemed to enjoy that challenge, resting their frosty Danish for a moment on the Colonial-design napkins.

"We have to get more state money or we'll drift into becoming a second-rate, semiprivate college," said the sailor.

"Why not live with that and build on it?" said the quiet, natural-looking lively female teacher of romance languages. "A poor state is a poor state. I doubt if that will change much. And we have private resources to tap—but I guess that does present the danger of forcing even greater wealth in the student body makeup. I don't know. . . ."

When asked if women fare well in this community, she said, "Administration, no; faculty, *yes*. The last two chairs of the faculty have been women, and they've done a marvelous job."

Another faculty voice helpful in understanding the University of Vermont was tucked away in a small windowless office near the chemistry labs. He was a young man, obviously in a hurry, and effusive in his praise of UVM. "Our top 10 percent could be matched against anyone's. Sure, the student ability ranges widely, but the cream rises and we certainly accommodate the top well. For example, I can't really separate my involvement with graduate and undergraduate students. We're all a family. Probably one-third of my publishing is done with direct assistance from undergraduate research. And it helps students to have the medical school right here on the grounds. The arrangement creates less inner confusion for me regarding teaching versus research—I'm doing both at the same time with the same people."

When asked for key words to describe UVM, the energetic teacher responded with no hesitation: "Quality academics; aggressive (student recruitment and the search for more funds); personal; high quality of life. But don't get me wrong—everything is not ideal here. Our freshmen differ; the Vermont students take a little longer than out-of-staters to get going, although they eventually end up with equal honors at graduation. And our departments are uneven too. Stronger areas are history, philosophy, allied health sciences, nursing, chemistry. We're weaker in math, agriculture, education, and anthropology. And, as you're probably hearing from everyone, we're weak in funding. But we handle our monies so intelligently! For example, each of the eight academic units must decide independently who will get significant merit increases in their departments—the range is from 6 to 10 percent. That leaves considerable incentive at the grass roots level because hard work will be noticed and rewarded. In short, we do a *hell* of a job here, particularly with undergraduates."

In a local dining room, permeated with the stench of booze from the previous night's graduation party, two more professors shared thoughts about the university. One was a mild fellow who directs instructional development, and the other was a rather aggressive professor of political science who chaired a key committee on re-energizing general education and had written a brilliant working paper for the faculty on that topic.

"There is an interesting, lingering tension here that stems from Vermont's being a land grant college (once called 'State Agricultural College') *and* a nearly private college of the liberal arts. Time and the legislature have had an impact on the relationship, but the latter concept has been taking over, to the point that the former is almost fully eclipsed," said the political scientist over cold brunch eggs. "Our COBE (Committee on Baccalaureate Education) group has found little selfishness of time among faculty and staff. We're moving right along with the goal of UVM's having a consistent general education program, regardless of one's major. Oddly, nursing is the specialized program which now takes greatest advantage of the university's liberal arts offerings. Other preprofessional zones are much more isolated and seem to prefer it that way."

The two agreed, on the whole, with others regarding UVM's strong and weak departments. "But business here has been caught with its pants down. All of a sudden, boom, all the kids want it. It will strengthen in time, I guess," one commented.

The mild fellow took every opportunity, while the political scientist was eating, to speak. "I'm familiar with Middlebury, Columbia, and others, and I just can't imagine a better *teaching* institution than ours. There is genuine interest in teaching undergraduates."

"And are they getting their money's worth!" added the other. "Take political science, my area. We only have two M.A. candidates, so all the students are undergrads—140 majors. Ninety-nine percent of the faculty's attention is given to the first-degree student. The average class size in our department is around forty—we can't have terribly large classes at UVM, because we have no rooms large enough to hold them." He showed me a table regarding class size at Vermont.

"Our students are bright, dutiful. I wouldn't call them 'intellectual.' But they can get excited now and then about an issue. James Watt, at the peak of his controversial career as secretary of the interior, visited. He brought out all our remnants of guerilla theater from the late sixties—it was good to see we could get fired up again. I'd say our student body is smart. But intellectual, no."

The two agreed that more should be done at UVM for the exceptional student. Honors programs are growing but not fast enough. "Students will reach the level we expect of them. But too often, the standard set for some individuals is just not high enough."

The quiet professor brought up a recurring theme. "People get along well together here—town and gown, gown and gown. Part of that is due to the expertise of the administration in centralizing authority while decentralizing responsibility. They know what they can do for the institution and where to draw the line so others won't feel excluded. The two top men—the president and vice-president—seem to like this place because

University of Vermont, Class Size, 1983*

| | Number of Enrollments | | | | | |
Discipline by College/School	1–10	11–20	21–30	31–50	51–100	100+
Agriculture	38	42	27	23	13	9
Allied Health Sciences	34	11	9	23	0	0
Arts and Sciences	269	384	264	170	94	69
Education and Social Services	174	270	126	41	4	2
EMBA	84	104	108	134	17	7
Environmental Studies	2	5	6	3	0	2
Home Economics	29	44	13	14	11	8
Medicine, Basic Sciences	32	7	2	9	1	2
Natural Resources	13	12	14	10	2	0
Nursing	25	0	6	8	0	0
Totals	700	879	569	433	150	99

*Includes traditional lecture and laboratory course. Excludes the evening division, military studies, and individualized courses such as independent study and reading and research.

it's manageable. We'll be lucky to keep both of them. But they've created a good secondary administration also. There are a few flaws on the landscape—the fraternity sex mores, the persistent money problem—but we're a strong community. Very strong."

Rarely does one hear such cheery reports about the administration from both faculty and students. Nonetheless, one anticipates gray sessions with administrators—they're guarded, poised in the middle to applaud and restrain both sides, rarely outspoken, rarely of (exposed) character. These expectations were not at all on target at UVM.

The dean of engineering, mathematics, and business administration mentioned technological growth in the town during the last fifteen years. IBM and GE have major plants in Burlington now. The companies help the university attract attention *and* funds for research and capital growth. But this dean is too busy at the moment reorganizing his division in the face of tremendous demand for undergraduate business and engineering to give priority to fund-raising. Business has become a separate unit. There is hope that attrition of faculty in less popular disciplines will allow business to pick up new professors, the "rob-Peter-to-pay-Paul" formula applied during tight times and faculty freezes. Business anticipates a quick jump from sixteen to twenty-five faculty members, so a watchful eye is peeled on upcoming retirees on campus.

Up the administrative ladder, a tough character emerged: the dean of the College of Arts and Sciences, which is easily the largest undergraduate division. He was joined by the assistant dean/director of student affairs who said nothing but "hello" and "goodbye."

This dean dresses Harvard; his office looks Harvard; he talks Harvard. And he talks fast.

"With the possible exception of Cornell, we probably give more liberal arts degrees than any land grant college in America—766 this year. But our faculty is second to none, more like faculties at Amherst and Williams than like those at other public universities. We concentrate on the under-graduate—there are only three Ph.D. programs in arts and sciences. But we do have diversity. And we have, among this faculty, a *passion* for teaching, even while immersed in research."

"The flaws?" he queried, cupping his hands on the desk after adjusting his rep-stripe tie. "Well, we need a more structured curriculum, a more even curriculum across the board. This is en route, thanks to COBE, or the Committee on Baccalaureate Education. And we need more faculty. The ratio of students to faculty is now 14:1, with particular strain on the senior members with high merit awards; they're popular and attract large numbers (although our largest class is only 350—that's in Psychology I). Also, our departments are somewhat uneven. The better ones are chemistry, philosophy, history, political science, classics, geology, and psychology. Communications was eliminated, but we have some other weak links: religion, physics, economics, most of the social sciences, and theater. With money and time, they can all be improved. The student body is bright, although some from the suburbs need a boost in motivation. Remember the enormous importance of the Vermont contingent here: this weekend at commencement all five of the top student awards are slated to be given to kids from Vermont."

The president of UVM, Lattie F. Coor, is a local celebrity. Everybody respects him and likes him! The director of admissions said he'd lay down in the highway if the president asked him to. Coor came to Vermont from the vice-provost's post at Washington University, St. Louis.

Lattie Coor's office looks like the director's quarters at a boy's camp. It's all wood—different kinds—a little rough around the edges, with some nice old pieces placed sparingly and an impressive carved crest of UVM over the fireplace. The president, well tanned, had a huge smile and a jolting handshake. He is a politician, an academic, and an obvious leader, with a down-home style.

After well-paced niceties, Lattie Coor got down to business. "Of course we're a Public Ivy. First, you must remember that we have a grand history. We're nearly 200 years old now. During the War of 1812, the campus was requisitioned to house American troops. During the Civil War, we were down to thirty students. John Dewey went here; so did Henry Raymond, the man who created *The New York Times* and *Harper's*. So did Justin Morrill, the land grant college originator in Congress. And here we are today, a survivor in excellent health. This year's graduating seniors will retire at age seventy around 2035—they will have spent half of their working lives in the twenty-first century. So we have history. And we certainly have presence.

"We're a series of paradoxes. We're *the* college for Vermonters, but half our students are from 'away.' Even though we're a Public Ivy in New England's view, we are Vermont. Fifty-nine percent of all high school graduates in our state who go to college, go here. Can any other state university say that? At the same time, we're able to draw a fabulous array of students from other states who arrive trying to look Vermont and act Vermont."

The president gave the impression he had given this speech before—the words were coming very easily. But he grew excited and leaned forward across the rough-hewn coffee table to continue.

"A second paradox is the intensity in the classroom for a place that has so much to offer outside the classroom. Our strong academics are a given. But also we have the *happiest* damn student body I've ever experienced. Again, it's the Vermont influence—work hard, but make certain there is human balance. We have 1,800 kids in the Outing Club alone! And 1,300 are active in the Phillips Brooks House service activities. 'Integration' is a key word here. And because of that UVM seems to please parents a lot. Kids get good academics but lead a wholesome, safe, happy, involved life when classes let out.

"The third paradox is our graduate and professional school quality for a place that concentrates on undergraduates. We have only fifteen Ph.D. programs—but that is just enough to keep the proper balance between graduates and undergrads. 'Integration' comes in again at this point: every graduate or professional program somehow involves the fast-moving undergraduate through common faculty, common facilities. We're a family, and all share."

Lattie Coor was talking faster now. And his gestures suggested a larger audience. Perhaps he was rehearsing for the next day's commencement ceremonies.

"Our problems? First, unevenness in the quality of students, although our exit standards are more consistent than our entrance standards. Also, I'm concerned about the unevenness of quality within the institution— college to college, I mean. We had to close the home economics program because it had slipped beneath our standards. Education and agriculture are now something of a problem, but we might well turn these around—the student demand just isn't there at the moment. Also, we have unevenness in advising. My goal is a comprehensive university with the environment and consistency of a small college: we're getting there, but we're not yet at the mark."

What about the seeming lack of student "electricity"? The cheery, relaxed president had a ready answer.

"Well, that's a common reaction probing visitors have here. Vermonters are wary, and will hold back. Smart! Also, remember that this is a mellow time of year—commencement. For the moment, all the big issues and campaigns are moved to the back burner. And finally, don't be put off by Vermont gentility. There is a style here that is difficult to pick up on, but it is warm and wonderful, once perceived."

Lattie Coor suddenly stood and turned on his big exit smile.

Resources

"UVM wouldn't be what it is today," many say, "without the financial wizardry of our vice-president for academic affairs." The title doesn't sound quite right for the man who is credited with keeping the place solvent and moving. But no matter: this is the money man, and given Vermont's rather paltry resources, he runs a tight and imaginative ship. Vermont gets the blue ribbon not for resources but for resourcefulness.

A wealth of studies under the vice-president's direction have documented UVM's financial plight. The goal is to impress upon the state legislature the need for more magnanimous spirit in funding their public university. UVM fares very poorly in state appropriation when compared to other states.

Although the university does well in federal appropriations and contracts, it must charge the highest out-of-state *and* in-state fees of any public university in America to make ends meet. And Vermont states frankly that out-of-state tuition exceeds the expense per student by several hundred dollars.

A direct and dramatic report by an Ad Hoc Committee on Finance to the board of trustees in 1982 was intended for notice by the state legislature. It pulls no punches. The report deserves more than passing interest because it is symbolic of the contest currently under way in many states between academics and the politicians. The Vermonters presented their case carefully and convincingly.

Serious consequences would be realized soon at UVM if the legislature did not undertake immediate "remedial action" for declining support, the trustees said. Reasonable tuition charges had been surpassed, and "staff compensation levels are beyond being merely embarrassing, and in some cases border on the unconscionable." The trustees stated suspicion that the legislature was unwilling to take notice of good management at the university but, instead, would continue to assume that the institution could "make do," regardless of how much state funding fell short of what was minimally required. The request hit hard at the excuse that Vermont is a poor state and cannot afford more for higher education, listing how much more other "poor states" were doing for education. The trustees succinctly dealt with the facts: UVM's share of the state's general fund slipped from 9.8 percent to 6.5 percent between 1969 and 1982, the largest decline of any major state fund recipient; that same period, the share of state support in UVM's total budget slipped from 27.4 percent to 16.1 percent. This support is last in the land in terms of state support for its public university. The national average is 40.8 percent. Some states provide as much as 70 percent of their university's budget.

Vermonters pay twice as much to attend UVM as they did a decade ago. The report warned that tuition could double again in five years if the state did not come to the university's rescue. In the interim, one group forced to come to the university's rescue, the report said, were the out-of-state students who "pay the full cost of their education and then some."

The trustees demanded an increase in the state's contribution to the university's budget until it becomes 22 percent of total income. And to add salt, the committee attached an appendix to their report by a professor of sociology. It dramatized Vermont's low position among "poor states" with respect to support for higher education.

> Even such historically poor and oft-labeled "backward" states as Mississippi (50th in per capita income), Arkansas (49th in per capita income), South Carolina (47th in per capita income), and Alabama (48th in per capita income) exceeded Vermont in their support for higher education by a considerable margin. . . .

> The University of Vermont has been the victim of this legislative hocus-pocus on more than one occasion in the past two decades. As regards the funding of higher education in Vermont, there has been, in my view, insufficient statesmanship and constructive leadership by the majority of those people in the Vermont Legislature who have the power to address the financial aspects of this matter.

The discussion crawls on. The governor consented to appear in front of the UVM Faculty Senate to face the hard questioning, but he was uncompromising. "I think it is important for us to like each other. . . . But if you think the people in the State of Vermont are likely to increase spending to any significant degree, and that therefore there's a solution to our problem, which is to simply increase appropriations here . . . I guess I will fail in square one."

The vice-president is credited with not allowing the university to fail in its mission, despite a poor *and* stingy state. He is responsible for the development of "other resources": the fat federal contribution, the highest "voluntary" parental contribution among colleges in the United States, and the development of an endowment that is not huge but places UVM well ahead of other Yankee Conference institutions in endowment per capita student.

The wonderful irony is that UVM, unlike most campuses today, shows clear signs of growth, even capital growth. The dazzling new wing to the library has been completed; and just as the finishing touches were put on the new Natural Resources Building, the equipment and crews moved in to completely renovate the three "shoebox" dorms. It appears there is a major building project every year at Vermont, not to mention the impressive maintenance of old buildings and grounds.

"The real savior," the pleasant but quiet vice-president says, "has been our reputation among out-of-staters. They keep coming—good ones— in droves. How long can we depend on them, given the demographic predictions today? As long as we're compared to the better private institutions in the East, as we now are, we'll be okay. In *that* context, you see, we're a bargain." He leaned forward to munch on a tired sandwich.

"Also, we must keep a clear head regarding our strengths and weaknesses. Agriculture, natural resources, and education are somewhat down now, while business suddenly zooms. We can't hide our heads regarding what people want and what they don't, what we can offer with quality and what we can't.

"Thank God for our location—three separate tourist seasons and a cosmopolitan town. The quality of personal life keeps people here—faculty, staff, and students. We're in good shape, thanks to the accident of where we are plus some careful, deliberate administrative choices of priorities. And we intend to maintain a watchful eye."

Admissions

Who gets in? The UVM admissions staff play their cards closer to the chest than those dealing with the institution's finances. That's understandable: in admissions they're rich, while in resources they're poor and have need for eloquent pleas.

The University of Vermont *Prospectus* says that secondary school record and rank, College Board SATs, recommendations, and "other pertinent information" are considered for admission. UVM does not have a pat formula—each candidate's accomplishments are considered in the context of his or her background, circumstances of life, school, and so on. Also, says the *Prospectus*, "Most prospective freshmen present at least sixteen high school units, including a minimum of four years of English, three years of mathematics, three years of social sciences, two years of foreign language, and two years of science. . . . Exceptionally well-qualified students may be admitted even though their secondary school records do not include all of the subjects listed above."

Actually, there are two admissions processes at UVM: one for Vermonters and one for those from "away." The *Prospectus* says, "Admissions will be offered to all qualified freshmen who are residents of Vermont." Qualified? According to the director of admissions, a young, lively Yalie (who trained for this job as an assistant football coach and assistant vice-president at Ohio State), this means "any Vermonter who has done reasonably good work in high school—has taken a decent courseload, ranks in the top 10 percent, and has a combined SAT verbal and math of 800 to 900."

The director is the kind of man who marries the job. He jogs miles to work, showers and changes at the office (the convenience of working in a converted Victorian home), stays late, and jogs home. And his accomplishments complement the effort. Due to the problematic state funding and at-home image dilemma, his priority had to be bolstering the Vermont contingent in the applicant pool. He and his staff have succeeded, but it has not been easy. It is not fashionable in the East to stay in one's own state for college, and some Vermonters think UVM too big, others think UVM too small; some think UVM too awesome and sophisticated, others question if it's up to their standards. And there is, of course, the problem of price—high for in-staters, with financial aid on the decline rather than on the rise. The latest lure to locals is a Vermont Merit Scholar Program, awarding no-need, "incentive" scholarships (some would say "bribes") to outstanding Vermonters, particularly those good enough to be wooed by out-of-state private colleges.

The out-of-state admissions situation is a different story. UVM is deluged with solid applicants. For the class of '85, there were 7,410 applicants for the approximately 1,000 out-of-state places in the freshman class. Of those admitted, 48 percent ranked in the top tenth of their high school class; the mean SAT verbal was 543, the mean math, 587.

UMV works hard for the impressive out-of-state applicant pool. Of the eleven "professionals" in the admissions office, seven travel and recruit, visiting over 400 high schools during the peak fall season, mostly in the other New England states, plus New York, New Jersey, and Maryland. The recruiters report that UVM's out-of-state image is strong, the prestige factor high. "We're a very respectable choice for the second and third quintile kids at the East's best prep schools. And let's face it: these are the schools where college images are manufactured," said one seasoned recruiter.

The director and his staff give an application at least two readings, each officer casting judgment on a 1 to 7 scale (1 = highest). The more popular the academic division at UVM, the higher a candidate's ranking must be to get the "You're In!" letter. Normally a 2 is required to make the grade in physical therapy, computer science, and business; a 3 to gain admission to engineering, arts and sciences, or nursing; at the lower end of the scale, 5's may squeak one inside agriculture and education.

The affable admissions director says candidly: "We'd like our rating system to be consistent, despite the division a student wants; but the consistency ends there—what level gets in differs significantly from college to college." Also, the director was quite up-front in saying that "Vermonters (of course), jocks, alumni sons and daughters, and minority students get extra readings. Basically, though," he added with a huge grin, "we're uncorruptible."

In the national context, UVM is in an enviable position in admissions. But the director is apprehensive regarding the near future. Other Yankee Conference institutions are starting to recruit hard, a new activity for most.

UVM's high cost, coupled with the not-so-bright financial aid picture, are the admissions office's No. 1 and 2 handicaps. But as long as UVM's stock remains high and the institution is grouped in the public view with the big and little *Private* Ivies, the cost is relatively unimportant. As one guidance counselor in Massachusetts said: "It's academically respectable, located in a wonderful spot, cheap compared to the private colleges, and all the kids who go there love it, as do their parents. Among today's youth, pessimistic about their future, UVM seems a bright flash of fresh air, just a good place to be, almost an escape."

UVM: low in resources, high in resourcefulness; high in academic and social vitality; high in selectivity, particularly among out-of-staters; "politically conservative, personally liberal"; a place for all seasons; painfully pleasant. The smiles stick; it is the home of granola chic, or "Let's-all-play-we're-really-from-Vermont."

University of Virginia

Charlottesville

"Yoo-Vee-Ay!" Conservative but liberal. Academic but recently athletic. Preppy but diverse. Southern but national. Elitist but inexpensive. Historic but new. Formal but rowdy.

Even Mister Jefferson would probably be proud of his "Academical Village" today. (He dreamed it, designed it, funded it, and led it.) The University of Virginia may well be the best combination of quality-everything that the nation offers in public undergraduate education.

History and Tradition

The story has to begin with Thomas Jefferson. He lives! He was influential then but he seems even more of a presence now. He's everywhere. They talk about him as though he'd just left the room and will return any moment. An outsider inwardly giggles about all this until a sturdy black scholar-athlete looks you in the eye and says, "Nothing in my life has moved me more than standing on the Grounds at dusk, realizing I'm sharing a vision with Mister Jefferson."

Thomas Jefferson conceived the idea of a university for Virginia before he was elected president, the local historians say. A letter written by Mr. Jefferson in 1800 outlines a plan:

We wish to establish in the upper and healthier country, and more centrally for the state, a University on a plan so broad and liberal and modern, as to be worth patronizing with the public support, and to be a temptation to the youth of other states to come, and drink the cup of knowledge and fraternize with us.

University of Virginia at Charlottesville

1) Size of Student Body

   Undergraduate __10,967__ Graduate __5,412__   Total __16,379__

2) 1983 Freshman Class Profile

   Class Size __2,539__   % Men __47__   % Women __53__
   Percent of Applicants Admitted __35__
   Average SATs: Verbal __575__   Math __600__
   High School Class Rank: Top Tenth __62__ % Top Quarter ___ %
      Geographical Distribution (% of class):
   In-State __60__% Middle Atlantic __83__ % New England __3__ %
   West __2__ % Middle West __3__ % South __9__ %
   Minority Students __10__ % of Class
   Financial Aid __34__ % of Class

3) Retention of Students

   __80__ % of freshmen graduate in four years
   __85__ % of freshmen graduate in five years

4) Ten Most Popular Majors of Graduating Seniors, 1983

   1. English
   2. Economics
   3. Psychology
   4. Business
   5. Engineering
      (not ranked in order)

   6. Chemistry
   7. Biology
   8. History
   9. Government

5) The Financial Picture (1982–83)

Annual Campus Budget	$ 158,259,036
1983–84 Tuition and Fees for State Residents	$ 1,586
1983–84 Tuition and Fees for Out-of-State Residents	$ 2,180

Revenues

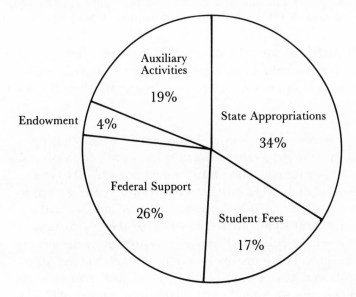

Expenditures

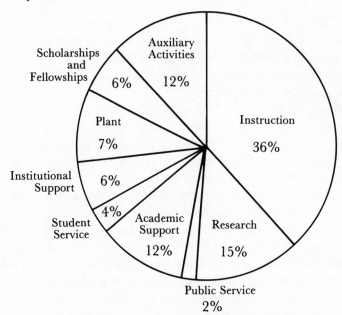

The Virginia General Assembly did not charter the university until 1819. Mr. Jefferson became the first rector and two other American presidents were members of UVa's first board of visitors: James Madison and James Monroe.

Although Mr. Jefferson is UVa's and UVa is Mr. Jefferson's, there are others who yearn for the association. A. Barlett Giametti, president of Yale, borrows from Virginia's founder in a recent annual report from New Haven:

> Jefferson saw education as essential to our life as a free people. "Preach, my dear Sir, a crusade against ignorance; establish and improve the law for educating the common people." (To George Wythe, August 13, 1786.) . . . Jefferson had not only an eighteenth-century rationalist's faith in the perfectibility of man; he had not only an aristocrat's enlightened concern for the less fortunate; he had not only a cultivated thinker's awareness of the educational principles of his humanistic heritage, he also had the American's fundamental conviction that "on the good sense" of an educated citizenry we could build and defend a country of liberty and justice. He was placing his faith in education as essential to a free and orderly society.

After Mr. Jefferson authored the university's mission, rendered the architectural plans and policed construction (partly through telescope from nearby Monticello), designed the curriculum and recruited the first faculty, his Academical Village opened for classes in March 1825 with a faculty of eight and a student body of sixty-eight.

But according to Professor Dumas Malone, UVa's Pulitzer Prize-winning author of the six-volume definitive biography of Thomas Jefferson (started in 1943, it was completed in 1981 by the nearly blind, eighty-nine-year-old historian), there is a moving, little-known, adjunct dimension to Jefferson's UVa period, actually his retirement years.

Professor Dumas records that there were "sorrows and troubles" in Jefferson's last years. Virginia was suddenly in bad times, partly because its land seemed worn out and eroded and its value had thereby declined. Many from the colonies were being lured to the west, where the land was reputedly better. There was general panic in Virginia in 1819, and Jefferson's financial difficulties were severe as a result. Coupled with this was the new commercialism that emerged after the War of 1812, a get-rich-quick aggressiveness which Jefferson did not like. His goal of creating an enlightened agricultural society seemed to be in difficulty. And so was his family. His daughter's husband went bankrupt, and Jefferson was forced to support his many grandchildren, one of whom married an alcoholic and died before her grandfather. This was a tragic time in Thomas Jefferson's life.

"Although the founding of the University of Virginia was probably the most successful event in the twilight of Jefferson's life, he didn't get what he wanted there either," reports Professor Dumas. The complete system of public education at all levels that he envisioned never quite materialized. Nonetheless, the university grew and kept the founder going. In a way, the development of the university was his great escape during this trying personal period.

Atmosphere and the Campus

Mr. Jefferson's "great escape" has obviously changed over 150 years, but at least three concrete reminders of the founder linger at UVa: his leadership in absentia, felt and acknowledged at every turn; the magnificent Grounds (campus) and historic Lawn (central quad) that he designed; and the national character of the student body, which he mandated.

Ada Louise Huxtable of *The New York Times* said the University of Virginia ". . . is probably the single most beautiful and effective architectural group of its kind in the country, or in the history of American building." Others agree. In 1976 the American Institute of Architects polled forty-six experts to nominate the most outstanding American architectural achievements of the past 200 years. Mr. Jefferson's design for the university's Grounds received more nominations than any other building or group of buildings.

The admissions office takes full advantage of Mr. Jefferson's architectural aesthetics. After candidates and parents had assembled in tired-looking Miller Hall, not of Jefferson origin, an admissions officer walked the large group toward the Lawn, heading toward the Rotunda.

The scene, in short, was breathtaking. Mr. Jefferson, the UVa *Record* says, had it all laid out by 1821: the Rotunda as centerpiece (a modified replica of the Pantheon in Rome), the Lawn with its ten Pavilions (originally classrooms on the first floor, professors' residences on the second) and fifty-four student rooms, six "hotels" equally spaced (once used as dining halls), and gardens behind each unit. The very green lawn stretches 600 feet south from the Rotunda and 200 feet across, with not a weed in sight. The classrooms and dining halls are gone from the Pavilions now, but seniors and professors still live behind the elegant stretches of colonnades. The Rotunda, the focal point of the university, was beautifully restored to Mr. Jefferson's original specifications in 1976, having survived a series of incarnations over the years, not to mention fires.

Inside the Rotunda, the drama continued to unfold: the tour group was paraded, on a spotless white carpet, around the bigger-than-life, floodlit statue of Mr. Jefferson to pay respects, then downstairs to a grand oval room with a colonial pewter chandelier and period chairs.

The young, serious admissions officer began his formal spiel to an awed group of prospective students and parents—a varied lot, hardly looking like the UVa stereotype of preppy and rich.

"As you now should know, the University of Virginia is the length and shadow of one man—Mister Jefferson—who spent the last years of his life solely on its development. This was the first truly public *and secular* university in the country and was intended to be national, not just Virginian, from the start."

After further tributes to the founder and his philosophy, the host outlined the current broad-brushed picture: a total student body of 16,000 with approximately 10,500 undergraduates; baccalaureate degrees in seven areas, doctorates in seventy-eight; a faculty of 1,500, over 95 percent of whom have earned doctorates; a combined library resource of 2,350,000 books, 10,000,000 manuscripts, and the largest microfilm collection in the country; and other "notable resources" such as a 2,000,000-watt nuclear reactor, a nuclear accelerator, a 500,000-volt electron microscope, two optical observatories, and the central facilities of the National Radio Observatory for Astronomy. He said that first-year students (freshmen at UVa) may apply for entry to the College of Arts and Sciences, the School of Architecture, or the School of Engineering and Applied Science. After two years of preprofessional study at Virginia or elsewhere, students may apply to the upper-division "professional" Schools of Commerce, Education or Nursing.

This session was strictly business, hardly a college sales promotion. The tour group was rather stiff, imitating the knowledgeable presenter, who said that UVa can be considered "selective" in admissions, with preference given to Virginians. A few brag-lines were carefully inserted, and most were memorable: Virginia has had more Rhodes scholars than any public university in America; at least two-thirds of UVa's premeds are annually admitted to med school (one-third of whom stay at Virginia for professional training); and UVa has an 11:1 student to faculty ratio.

One father relieved the intensity of the gathering by asking if it was true that Virginia, as rumor would have it, is "P-squared: Party and Preppy." With an oh-so-slight smile and his usual composure, the striped-tied leader responded that *Playboy* magazine had listed the "Top 10 Party Schools in America" and had not included UVa, although it had added a postscript saying that *one* institution—Virginia—was in a class all by itself. He also confessed that the film *Animal House* was too "toned down" to have been shot on Virginia's fraternity row, but that the fraternities, though still important, had faded from their rowdy pinnacle of the pre-1970 era when UVa was all male. Following a few more pleasantries and rather forced questions from parents, the group broke up. Some continued on a tour of the campus (oops—the Grounds) with a student guide, a sophomore.

Both the admissions presenter and the student tour guide helped dispel—quite by design, probably—the down side of UVa's image. Both were understated, studious types, respectful of Virginia's academic traditions but willing to discuss the lighter side of college life when asked.

UVa's campus-beyond-the-Lawn is disappointing, only because the dramatic portion designed by Mr. Jefferson builds such high expectations. It *is* attractive, fairly compact, green, with a few slight rolls that relieve the monotony of very forgettable brick buildings—mostly dorms and scattered functional boxes. Massive Alderman Library is impressive, as is the ambitious Clemons undergraduate reading library, just opened. Newcomb Hall, the Union, with its popular pub called the Pav, is drab and behind-the-times. On the whole, the Grounds are well maintained, with one maddening idiosyncrasy that locals excuse as part of "tradition." It seems countless secret, honor, and service societies have sprung up at Virginia over the years. A few of the more prominent, including the "Seven Society" whose members remain anonymous until death but give generously to the university throughout life, and two service groups whose members are well known—"Z" and "The Imps"—have the license to paint their silly names, usually neatly and in stark white, in prominent places throughout the Grounds, blatantly defacing some of Virginia's finest old serpentine brick walls and walkways.

There is order to the Grounds: six major academic areas have their buildings in clusters, combined in a hodge-podge of the old and the new, the old always being the more conspicuous; Cabell Hall is an example, a Stanford White–designed building at the opposite end of the Lawn from the Rotunda.

Adjacent to the campus is "the Corner," a rather seedy little gathering of essential shops and eateries, disappointing for a university the size and style of UVa. Charlottesville, a town of 62,500, 110 miles from Washington and 70 miles from Richmond, is not much better: it sports a new fashion mall, a fairly bleak "refurbished" downtown section, and segregated neighborhoods, but it is tidy throughout.

Admissions

Although the modernists have compromised Mr. Jefferson's Grounds by not coming close to the architectural standard he set, they have not compromised his insistence on a national student body. UVa says it up front in *The Record* (known as the admissions "viewbook" at many institutions):

> Unlike many state-supported institutions, the University of Virginia follows a practice of selective admissions and seeks qualified students from throughout the United States. The basic goal of the selection process is to provide a capable, diverse, and enthusiastic student body. The University intends to remain Virginia's national university.

It has. At least 35 percent of the UVa freshmen are from out of state, sometimes close to 40 percent (as compared to approximately 10 percent out-of-state students at the Universities of California, Connecticut, and Illinois). The University of Virginia's policy has not gone unnoticed by critics within the Commonwealth. A spunky little paper called the *Tidewater News* editorialized boldly on the issue recently:

> Stung by the awakening of a state fed up with an admissions policy that denies so many of its qualified residents a place in their own state university, the University of Virginia has launched a counter-offensive. . . .

> Enough of this nonsense. Legislatures in other states have solved similar problems with their own errant academicians by imposing mandatory in-state student admission percentages. . . .

> It is time for the General Assembly and the people of Virginia to reclaim U. Va. as an educational asset for its citizens. It is time to reject the pretentious notions of those who have no qualms about using public money to pursue their own goals and to make the curious claim: U. Va. is the nation's only *private* state institution.

UVa responded by quoting Mr. Jefferson's ". . . and to be a temptation to the youth of other states to come, and drink the cup of knowledge and fraternize with us" line, and also by quoting a mission narrative from the Commonwealth's *Virginia Plan for Higher Education, 1979*: "The University of Virginia, founded by Thomas Jefferson in 1819, is a major comprehensive state university of national character and stature."

In fact, UVa's president, Frank L. Hereford, Jr., launched a series of letters to alumni and friends, highlighting this very aspect of the university: "Mr. Jefferson made powerful arguments to gain state support for a uni-

versity that was to be innovative in scope, national in character . . .",
President Hereford said. Almost half of the students who attended the
University of Virginia during the thirty-year-period following the Civil War
came from other states, mostly from the South. The Southern character of
the university was diminished after the turn of the century when New York
became the second largest supplier of students to the university, a position
it still holds. According to President Hereford, the General Assembly of
Virginia recognized the value to the Commonwealth of sponsoring a fully
comprehensive university of national character, similar to the private institutions that exist in neighboring states—Duke of North Carolina, Johns
Hopkins of Maryland, Vanderbilt of Tennessee are examples.

President Hereford made a strong point of the value to Virginia and
UVa itself of having out-of-staters who return to other parts of the country
following their graduation. He indicated that approximately two-thirds of
the Virginia endowment has been derived directly from out-of-state alumni.
He cited Virginia's national impact by having alumni in wide-ranging state
senates or legislatures, not to mention the United States Congress. And
last, he cited the good fortune of the Commonwealth of Virginia in attracting many out-of-state undergraduates as full-time Virginia residents.

Controversies such as the in-state/out-of-state issue have allowed UVa's
dean of admissions to step into the limelight. That is UVa's good fortune.
There is not a more highly respected admissions professional in the nation.
This man is different from other admissions directors today; while most
focus on enrollment planning, marketing, and improved sales campaigns,
the UVa dean remains what he has been—an academician, an associate
professor of English, and a political lobbyist for higher education. He speaks
sensitively and well. In response to the *Tidewater News*:

> Simply stated, the University's policy is that we offer admission
> to Virginians whose records indicate that they are in every rel-
> evant respect prepared to compete successfully in the program
> requested with the average student currently enrolled here,
> and to graduate on time and on track. After accommodating all
> qualified Virginians, we offer admission to the strongest non-
> Virginians who apply.

The good dean is less than scholarly behind the wheel. What does a
guest do when a somber professional pulls up in a small blue bug, leans
out and asks: "Do you get car sick? If not, would you risk driving a half
hour with me to Shenandoah Park? Great views there, and the best mountain trout you've had for years."

Off in a puff of dust, the elderly VW rolled, bumped, hairpin turned, and sped through gorgeous hills and horsey country with poverty patches more lastingly impressive than the fox-hunt crowd's scattered elegant encampments. As we approached the spacious park at dusk, deer were silhouetted against the fields, with backdrops of blues and purples. The pastoral magnificence settled the stomach and enhanced the appreciation of what the UVa family can enjoy close by.

The dean talked UVa more than admissions, but the two were one in his mind. He had plenty to say, and what he said was compelling, probably on target. This man always seemed to be in front of a class underscoring a point or perhaps running for office. He was the aspirant-to-college-president type, horn-rimmed glasses and all.

"There are a few 'givens' you must accept before you can understand the subtleties of UVa," he said. "First, the magnificence of the Grounds and the facilities in general. Second, our self-satisfaction: it is very important and undergirds much that happens here. Third, our enormous variety of students. Granted, they all look alike within two months after arriving in Charlottesville, but they are wonderfully different from each other in background, style, and purpose. Fourth, our own vocational traditions: students here traditionally work toward business or law. Why not medicine, like any normal college's student body? I really don't know. And finally, the unevenness of our quality. I am reluctant to confess it, but we are inconsistent at Virginia in standards of excellence. Unevenness of departments just isn't allowed at a place like Berkeley, but it has sneaked up on us at UVa. Don't get me wrong: we're strong, particularly in our program for undergraduates. But greatness across the board eludes us."

The dean paused for wine. When he sipped, he gulped, impatient to continue.

"But how do you really judge the quality of an undergraduate program or department? For example, one of our easiest majors here, supposedly, is speech communications. You should see the conversions that program produces! Kids learn to 'present themselves' with extraordinary effectiveness. Who cares if the Ph.D.s there aren't top-rated in their field in the nation? They are superb *teachers*, and the need that is addressed is significant."

Time and again, the dean's comments underscored pride in an undergraduate program that met the needs of a diversified student body, not just the mainstream who enter well prepared, zip through, and ease into a top professional school at graduation. He often referred to the well-being of minority students.

During the ride home, the dean addressed the minority issue directly. It is not well known, even within the admissions profession, that UVa has one of the most successful black recruitment campaigns of any selective college in America, public or private, resulting in a high percentage of minority freshmen. Ten to 13 percent of the freshmen entering UVa during the last four years were black, making Virginia one of the all too few highly selective institutions that have enrolled blacks at a rate comparable to their representation in the total population. The admissions dean said that, once again, Thomas Jefferson had pointed the way:

> Laws and institutions must go hand in hand with the progress of the human mind. . . . As new discoveries are made, new truths disclosed, and manners and opinions change with the change of circumstances, institutions must advance also, and keep pace with the times.
>
> Mr. Jefferson, 1816

Mr. Jefferson aside (one cannot notice without raised brow his slave quarters at Monticello), it is UVa's dean of admissions who has successfully recruited blacks for a seemingly unlikely place. And he has done it through academic channels, not through "more effective marketing." Noting that minority-oriented high shools in Virginia were too often characterized by uninspired teaching of the basic disciplines, he led a series of workshops, school to school, to enhance the teaching of English and advanced mathematics. High school teachers, in turn, pushed UVa's name to promising students in the enriched courses. Little by little, the number of black students referred to UVa grew, paralleling appreciation for the admissions dean's contribution to secondary school quality in less affluent areas.

Admission to the University of Virginia is *highly* selective, regardless of what the presenter in the Oval Room of the Rotunda called it. The dean supervises a thorough review of each candidate. There are nine readers, each passing judgment on about fifty folders per day. The reading starts with the assistant directors; folders then move up the line to the associates, and finally they are read by the dean himself, in every case. The competition for the out-of-state 35 to 40 percent segment of the class is the toughest.

All applicants are advised that their chances for admission will be enhanced if they pursue the most rigorous course available to them in their respective schools, especially in their junior and senior years. Virginia recommends that students take all five core subjects—English, foreign language, mathematics, natural science, and history—each year, and in the most advanced classes available. Applicants are told that they should rank in the top tenth of their class if they are attending a "heterogeneous public high school," or in the top third of the college-bound group, should they be attending selective college-prep schools. Students are requested to present samples of their writing that are "fluent, logical, grammatical, and well organized." Also, some demonstration of leadership and some service in extracurricular affairs are desirable. Students are expected to be well recommended by teachers and counselors and to show high competence on tests of reading, vocabulary, and arithmetic skills. Candidates for admission are told: "The goals pursued by the Committee on Admissions have been at least as much pragmatic as philosophical: we want to admit students who succeed here; we want to foster real excellence in Virginia's schools; we want to do our part to maintain the flow of literate, thoughtful, professionally competent men and women from our undergraduate schools to Virginia and to the nation."

UVa, unlike the University of California and a handful of other selective public universities, does not admit by formula or computer. Virginia's process is more thorough, more flexible, and, granted, more subjective. The *Record* says: "Recognizing that superior academic performance and promise do not necessarily guarantee success or happiness at any university, the Committee tries to understand each applicant in personal terms, and accordingly seeks evidence of good character and social habits, facility in self-expression, leadership, commitment to service, and any other predictors of probable contributions to the University community. The University actively seeks the well-rounded student."

The scholarly dean of admissions is not immune to the lighter side. When asked the funniest thing that had ever happened to him "in the line of duty," he lit up. One day he was interviewing a young woman who thought her credentials for admission were more compelling than the dean seemed to be acknowledging. Frustrated, she decided on a course of action to impress this all-important authority.

The dean smiled wryly as he continued the saga. "I had turned my back to her to pick up a brochure. Then the phone rang, and I became engrossed in that conversation, my back still to the candidate. On wheeling around, I was stunned to see her sitting there with an inviting look, both breasts bared." The dean blushed in even recalling the story. "I excused myself, walked straight to the library, and buried my head for about two hours. Later, the real problem emerged—what to do with her application? She was an above average candidate. We finally put her on the waiting list and, as an institution, conveniently forgot about her. But she is etched in *my memory!*"

Student Life

What are the students like who survive the rush on Virginia's front door? It is easy to meet and talk with them around the Grounds or at pubs adjacent to campus. One of the latter produced a group ever so loyal to the place, ever so alligatored and nice-looking in a Saks-Fifth-Avenue-front-window sort of way, obviously bright but with little to say. Their theme of the evening was "interpersonal relationships": "UVa is strong in many ways, but particularly in nurturing interpersonal relationships."

Q: "Is UVa's public image on target?" A: "No! It's the rest of the world that is stuck up. Yes, we party hard, but only after we study hard. The partying nurtures knowing and understanding each other—you know, interpersonal relationships."

Q: "Is UVa as strong academically as its reputation indicates?" A: "Yes, if you like your studies tempered with a joyful college life. At dull William and Mary, studying is *everything*. At UVa, where the academics are as strong if not stronger, studying is *part* of college."

Q: "What academic programs stand out as particularly good, particularly demanding?" A: "For entering students, the Echols Scholar Program in the College of Arts and Science. About 125 kids in each entering class are chosen for it, and they really have to be *super* smart. They are exempt from distributional requirements and even from picking a major. It is full of independent study, tutorials, and free choice of the curriculum. They're not exactly your well-rounded Wahoo types, but they *are* respected."

The beer flowed freely with this little group, and so did the smiles and good manners.

"Engineering is rugged. So are English, chemistry, biology, physics, government and foreign affairs, history, and accounting. The guts are anything in the Education School, also psychology, speech, and a smattering of others. The place in general keeps you on your toes academically. It is tough to get top grades, but it's even tougher to flunk out."

The group was proud of UVa's national character. On the other hand, they fared poorly in responding to which other universities in the nation might qualify for Public Ivy status. They didn't want to guess—largely, it seemed, because they didn't care.

The one topic of the evening that stimulated the group was UVa's Honor System. At issue: should the university continue to expel any student caught "lying, cheating, or stealing?" The Honor System is a basic ingredient of UVa life. Initiated in 1842, it has always been so. President Hereford underscored the lingering importance of the Honor System in a letter to alumni and friends:

> Throughout its history the Honor System has been a living system which has undergone modifications and revisions as tides of sentiment regarding social justice and equity have shifted. However, three features of the Honor System have remained steadfast:
> —the Honor System remains based on the concept that the

presence of one guilty of lying, cheating or stealing will not be tolerated.

—the Honor System remains under the authority of the student body through its elected representatives with no appeal to the faculty, administration, or Board of Visitors.

—the Honor System continues to rely on the acceptance by each individual in the student body of his or her personal responsibility.

It seems to work. As one student said: "It breaks down occasionally, but I left my door unlocked virtually every day for three years in the dorms and was never ripped off!" Another commented, "I'm afraid it could be eroding, but it does work better than I would have thought possible. This does not mean there is no cheating, but rather that honor is the rule rather than the exception."

An exception created one of the latest stirs on campus: an athlete was caught stealing Cokes from a broken dispenser. Wasn't it a little stiff to *expel* someone for that level of crime? Wouldn't a one-year suspension for first-time offenders make more sense? After months of discussion and position papers, the "single sanction" (immediate expulsion) won again in a student vote, 3,216 to 2,670. Virginia kept its Honor.

But a student *can* lie about his or her age to get a drink at UVa. The "party" part of UVa's reputation remains intact. Despite some recent efforts by the administration to diminish this tradition by suggesting "alternative beverages," the heavy partying continues. Wild times continue on Rugby Road, and "Easters" weekend annually draws tremendous crowds. There are a few well-attended formal balls, and less elegant occasions are frequent and always full.

Times do change, of course. The "Wahoo" (from a campus cheer) men's "roll down the road" to search for women at Mary Washington, Hollins, Randolph-Macon, and Sweet Briar colleges has slowed since, in one short decade of coeducation, UVa has accomplished a near 50:50 ratio. The required coats and ties of the all-male era are gone, and so is the locker-room atmosphere of the place—except for Rugby Road, where the Greeks are still at it. Thirty percent of Virginia's men join fraternities; 20 percent of the women join sororities. As the yearbook records:

The Greek system thrives at the University with 37 fraternities and 15 sororities. The fraternities hold the last remnants of "Old U-ism"—that traditional aspect of the University which is so attractive to some and so offensive to others. Big party weekends, trips "down the road," gatoring and preppie clothes epitomize the stereotypical Old U fraternity, but not all fraternities fit this mold. Service activities also have their place among the fraternities, though in varying degrees. The black fraternities devote their efforts entirely to service activities. . . . While fraternities represent, to some, the last bastion of conservatism and elitism, they are a dominant force in the social and service life of the University.

As at many other colleges and universities, some undergrads join the Greek system at UVa to find housing. The university is apologetic about its housing situation. All freshmen live in coed dorms which seem to function better than they look. Students eat in massive cafeterias, although there are options on meal contracts. Upperclassmen must enter a lottery for dorms or the university apartments on the outskirts of campus. The exception is that elite little group of fifty-two "Lawnies," fourth-year students "who have made special contributions to the university community" and who choose to live in the prized but cramped single rooms behind the Collonnades on Mr. Jefferson's original Lawn. (They can be seen during the wet weather dashing down exterior cold brick corridors to common johns and, in spring and fall, rocking proudly in their uniform straight-backed chairs on the historic grasses.) In total, UVa can house approximately 30 percent of its student body, but it has set a goal of accommodating 50 percent through new housing units. "This will require the reproduction of 60 percent of the existing student housing units. But the University has no other choice if it expects to retain any sense of community or cohesion, much less, any vestige of the Academical Village envisaged by its founder," President Hereford has said.

Another element of change which some attribute to the current president (who gets mixed reviews; "He'd just as soon see us all male and very straight again" was the impression of one young man on campus) is success in athletics. For years "the University considered *victory* disturbing . . . ," reported Frank Deford in *Sports Illustrated* (September 15, 1980). "So cherished is defeat in the Virginia tradition that its fondest sports memory is of a loss. It was 1941, the year The University . . . nearly had its only perfect football season. The Wahoos were ahead of Yale 19–0 at the half but lost 21–19. And here's the punch line the alumni really savor: not only was it Virginia's lone defeat, but it was also Yale's only victory . . . Virginia athletics have always reminded me of British foreign policy, with a magnificent history of honorable failures."

At some point in the mid-1970s, the athletic director appealed to the president saying, "If we're going to keep on fielding teams, mightn't we also try to win?" The president said okay, the monies were increased, and the rest is a new chapter of UVa "tradition." As the president proudly stated in his 1980–1981 annual report:

> Our athletic program had its greatest year. The men's and women's teams as a group had winning records in Atlantic Coast Conference competition for the first time since the University joined the ACC in 1953. . . .

The football team is having a winning season for the first time since 1968, the men's basketball team recently won the National Invitational Tournament, and the lacrosse team regularly goes to the finals of the NCAA. Women's teams in basketball, track, cross country, and tennis are doing just as well. An important postscript: Wahoo-recruited athletes match the overall student body in retention: 67 percent graduate in four years, 75 percent in five.

Deford, in *Sports Illustrated*, concluded: "Yes, losing isn't everything. And good Lord, after all those years of world-class practice, can you imagine the Victory Party they could throw at The University?"

In fact, the fever to win has grown so intense at UVa that the faculty chairman of athletics is now playing with history just to honor the jocks:

> In an ironic way, it is the athletes here today who most resemble the ideal of the old-line Wahoos. Those men came here to learn how to be responsible, to be role models, so they could leave as gentry, as leaders of the Commonwealth. The athletes may come only as that, as athletes, but by the time they leave, they have learned to respond in many ways to this beautiful place. And that's what the liberal arts are all about.

It would not be fair to move from a discussion of campus life at Virginia without mentioning student activism, an important new dimension at UVa which did not pass with the early seventies. Again, Mister Jefferson is credited for stirring activity:

> The spirit of resistance to government is so valuable on certain occasions, that I wish it to always be kept alive. . . . I like a little rebellion now and then. (from a letter to Abigail Adams, 1787)

There was rebellion at Virginia, as most everywhere else, following Cambodia and Kent State. Police arrested student demonstrators (even on the Lawn!), and undergraduates occupied the ROTC building, staged a massive "honk in," and called a strike. The Charlottesville Activists' Coalition (CAC) remains active. One result is that levels of radiation emitted from the university's reactor have been reduced. There is a continuing drive, spearheaded by the Black Student Alliance, to improve UVa's dismal record of hiring black and female faculty and staff members. There have been campaigns against draft registration and in support of ERA. When Vice-President George Bush attended "Final Exercises" (graduation) in 1981, he was met by graduates in white armbands to protest the Reagan administration and by an associate professor of history carrying a banner that read: "Get us out of El Salvador, By George. No more Bush league wars!" There were even handbills at commencement endorsing vegetarian diets. Although pooh-poohed by many, if not most, Virginia undergraduates, the CAC probably won't go away. The liberal Mister Jefferson may have the last word, after all, at his reputedly conservative university.

Academic Programs and Staff

"Liberal learning" is a force at UVa. One is not as overwhelmed by the intellectualism, however, as by an atmosphere combining tradition and seriousness with quite adequate doses of social relief.

Getting a handle on the faculty of Virginia who are directly involved with *under*graduates is a difficult assignment, as at other universities with shared undergraduate/graduate appointments. But at UVa one develops the sense, in talking with both students and teachers, that undergrads do profit directly from strong graduate divisions. Part of this happy situation simply relates to size—both levels of the student body are relatively small—and to geographical proximity—everyone is part of the same Grounds (the Medical School and Hospital, for example, are within stone's throw of the Lawn).

A mathematician who was recently appointed vice-president and provost, having been dean of the faculty for years, is the principal administrator of academic affairs. He possesses a wealth of knowledge regarding the University of Virginia.

According to the provost, UVa opened with Jeffersonian leftist tendencies in the classroom and stayed afloat with mild success until the South fell on hard times in the 1860s, straining the university's health and spirit until 1900, when the first real president came on board. There was slow growth until the 1950s, when dramatic change entered with President Darden who "democratized" the university. During the sixties and seventies there was considerable growth *and* academic acclaim, as the university changed from small to "moderate-size." The provost feels that the national character of the institution has been a basic advantage to UVa's visibility among quality institutions in the country, both public and private, from the start, as has the well-known Honor System. He cites the large endowment as important to UVa's prominence among public institutions, as well as consistency of quality in the student body. But more than anything else, the vice-president/provost feels UVa deserves top billing among public institutions for the consistency of the quality of its faculty.

President Hereford agrees. In his letter to the UVa family, "in celebration of the 238th anniversary of the birth of Thomas Jefferson," he said:

> It has been said that distinguished teachers attract distinguished students. I believe that it is equally true that distinguished students attract distinguished teachers. . . . Paralleling the achievements of our students, it is easy to cite examples of the outstanding achievements of faculty members during the past several years: —Biographer-in-Residence Dumas Malone received the Pulitzer Prize in History for his monumental biography of Thomas Jefferson; only a few years later Associate Professor James A. McPherson won the Pulitzer Prize in Fiction. —Over a four-year period Commonwealth Professor of French Roger W. Shattuck, Professor of English Douglas T. Day, and Lecturer in English Mary Lee Settle won National Book Awards. —Vice-President for Health Affairs William H. Muller, Jr., became the first surgeon ever to hold the presidency of the American Surgical Association and the Southern Surgical Association simultaneously; five years later he was elected President of the American College of Surgeons. —Edgar F. Shannon, Jr., former President and now Commonwealth Professor of English, was elected national President of Phi Beta Kappa.

Resources

Hereford also points out that the distinction of the faculty has been apparent in their outstanding success in competing for private and state funds for research support. While there has been little increase in federal support for academic research in recent years, the number of grants awarded to Virginia faculty members has increased approximately 15 percent per year.

Hereford is particularly proud of the number of endowed chairs at UVa. There are 150 endowed chairs supported by approximately $28 million in endowment principal. Much of the support for the chaired professors has come from the state's Eminent Scholars Program through which the Commonwealth matches gifts specifically designated for attracting and retaining Eminent Scholars. "Without any question," says President Hereford, "the University's endowed professorships constitute our greatest single asset in providing an outstanding faculty."

Among public institutions, Virginia is wealthy, thanks partly to a generous endowment developed from private sources. In his 1981 annual report, President Hereford indicated the trustees had approved an operating budget of $303.6 million for the 1981–1982 fiscal year. At that time, he indicated that the market value of the endowment was $225 million, with a 28 percent "return" for the year. The figures did not incude endowments held by alumni organizations and related foundations.

One obvious signal of UVa's financial well being can be seen on campus. New buildings keep rising and renovations of the old take place on schedule. In the past several years, a $2 million complex at the Darden School (business), a $10.8 million Primary Care Center, a four-level garage and a $600,000 Central Electron Microscope Facility at the Medical Center, the $5 million Clemons Undergraduate Library, greatly expanded seating—from 24,000 to 36,000—at the football stadium, and a 9,000 square-foot addition to the physics building have been completed, as have major renovations at Newcomb Hall (where the Union is housed) and at Peabody, an adjacent administrative building. Under construction: an eighteen-hole golf course at "Birdwood," near the Grounds—"We expect a championship rating"—and soon, a $16.4 million housing project to accommodate 650 students.

All that development obviously means a generous state legislature and/or a loyal alumni body. UVa has both. In terms of percentage of revenue spent on higher education, the Commonwealth of Virginia usually ranks well above average in the nation. And that endowment! UVa is second in the nation among public universities in private endowment, twenty-first among all colleges and universities. As a result, less than one-third of the university's operating monies must come from public funds.

Virginia not only has loyal alums, it has important alums. One UVa alumnus recently succeeded another as president of Chemical Bank in New York. The seven alumni in the United States Senate are second in number only to Harvard's. Bowie Kuhn, former baseball commissioner, is an alum, as are Louis Auchincloss and Erskine Caldwell, two of America's best-known novelists. Woodrow Wilson graduated from UVa, as did W. W. Yen, prime minister of China during the early 1900s. The recent governor of the Commonwealth, Chuck Robb (Lyndon Johnson's son-in-law), has a degree from Virginia's law school, as does Franklin Roosevelt, Jr., Edward Kennedy, and former-senator Hugh Scott. Much earlier in history, Walter Reid and Edgar Allen Poe took UVa degrees.

One gets a taste of zealous Wahoo loyalty by talking with just one or two alumni. A class of '42 Charlottesville citizen, a successful businessman, is now a member of UVa's sixteen-member "board of visitors," or trustees. He's a ruddy fellow, down-home, open-faced, and fiercely loyal to UVa.

"I turned down Princeton to attend Virginia, even though at my prep school you were *supposed* to go to Princeton—there's a southern tradition up there, you know. But I sure made the right choice. Hell, I doubt if Harvard, Yale, *or* Princeton can come close to our quality of education for undergraduates today. And we look at the 'whole boy' in the admissions process: we pass by some 4.0's who offer nothing else. We have breadth of curriculum for a small university, a top-flight faculty, strong student aid, and a real conscience when it comes to recruiting athletes—unlike some of our competition in the ACC. And we have loyal alumni, very loyal alumni."

The salty trustee leaned far back in his swivel chair, far enough to rest on the cluttered roll-top desk in his congested farm equipment office. He smiled a little, guarding his words carefully. "Not all of us have agreed, of course, with everything that has happened along the way. Each president has made a different kind of contribution. In modern times, Darden democratized the place; his contribution was consistent with the GI Bill of his era. He also built buildings. Shannon, after Darden, built the faculty and did a damn good job coping with campus disruption in the Vietnam era. And now we have Frank Hereford. He's trying to bring the alumni back into the fold, the ones who were irked by campus activism in the late sixties and seventies. And he spends a great deal of time with the legislature on financial matters. Even with our good endowment, we're still going to need public money, you know. But all in all, what a place! And it wouldn't have happened, of course, if it weren't for Thomas Jefferson. Have you heard what John Kennedy said when he entertained Nobel laureates at the White House? That 'no equally extraordinary collection of talent and human knowledge had dined in the White House since Jefferson dined alone.' "

Although "Mr. Jefferson" has a lingering presence at UVa and strengthens the pride of its donors, Colgate W. Darden, Jr., is probably most responsible for the university as it is today. He was president from 1947 to 1959, following a distinguished political career as a member of Congress, U.S. representative to the United Nations, and governor of Virginia. (It was Darden who was instrumental in reopening Virginia's public schools after they had been closed to avert desegregation.)

Darden was not popular on the college campus. As governor, for example, he had suggested that fraternities at state-supported schools be closed down. But William and Mary chose him as rector following his term as governor. One year later he turned down the offer of a U.S. Senate seat to become president of UVa. Those who knew him best felt it was a high priority for him to turn the elitist school that acted as if it were private into a first-rank public university that served the nation, but Virginia first. He came to UVa when fraternities dominated student life, private school graduates greatly outnumbered public school graduates, dormitories were scant, tuition for in-state students was the second-highest in the country, and the college had the reputation of being a cinch to get admitted to. Darden wanted to change almost all of that.

During President Darden's administration, the campus skyline dramatically changed, with $22.5 million worth of construction. In the days of a tough Byrd machine, he convinced the legislature to provide more money for public higher education—for construction, for student aid, for salaries, for research. He fought for a Union Building, belligerently opposed by the majority of students who thought the demise of fraternities was the hidden motive. He upped academic standards, started requiring College Board scores of candidates for admission, and challenged the "gentlemen's C" (which some say originated at UVa). He convinced the Commonwealth of Virginia to match private funds for an eminent scholars' program and to *assure* the university of permanent monies. He started the South's first business school, and he personally supported some needy students, not to mention the first seeds of the civil rights cause at UVa. Darden's associates said his efforts had one end—to make UVa the school its founder, Thomas Jefferson, had intended it to be. He wanted Virginia to be one of the top universities in the United States.

In this reviewer's opinion, it is.

William and Mary College of Virginia

Atmosphere

"What *other* college is part of a $100 million museum that serves as a national shrine?" exclaimed a William and Mary sophomore dressed in federal skirts, as she served up entrees in a rather expensive Taverne in Colonial Williamsburg. "That's why every Mom and Dad would like to put their kid here: it's Americana elegance, doggedly serious, highly selective—and, perhaps most important, it's a nice place to visit. But after a while, believe me, 'playing history' wears thin. Williamsburg is mecca for a sophisticated tourist for a week. For four years of college, though, it's dull as Colonial bean soup. But I'll grind through, like the rest of them."

Dull? Perhaps. Well, probably, in fact. But that's a small price to pay for exposure to the superb ingredients this institution assembles. For example, William and Mary can make a good case for being the most selective public college in America. Its size—4,400 undergraduates, 1,600 graduates—is ideal, the envy of a good many prestigious private colleges. Its setting—in historic, charming Williamsburg—and its own lush campus of distinctive Colonial, Georgian, and modern buildings, provide the stuff calendars are made of. Its academic program, focusing on liberal arts and the sciences, is no-nonsense, followed by impressive placement in graduate schools and jobs. In a recent year, for example, William and Mary placed 70 percent of its premed students in medical school; the comparable figure that year at UVa was 61 percent.

Beneath William and Mary's sedate and gracious facade are a few problems, of course: somehow the money ends up more in facilities-that-show than in increased faculty-salaries-that-don't; women and minority

William and Mary College
Williamsburg, Virginia

1) Size of Student Body

Undergraduate __4,731__   Graduate __1,572__   Total __6,303__

2) 1983 Freshman Class Profile

Class Size __1,107__   % Men __47__   % Women __53__
Percent of Applicants Admitted __37__
Average SATs: Verbal __595__   Math __615__
High School Class Rank: Top Tenth __55__ % Top Quarter __81__ %
    Geographical Distribution (% of class):
In-State __65__ % Middle Atlantic __21__ % New England __4__ %
West __1__ % Middle West __3__ % South __69__ %
Foreign __2__ %
Minority Students __3__ % of Class
Financial Aid __18__ % of Class

3) Retention of Students

__80__ % of freshmen graduate in four years
__85__ % of freshmen graduate in five years

4) Ten Most Popular Majors of Graduating Seniors, 1983

1. Business
2. Economics
3. Biology
4. English
5. Government
6. Psychology
7. History
8. Mathematics
9. Computer Science
10. Chemistry

5) The Financial Picture (1982–83)

Annual Campus Budget	$ 31,000,000
1983–84 Tuition and Fees for State Residents	$ 1,776
1983–84 Tuition and Fees for Out-of-State Residents	$ 4,690

Revenues

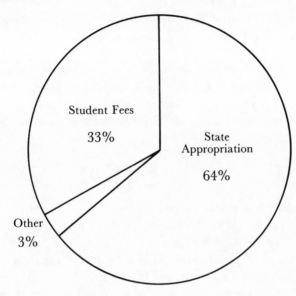

Expenditures

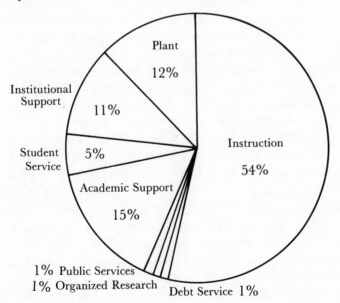

professionals are inadequately represented; "moderation" is a bit too much the password in all quarters; and there is no place nearby for students to raise hell, even to whoop it up a little. But the negatives, though real, are dwarfed by the very Ivy look, character, and quality of this unique institution.

"William and Mary is America's best kept secret," says one faculty member. Well, almost. Word has been getting around, however slowly, that prestigious William and Mary is public, not private. That means affordable, and that means crowds. But the prestige has always been there. Dramatic beginnings paved the way.

History and Tradition

William and Mary was the second college in the American colonies. Harvard was first, in 1636; then came William and Mary in 1693, before Yale in 1701. The charter was granted by King William III and Queen Mary II when a movement emerged in England to create a college in the colony of Virginia to train young men and clergy for the Church of England. The site of Williamsburg was chosen after initial construction near Richmond was destroyed in an Indian massacre in 1622.

A who's who of American history paraded through the young college's historic Christopher Wren building. Three presidents—Jefferson, Monroe, and Tyler—attended, as did sixteen members of the Continental Congress, four signers of the Declaration of Independence, and, through the years, over thirty U.S. Senators, sixty members of the House, and twenty-seven governors of ten states. George Washington received his surveyor's license from William and Mary and became, after serving as president of the United States, the college's first American chancellor. But with American independence from England and the consequent severance of the college's royal patronage, William and Mary's future was in doubt. It struggled to stay open through the Civil War, and it did close in 1881 although, as the College Visitor's Guide records, "The symbolic ringing of the College bell kept alive the Royal Charter." Virginia granted $10,000 for William and Mary's reopening in 1888. In 1906, all-male William and Mary formally became a state institution with a board of visitors (now numbering seventeen) appointed by the governor. Women were first admitted in 1918.

Although William and Mary had a heady beginning, the college floundered for many years. Until, that is, two fiftyish men met on a Williamsburg street corner in 1926. One had a vision, the other a fortune. Happily for William and Mary College, the latter funded the former and the college was swept by this liaison to stability and eminence.

The man with the vision was the Reverend W. A. R. Goodwin, rector of the local Episcopal church, who dreamed of turning back two centuries at Williamsburg and restoring the town to its eighteenth-century appearance. One hundred million dollars later, and by the time Reverend Goodwin died in 1939, John D. Rockefeller had accomplished the feat. But the role of the college cannot be overlooked in transforming Williamsburg into a living national museum.

William and Mary's president, Julian A. C. Chandler, inaugurated in 1919, had high aspirations for his struggling institution. He knew the work of Reverend Goodwin in restoring churches. In 1907, for example, on the three hundredth anniversary of the establishment of the Episcopal church in America, Williamsburg's old Bruton church was rededicated. Thanks to Goodwin's energy, research, and fund-raising, it had been restored to its Colonial pattern—that is, as the church had been in 1779 when Williamsburg ceased to be Virginia's seat of government. Then Goodwin moved to New York to revitalize St. Paul's Church in Rochester. But in 1923, President Chandler lured him back to Williamsburg as professor of biblical literature and religious education *and* director of endowment at William and Mary College.

From the moment of Goodwin's arrival at William and Mary, it seems, he and Chandler eyed Rockefeller's fortune as the means of returning Williamsburg, and with it the college, to "the original." After several years, Rockefeller, who had played an important role in the restoration of Reims cathedral and the palace and gardens of Versailles, visited Goodwin, toured Williamsburg, and saw the tawdry eighty-eight Colonial dwellings that remained within the limits of the town. Soon after, he secretly commissioned Goodwin to have drawings made for the renovation of the Sir Christopher Wren Building at the college, and preliminary drawings for the restoration of the town. Impressed by the plans, and agreeable to the enormous project but insistent that his identity remain hidden, Rockefeller commissioned Goodwin to start buying up old houses throughout Williamsburg. The villagers knew that *someone* was backing the poor clergyman in his buying mania—Henry Ford and George Eastman were the rumored angels. But as decrepit buildings soared in price, the news had to break: John D. Rockefeller was buying up the town. Rockefeller acknowledged his involvement and announced: "I've heard of people being taken for a ride. Dr. Goodwin only took me for a walk."

The elegant village that was raised from the dead and now draws over a million tourists a year to restored homes, public buildings, craft shops, and gardens, represents the removal of approximately 600 buildings, the restoration of nearly 90, and the reconstruction of others from records which researchers uncovered in England or America. One of the most popular and familiar sights in Williamsburg is the crown jewel sitting at

the top of Duke of Glancester Street: the College of William and Mary's
Wren Building, the oldest academic building in America (1695), the survivor of two wars and three fires.

The director of admissions at William and Mary knows just how to
use the magnificently restored Wren Building. Twice a day, a caravan of
prospective students and parents wend their way from the admissions office
to the historic edifice, pausing first on the herringbone brick walkways
lined by white fences to let the group ooh-and-aah at the Colonial gardens
of the president's home, and then at the old marble tablet on the Wren
Building itself. The tablet's claims for William and Mary College are worthy of respect:

> Chartered February 8, 1693 by King William and Queen Mary
> Main Building by Christopher Wren
> First College in the United States in its antecedents,
>   Second to Harvard in actual operation
> First College in the United States to establish an
>   intercollegiate fraternity, Phi Beta Kappa, December 5, 1776
> First College to have the Elective System of Study, 1779
> First College to have the Honor System, 1779
> First College to become a University, 1779

Academic Programs and Staff

Forgetting tradition for the moment, although reminders hit one at
every turn at William and Mary, what is the character of the college today?
The faculty and administration like to talk about that.

"We're on a par with the best small private colleges—Carleton and
Colgate, for example," said the chairman of the Religion Department who
used to be dean of the undergraduate program. The preppy, penny-loafered
professor was sitting in a cement block, pastel office on the modern part
of the campus, which suggested Iowa State more than Colonial America.
"It's our faculty. They're responsible for the 'work hard' reputation of the
place. A recent study revealed the average faculty workweek here is fifty-
nine hours, the highest in the state. And we're academically conservative.
We still have a five-course load per student each semester, and probably
we're the last college in the nation to introduce a pass/fail option, for one
course in each of the junior and senior years. If any one wonders about
our standards, he should look at our grade distribution—no grade inflation
here! And the students take it, although they do complain that too much
of the load is 'busy work.' Are they right? Probably, in some disciplines."

The energetic professor, author of two books on Christian thought and winner of the Brass Prize for a paper on Matthew Arnold, continued. "Like any college, we have our weaker areas and our stronger areas. Psychology, sociology, music, and education are often considered 'guts' here; the sciences and history are considered our forte. That lising is incomplete, but popular. But remember: unlike almost all other public institutions, and most private ones, we have *no* teaching assistants [graduate students substituting for professors]. So professors know their students fairly well and have a reputation for actually *enjoying* them.

"Problems? Of course we have them. Our small, very special town isolates us. The students, as a result, are not very active politically. You won't believe this, but one junior girl said she didn't know there had been an assassination attempt on President Reagan until the next day.

"But *what* a place, really, thanks largely to John D. Rockefeller. . . . We often forget to credit him."

The current dean of undergraduate programs teaches classics. She went to Vassar. She sits in the office one expects all faculty at William and Mary to have: in the Wren Building with a huge fireplace, tall ceilings and an Oriental rug, but no pictures on the walls ("They won't let me"). The dean is rather pale and somber. Perhaps it is because she is the only woman among the twenty-two people working in the central administration.

"Yes, it's lonely. Only 10 percent of all our faculty are women; even that percentage is inflated by the large number of women in physical education. But William and Mary's strengths far outweigh this shortcoming.

"Why do we deserve the label Public Ivy? Largely, I guess, because of our high student selectivity. Certainly not because of our faculty research, although that is growing—the School of Marine Science just relocated here, and it is all research. I guess we're Ivy in that we *concentrate* on the undergraduate and on liberal arts. We have kept traditional emphases and the core curriculum intact, despite social pressures over the years to change. And we're determined to avoid grade inflation. We have rather small classes but a broad curriculum."

The dean shifted slightly in her high-backed chair, but this was not an animated lady. What she said, however, was said with precision. And she is a team woman.

"When President Graves came here over a decade ago, he healed the place with good managerial skills. All the units had been at each other's throats. But even he is constrained by a very conservative board of visitors. Yes, we are conservative, probably an honest representation of our state. But that doesn't really hurt us. The one thing that does hurt us is the low faculty salary scale. It is beginning to be felt at every turn."

In a tidy, sparse office in the stately Georgian section of the campus, the dean of the Faculty of Arts and Sciences was earnest in his analysis of the college. He looked and talked like a professor. In fact, he admitted that he longed to return to full-time teaching and soon would.

"We're very traditional here, curriculum and all. And we're stable— perhaps too stable. How can our faculty get up morning after morning and be excited about doing the same thing each day, year after year? A decade ago, there was so much movement here! Now we are 72 percent tenured. Since our average faculty age is in the low forties, they'll be around for a while. Part of the stability is due to our president, who has been a superb manager. He is a 'President of Consolidation' rather than a 'President of Growth,' and he supports others who will keep the place in good order. Look what he has done to the facilities—we have remarkable renovations and upkeep. But he may lack an educational philosophy. He's sort of an academic cheerleader. When he came, we definitely needed that.

"I'm a facilitator too, not an educational philosopher. Our departments are autonomous—they stand alone in philosophy and movement. Actually, they have too much autonomy. For example, we'd probably have more minority faculty if departments were less autonomous and the president were more than a manager." The dean, thoughtful and obviously committed to the place, stood and walked around his office.

"But don't get me wrong. There is real strength here. In history, physics, philosophy, government, religion, you won't find better undergraduate programs in America combining serious scholarship with strong teaching. In math, sociology, arts and music, and education, our strengths, quite frankly, are less compelling. But we concentrate on good teaching throughout. And we concentrate on undergraduates—that alone probably sets us apart from our peer group of superb public institutions like Virginia, Berkeley, Michigan, and Texas."

Also setting William and Mary apart from larger scale universities is unanimity of purpose, a consistent agreement among staff and faculty on the mission of the college. Few public institutions defend the liberal arts so directly and with such clarity. In the admissions office's viewbook a professor is quoted as saying:

> To think of the liberal arts and sciences as a mere cultural luxury
> is not only misguided but tragic, for in our technological culture
> what is a salable skill at one brief moment may be obsolete and
> economically gainless a short time later. A curriculum built on
> what is immediately salable will have to change incessantly and
> colleges that attempt this will always be chasing the latest fad.
> In actuality, the liberally educated person has the most salable
> of skills—demonstrated by the fact that he or she is a person of

critical imagination and flexibility, a person who has learned how to learn. . . .

President Thomas A. Graves, Jr., in a recent, endless annual report, demonstrated his cheerleader skills for the cause of liberal learning:

I hope that all of our students will leave William and Mary with the capacity to communicate well, orally and in writing, and to read with understanding, imagination, and wonder. . . . Liberal learning involves relationships, abstractions, values, ideas . . . Liberal education instills in a student the confidence to take initiative, the courage to be curious, the will to experiment and to make mistakes and thus to learn again. I do not know how or whether one can teach faith or morality or values. But I hope that out of a William and Mary liberal education will come men and women with faith—in themselves, in their country, in their world.

The liberal learning emphasis at William and Mary is real, and it is traditionally structured. The college offers three undergraduate degrees: bachelor of arts, bachelor of science, and bachelor of business administration. There are twenty-seven undergraduate fields of study, and preprofessional programs in conjunction with William and Mary's Schools of Law, Business Administration, Marine Science, and Education.

Prior to choosing a major, each student must satisfy underclass requirements and prerequisites. In this area, William and Mary shows off its conservatism and its standards. An undergraduate must demonstrate high proficiency in writing or take catch-up English 101; if a student has not completed four years of a single foreign language in high school, he must make up the deficiency on arrival at William and Mary; and each student must take two years of physical education unless he or she is participating in a varsity sport or demonstrates "exceptional skills." Also, students must complete the "area-sequence requirements," or eight courses distributed among the humanities, social sciences, and natural sciences. The major or "concentration" itself requires from twenty-seven to thirty-six hours, depending on the department.

There are "special programs" at William and Mary. The Honors Program, for example, is strong. In over half the departments, students have the opportunity, through independent study and distinguished work on a thesis or advanced project, to be awarded a degree with honors, high honors, or highest honors. A series of preprofessional exchange programs fill the gap for some majors *not* offered in Williamsburg. A student wanting engineering, for example, can take three years in liberal arts at William and Mary prior to two years in engineering at Columbia, RPI, or Washington University of St. Louis, graduating with two bachelor's degrees. "Asia House" is an on-campus, coeducational residence for undergraduates studying that area of the world. A Washington program offers a series of seminars in the nation's capital, three hours away. There are semester or one-year programs abroad in England, Scotland, Germany, France, the Philippines, and Spain. And Army ROTC is available.

William and Mary takes considerable pride in offering small classes with only professors teaching, and in checking grade inflation. The student/faculty ratio is 15:1. In a recent semester, 52 percent of the classes enrolled 20 or fewer students and 38 percent enrolled 21 to 70 students. The largest lecture course enrolled 283 students.

The catalog states that only 23 percent of the grades given undergraduates at William and Mary are A's. The grade point average of a recent senior class was 2.87 on a 4.0 scale. "A grade of B still signifies very good work here, and a C, which today represents about 26 percent of all grades, is considered by the faculty to mean quite satisfactory work," reported one dean. Approximately 10 percent of the grades are D's and F's.

The retention of students at William and Mary must be underscored—they graduate at a higher rate than students at most "elitist" private colleges. William and Mary reports "the highest graduation rate of any state-supported university in Virginia," a gracious way of saying "higher than the University of Virginia." Approximately 75 percent of the entering freshmen graduate within four years. Even with the handicap of a tough grading system, students stick here.

After the demanding distributional requirements are satisfied, a large number of students concentrate in the business and science fields at William and Mary. One might think a business major mentality would sweep the student body despite the viewbook's or president's declarations regarding liberal learning. That tone is clearly present, but the liberal learning personality seems to prevail, with a heavy dose of creativity.

Resources

Whether William and Mary can maintain its current academic strengths depends upon funding in the near future; particularly crucial is an increase in faculty salaries. President Graves said:

> Although we have made a lot of progress on faculty salaries, it continues to be our number one problem. . . . It's a preoccupa-

tion, it has to be, when individual faculty members are just making ends meet. There is no doubt in my mind that this preoccupation is going to mean that they will devote less than all of their energies toward teaching.

The president has attempted to raise increased private funds for the faculty salary pool as a supplement to state monies. Also, there has been some shuffling of unrestricted funds within the university's budget over to the faculty salary pool. These adjustments, of course, have not been made without sacrificing or tightening other activities and programs of the college—but priorities have had to be honored.

In late 1979, the governor of Virginia elevated William and Mary up to a new collegiate "peer group" for comparable salary scaling, a group that includes such institutions as the University of Vermont and the University of New Hampshire. That meant an increase in money from the state, which has complemented the increase from private funding. Alumni support of William and Mary is consistently rated among the top ten in the nation among comparable public institutions. Nonetheless, President Graves gives bleak warnings:

> Whatever improvements have been made can hardly be called progress if the cost of living, for individuals and families, is rising even more rapidly than are the average annual increments. . . . Given the fact that we have not reached the limit of the authorized salary average with state funds, the fact that we have moved into the salary pool virtually all internally available private funds, and the possibility of a recession that will inhibit our raising of new private funds, we should not be sanguine that the salary increments for the near future will measure up to those provided for the near past. I am committed, however, to continue this effort with all the resources we can muster; the excellence of William and Mary is at stake.

Student Life

A nearby, drab pub and a fast food eatery provided the backdrops for students eager to talk about their college life. The small groups incorporated a host of different students: a bubbly blond who was preppy but longed to be different; a defiant, articulate, deadly serious Baptist woman who was most unhappy with W and M; a dashing, large, blond fellow who had transferred from Randolph-Macon, an ace swimmer and fraternity man who didn't say much but gagged late in the conversation upon hearing the word "homo"; a slight young man, a leader, from a small town in Virginia, who held everyone's attention as he spoke with authority; a sorority type—another blond—who thought everything about the place was just nifty-keen; a good joe who drank the most beer, was bright, thought the place was okay, had joined a fraternity but was not gung-ho, studied English, and aspired to a Ph.D. at Duke. Highlights of their animated discussion:

> "We're bred to believe we're best. And I think we really are the equal of Yale."
>
> "If we're so good, why isn't our graduate placement as good as Yale's?"
>
> "The vast majority of us were not challenged by high school. For that reason, we're willing to work hard here. The job market and grad school are next. Nonetheless, we're a complacent crowd—work a lot, play a little, and that's it."
>
> "The key word here, though, is 'I can conquer.' "
>
> "And this is a wonderful place to grow."
>
> "Are you *kidding?* This place is *stunting* to social growth."
>
> "Well, I just feel growth is *working.*"
>
> "Work, fine. But there is so little excitement with *ideas* here. Isn't that what a college is supposed to be all about?"
>
> "Yeah, I guess there is a bit too much emphasis toward the practical—the Business Major Mentality."
>
> "I wonder if William and Mary alums do much to change the world? . . ."
>
> "Hell, I don't want to change the world. I want to be successful. *Then* I'll have time to make a few little changes." (Chuckles all around.)
>
> "Nothing wrong with learning the facts of life in an ivory tower before getting involved . . ."
>
> "Well, we do get involved, here, a little. Remember all the service programs we have."
>
> "And the Jesus movement. Hell, the Jesus people here—particularly the Baptists—are a Greek system unto themselves."
>
> "We're so ivory-towered at William and Mary that 'girls' aren't even called 'women' yet!"
>
> "And we're so small that there is no anonymity. Everyone is sort of in a mold. This place has aggressive sameness."
>
> "But let's face it, it's fun. There are *eighty* teams in intermural basketball. And the Greeks are becoming more active, more fun."

"Complain over beer—we do it all the time. But we stay. We
know it's good."

William and Mary students talk a lot about hitting the books and
getting ready for graduate school and/or the job market. But other issues
do emerge that create some excitement: the value of Greek life; low minority
representation in the student body, faculty, and administration; spats over
commencement speakers. One issue *captured* William and Mary recently.
Predictably, it related to the college's view of itself—the furor was not in
response to an issue of the nation or the world. It concerned, of all things,
the football stadium. At issue was whether to significantly expand Cary
Field; this represented a symbolic choice between brawn and brains at W
and M.

"Brains" won. The football stadium was not expanded, although it
did undergo a facelift. And just as well. Athletic teams at W and M seem
to wait quietly for those who want them. There is little student excitement,
little fervor. "Who has *time*, when the books are so all-consuming?" one
hears as a monotonous ritual chant at this place.

Actually, the athletic facilities seem superb for a college this size: the
well-scrubbed 15,000-seat football stadium, a modern 10,000-seat basketball facility, fourteen tennis courts, two pools. And winning in some minor
sports does seem to be a source of pride at W and M. Also, there is
considerable enthusiasm for recreational and intramural sports. Women's
athletics are gaining a front-and-center spotlight, thanks to good coaching
and good results.

There are intercollegiate teams in fifteen sports for men, thirteen for
women. The trappings for football are big-time: Division I of NCAA,
competition against such now-and-then powers as UNC, Pitt, Harvard,
Navy, Wake Forest, and North Carolina State. There are athletic scholarships: thirty full scholarships per year for football and a few others for
assorted sports, for both men and women. But it is the alumni, not the
students, who are most gung-ho for football and the sports program. There
are more private dollars raised annually for athletic scholarships than for
the entire annual fund, reports the director of admissions.

The waitress in the village Taverne had a lot to say about student
life. "In short, it is subdued," she explained. "We go to 'Easters' weekend
at UVa for our big excitement of the year! You can't legally drink in
Virginia, see, until you're twenty-one. That means lots of beer and some
hard stuff on campus, but not out in the public places. The town keeps
threatening to crack down on the college because so many minors are
drinking—and the parents would probably support that. Meanwhile, the
president and deans say we're on our own, so we get by with what we can.

"The big complaint is that there are so few places to go around here. The Dirty Deli, the Green Leaf Cafe—that's about it, close by. Worse yet, we can't have cars until we're juniors. Most students can't afford all the classy nearby tourist traps and they're too sedate in Williamsburg, anyway. But does it make any *difference?* Everybody studies here on Saturday night. My part-time job has become the best part of my social life. Tourist-watching, believe me, is good fun."

William and Mary does have the usual spate of extracurricular activities: a variety of student government opportunities, musical and dramatic groups, a prize-winning yearbook and a substantial newspaper, an FM station, debating, a film and concert series, and so on. These traditional clubs and groups seem well peopled and active.

Housing is good at William and Mary. Many of the facilities are well above average, if not downright showy. Approximately 80 percent of all undergraduates live in dormitories; freshmen are required to, but new upperclassmen are subjected to the lottery system. There are coeducational dorms, and almost all living sections set their own rules and regulations. There is "a little" cohabitation, but it is frowned upon, and not just by the authorities.

The Greeks are smirking about their revival at William and Mary. About one-third of the students belong, and the number going through rush has greatly increased over the past few years. There are twelve national fraternities (ten with residential houses) and ten national sororities (nine with houses). Due largely to the drab social life in the campus environs, the fraternities and sororities become hubs by default. A recent yearbook records the typical pledge dance:

> By the band's second set, things had warmed up considerably. Out in the hall, someone had broken a beer bottle and a girl was looking for her shoe. The ballroom was hopping. . . . People climbed on each others' shoulders, waved bottles, whipped their dates in tight circles, spilled drinks, lost earrings, knocked over chairs . . . By midnight, two girls in white dresses were throwing up in the ladies room and another was wailing at her reflection in the mirror. A jacketless, shirtless, dateless gent danced down the hall wearing several yards of crepe paper.

The dating game is at a low ebb here. "What's the difference between a William and Mary coed and the garbage?" goes a local yarn. "I give up. What?" "The garbage goes out once a week." The frats and sororities spark a little dating activity—very little, some would say. "Sorority dances are the only two dates I have a year—and I get those by looking through the yearbook!" The yearbook documents the issue:

> According to a recent survey about 28 percent of our students date one person . . . 50 percent did not think there was enough dating; 32 percent thought there was . . .

> The dating situation is bad. You never get to know people— guys take no initiative. Are they shy or *what?* Maybe they're going through a midlife crisis. . . . Too many beautiful girls and too few guys to ask them out. And many of them have ego problems because all the girls are chasing them.

> Lack of places and activities is my major complaint. Williamsburg has a lot to offer tourists, but the colonial atmosphere isn't conducive to students and dating. . . . There's nowhere to go in Williamsburg like there is in your typical college town.

For a growing number of students at William and Mary, life beyond the classroom centers around religion. At last count, there were sixteen recognized religious organizations on campus. Nearly 10 percent of the student body belongs to the largest, the Catholic Student Association. The Catholics have four formal worship services a week, informal Bible study, and workshops. They publish a newsletter which is circulated nationally, sponsor field trips for study and fun, and field a champion soccer team. Other denominational groups are strong and active.

"Jesus has had a big impact on our campus recently," said the waitress at the Taverne. "I didn't mind it until the under-the-door proselytizing notes started arriving. But we need more tolerance of people who *stand* for something at William and Mary, so I'll watch and not complain. If the campus can handle our fledgling little gay group—and that is iffy—we can certainly tolerate all the new Jesus people, not to mention the Greek renaissance."

Admissions

When the director of admissions finished a short presentation and film for candidates and parents in the Wren Building, he asked for questions. The queries from candidates and parents gave clues to W and M's public image. "Is William and Mary all work and no play?" "Why do Virginia parents traditionally want their daughters to go here, but less so their sons?" "Why don't William and Mary football teams win?" "What does a graduate *do* with a liberal arts major?" "Why no engineering here?"

"Is it true the fraternities and sororities are resurging in popularity?" "Do you have to be an egghead to be happy here?" And finally, after all the curveball, but mannerly, questions had been asked, the one question everyone seemed to have in common came from a bold mother: "What can we *do* to get Joan in here?"

William and Mary is reserved, serious, and sensitive when talking about admissions policy. Before studying raw statistics of the new freshman class, the candidate is invited to consider the following:

> Remembering that the statement of admissions policy pledges the College to its responsibility as a State University as well as to the search for diversity and continued academic excellence, our class profile information does not imply cutoff levels. . . . We ask that you read and interpret this information in the spirit in which it is presented—a vivid picture of the means and extremes—what happened statistically in admitting this class to the College of William and Mary—remembering always the latitude portrayed.

A few highlights from William and Mary's admissions statistics: the college is selective indeed for Virginians, but nearly impossible for out-of-staters, particularly women; W and M matriculates an unusually high percentage of out-of-staters for a public institution; nonresidents profile considerably higher than residents, although both profiles are strong; women admitted to William and Mary rank significantly higher in their high school classes than men (87 percent of the women were in the top fifth versus 69 percent of the men).

William and Mary operates like a private college in selecting the new class. There are no precise formulae applied and there are no specific prerequisites except the SAT (though three achievements are "strongly recommended"). The director of admissions states the policy compellingly:

> Although all are invited to apply, the College must be selective due to the large number of applications received each year. In this process of selection, two important considerations are the potential benefit of the College to the student, and the student's potential contributions to the College community. Although a secondary school diploma is generally required, no specific program is prescribed as an absolute prerequisite for admission. . . . Successful William and Mary students have tended to perform well in pre-college years, both scholastically and on

standard examinations. Many have wide-ranging interests; many others have intensely developed a single special interest or talent.

The application process is personal; the decisions are subjective. The application requests three essays: what contributions you think you can make to William and Mary, which of your academic interests are most significant and why, and anything else you want to say to make this process more personal and your own case more compelling.

The small admissions staff spends the fall representing William and Mary at College Nights throughout Virginia, with a little travel outside the state—in a recent year, to North Carolina and prep schools in New England. Once the "recruiting" is over, the reading begins. The four staff officers do the job by pushing folders from one professional to the next: if two readers agree (up or down), that's it. If not, a third reader mediates. If there is still uncertainty, the folder heads to a Committee on Admissions which reviews a few "muddy middle" cases, about twenty-five each year. Out-of-staters must jump the highest hurdles (scoring 2 or better on the admissions officer's five-point scale). Strong athletes, students with other exceptional talents (music, for example), minorities, and sons or daughters of alumni are given particularly generous ratings if the academic credentials are "safe." Perhaps the rather nonobjective William and Mary system is best explained (or defended) by this statement from the director:

> While high school academic records are important, the College maintains an admissions policy that tries to attract students with other qualities as well: motivation, tenacity, imagination, and character. In each class the College seeks men and women of special talents and abilities in such fields as music, drama, science, the arts, and athletics. The admissions process weighs the broad interests of the applicants by considering their extracurricular activities. In addition, the College seeks to increase the variety of its student body by including students of different minority backgrounds.

The Campus

One cannot depart from William and Mary without paying final respects to the campus itself. Granted, "America's most charming town" sets the stage well, but the campus, on its own, is breathtaking. The huge, deep green magnolias sprinkled through the 1,200 acres; Lake Matoaka; the sunken garden in the Georgian section; the historic buildings in the Old Colonial section—not just the Wren Building, but the Brafferton (1723) and the President's House (1732) and others. Less atmospheric, but perhaps more important, is the functional and comprehensive "modern" campus which jolts William and Mary out of its historic fix.

This is a special place. President Graves, who looks and speaks as though he is prepping to be an American ambassador abroad, is almost teary as he says:

> Then there is William and Mary. There is not another state university like it in the nation. It is a credit to the state system of higher education in Virginia, of which we are proud to be a part, that only here could a William and Mary thrive. Only here could William and Mary have the confidence which we currently enjoy.

He's probably right. This strange and wonderful little place, with its tough liberal arts emphasis, its generous delegation from around America, and its charming atmosphere, is a tribute, in large part, to the leadership of the Commonwealth of Virginia.

William and Mary is also, as the dean of students said succinctly, ". . . a unique interlude for four years. America, there really *is* an Ivory Tower."

The Best of the Rest

University of Colorado
at Boulder

Georgia Institute of Technology
at Atlanta

University of Illinois
at Urbana-Champaign

New College of the University of South Florida
at Sarasota

Pennsylvania State University
at University Park

University of Pittsburgh

State University of New York
at Binghamton

University of Washington
at Seattle

University of Wisconsin
at Madison

University of Colorado

Boulder

Academics

Importance of the Liberal Arts

CU Boulder is divided into five colleges: the College of Arts and Sciences, the College of Business and Administration, the College of Design and Planning (emphasizing environmental design), the College of Engineering and Applied Science, and the College of Music. Within these undergraduate divisions are approximately 100 degree programs.

The College of Arts and Sciences is easily the largest, enrolling 48 percent of the undergraduate student body. "The objectives of the College are based on the belief that all students, no matter how specific and professional their aims, should have sufficient knowledge of other areas to be able to see their own disciplines in proper relationship to other disciplines," states the viewbook.

Although some of the technical areas seem to be Colorado's strongest, the liberal arts offerings are good and improving. The English department has one of the strongest creative writing programs in the nation, and the Philosophy department a unique "public policy emphasis." Beside idiosyncratic strengths in humanities and the arts, the College of Arts and Sciences is most prominent for biology, physics, and psychology.

Strong Departments

Thanks to a Sciences Developmental Program of the National Science Foundation in the late sixties and early seventies, a firm

University of Colorado at Boulder

1) Size of Student Body

Undergraduate __17,985__ Graduate __4,191__ Total __22,176__

2) 1983 Freshman Class Profile

Class Size __5,664__ % Men __53__ % Women __47__
Percent of Applicants Admitted __77__
Average SATs: Verbal __508__   Math __471__
High School Class Rank: Top Tenth __28__ % Top Quarter __66__ %
   Geographical Distribution (% of class):
In-State __61__% Middle Atlantic __6__ % New England __4__ %
West __79__ % Middle West __8__ % South __3__ %
Minority Students __10__ % of Class
Financial Aid __31__ % of Class

3) Retention of Students

__24__ % of freshmen graduate in four years

4) Ten Most Popular Majors of Graduating Seniors, 1983

   1. Psychology   6. Environmental Biology
   2. Finance   7. Environmental Design
   3. Political Science   8. Marketing
   4. Economics   9. Communication
   5. Journalism   10. English

5) The Financial Picture (1982–83)

Annual Campus Budget	$ 189,136,262
Percent of Annual Budget from State Appropriation	21
1983–84 Tuition and Fees for State Residents	$ 1,316
1983–84 Tuition and Fees for Out-of-State Residents	$ 5,096

foundation for excellence in several scientific departments was laid: physics, astrogeophysics, mathematics, psychology, and engineering. In addition, the molecular, cellular, and developmental biology department has become one of the finest in the country. If admissions selectivity is used as a gauge, the undergraduate professional colleges of engineering, business, and design and planning are very strong. Due to legislative budgetary restrictions, however, these selective colleges cannot expand and will become even more choosy in whom they accommodate.

Largely due to the decline of student interest, the social sciences have generally weakened. And the foreign language departments are not known to be particularly strong, although some individual teachers are given high marks. CU students feel there are general weaknesses in communications, physical education, and some areas of English.

Class Size and Faculty Accessibility

Twenty-four percent of all classes have fewer than 10 students, 59 percent have 10 to 49 students, 19 percent have 50 to 100 students, and 7 percent of all classes have more than 100 students. Since CU statistics include undergraduate *and* graduate classes, lower level undergraduate are traditionally exposed to the "over 100" category, and often complain loudly. Psychology classes are traditionally huge. But one student has found the key to small class access: "If you sign up for classes offered early in the morning or late in the afternoon, you're assured of a lean group and good faculty give-and-take." On the whole, CU professors are considered approachable and accessible.

Who Teaches Undergraduates?

With a student/faculty ratio at Colorado of 18:1, students quite often find themselves in the audience of a professor, not a teaching assistant. Graduate students generally lead recitations and discussion groups.

Are Most Listed Courses Really Available?

The most crowded majors are business, engineering, and geology. If a student has not passed the stringent requirements for initial admission to these programs, he or she is almost always prevented from enrolling in individual courses.

Students who preregister at appropriate times and pay preregistration deposits seem to have little trouble getting the courses they want. CU claims that 85 percent of all course requests are met at the exact place and time originally requested by students. More impressive: 94 percent of the requests for specific courses (as opposed to specific times) are honored.

The Library

Because of a stingy state legislature, the once-heralded Boulder campus library has slipped in holdings and in status. Private rallies and fund-raisers have been held to "save the library" and even the legislature is promising recovery funds soon. Nonetheless, the CU libraries constitute the major research collection in the Rocky Mountain Region. Norlin Library and its branches at Boulder house over four million books, periodicals, and microforms. Interlibrary loans in the region allow access to over eight million volumes and related materials. Regarding library sources and policies, students seem to have few complaints.

Honors Program for Freshmen

A small honors program in the College of Arts and Sciences offers special educational opportunities for the academically very talented. But two residential units, Sewall Hall and Farrand Hall, offer superb "personal academic exploration" programs to 330 and 400 freshmen respectively. Both programs include seminars, interdisciplinary courses, and an emphasis on student participation. The truly motivated student can find the "tone" of a small liberal arts college in Sewall and Farrand while attending a large public university.

Campus Life

Housing

There are loud complaints regarding overcrowding and excessive noise in CU housing. Freshmen are assigned a place in the university residence halls, but then the trouble begins. There are always waiting lists for upperclassmen, as off-campus housing can be difficult to locate. In all, 34 percent of the undergraduates live in campus residence halls. Unlike the lottery systems elsewhere, a first come, first served system is in effect here. The residence halls themselves differ: there are single sex and coed dorms, traditional halls and high-rise facilities, some centrally located, others remote. A variety of special amenities from free tutoring to exercise rooms to study skill workshops to darkrooms can be found in one dorm or another. Due to the magnificent locale of the campus, some outdoorsy students prefer to live elsewhere and a few do indeed find mountain retreats that are reasonably accessible to campus.

The Environs

As one student says: "Imagine! Majestic Rocky Mountains, lush, green, fertile valleys, cosmopolitan suburbs, a culturally diverse town, environmental consciousness, vibrant and colorful seasons, a home of poets, musicians, artisans, and students. *This* is the CU's setting!"

Boulder is about thirty-five miles northwest of Denver, with spectacular scenery and ski areas nearby. Many of the 80,000 people who live there are health and environmentally oriented, with a good many artisans. A few manufacturing firms produce everything from missile components and computer softwear to skiwear and health foods. Aside from a few winter blasts, the climate is relatively mild and pleasant, and the mountains are always within view.

Local Hangouts

As on many campuses, the student union, here called the University Memorial Center, is the hub. And CU's Center is a good one, with nightly films, expansive games areas, and the Alfred Packer Grill, named after Colorado's outlaw folk-hero cannibal. The drinking age in Colorado is twenty-one so there are a lot of 3.2 bars catering to the underage, including two on campus (the Connection and the Alfred Packer). For those of legal age, there are many watering spots on the downtown pedestrian Boulder Mall (Pearl's, the Walrus, the New York Deli, and the Blue Note are busiest). The Mall itself is a favorite hangout for both students and faculty, and the huge campus Recreation Center is for the more active.

The Greeks

There is a renaissance in the Greek system at Boulder. After a severe decline in recent years, the system is now growing once again, but still only a minority of the undergraduates partake. Approximately 12 percent of the undergraduates have joined the sixteen fraternities or ten sororities. But CU anticipates considerable growth: a 30 percent jump in the next several years, partly because of the tight housing picture. Although the Greeks are visible on campus promoting homecoming festivities, some political activity, and alumni-related events, one student reports: "If a decent social life is your reason for going Greek, don't. The good life at CU is quite available without joining a fraternity or sorority." And the good life at Colorado ranks respectably among the nation's private and public colleges.

Athletics

Since the late seventies, CU's intercollegiate athletic program has been under a microscope, both locally and nationally. Budget difficulties, controversy over the hiring of a football coach, a consistently losing football team, and an NCAA investigation have combined to cast a shadow over the traditional program. Now the budget situation has somewhat improved, the controversial coach has been replaced, and the NCAA investigation has been concluded with a minor sanction imposed. The outlook for athletics is upside.

With less than a gung-ho attitude toward the intercollegiate program in recent years, Boulder students have rallied to intramural and club sports. And the great outdoors keeps many involved without any organization at all.

Drugs/Booze/Sex

Whether Boulder has really earned the reputation of being a place "where hip meet to trip" is questionable. There are heavy fun-lovers at CU, true. But the lure of the clean outdoors, the shared goal of good grad school and/or job placement, and the threat of suspension or expulsion by campus administrators who are well aware of the institution's reputation have substantially curbed excesses in the use of drugs and booze. No doubt about it, though, a student can have a good time at Colorado, and most do.

Student Stereotypes

Colorado is much more diverse than its "rich kids' party school" reputation would have it. O.P. shorts, button-down shirts, Levi's, and Grateful Dead T-shirts are in abundance, as on most American campuses. And although students are less politically active than they were a decade ago, there are spurts of enthusiasm and protest when issues directly affect them—cuts in student aid or library funds, for example.

The Tolerance Level

One undergraduate says: "Students seem sympathetic to the right or are radicals for the left. Very few middle-of-the-roaders here." And as one senior said, "It is easy to be different in Boulder, easier than *not* being different." The university and the town are cultural melting pots of different ethnic, religious, and social groups. You're welcome to be yourself, to do your own thing, and no one will even give you a second glance.

Food

CU recently won the prestigious "Ivy Award" from *Restaurants and Institutions* magazine. That's quite an honor for a university food service required to prepare 15,000 meals for approximately 5,700 dormitory residents each day, not to mention stocking campus fast food, salad, and yogurt bars. "Boulder," says one sophomore, "is the last great health food mecca. Vegetarian food is basic here. Our *real* men almost always eat quiche!"

Cars and Transportation

Even freshmen can have cars at CU, but fewer than 20 percent of the student body feel it is necessary. Everywhere a student needs to go locally—from campus to the downtown Boulder Mall to the University Hill residential area—can be reached by bike or in a pair of Birkenstock sandals. For those who feel they must zip off to Aspen or Vail every weekend, a car is necessary. But there is plenty happening in Boulder worth staying for.

Life After College

Post-Bachelor's Placement

Although over 500 companies recruit annually on the Boulder campus, the university is short on placement statistics because so many students "operate on their own." A senior indicates that saying the campus career placement office keeps a low profile is an understatement. But the same student has heard few gripes regarding life-after-the-Boulder-B.A.

Alumni Stars

CU Boulder has graduated a curious conglomerate of celebrities: Byron White, Justice of the U.S. Supreme Court; actor Robert Redford; three astronauts; band leader Glenn Miller; pro football player Cliff Branch; jazz pianist and composer Dave Grusin; and Hale Irwin, professional golfer.

Admissions-Related Topics

Image versus Reality

Due to the idyllic recreational setting, an oft-projected image of Colorado is that of a wealthy kids' playground with little emphasis on academic quality. Although the mountains and the fun environs are there, CU supports a substantial and demanding academic program. Students are not disappointed with what they find here, even on the serious side.

What Elements Most/Least Draw Students?

Most attractive elements: Parents and prospective students seem awed by the on-campus Italian Renaissance architecture, the green of the campus grounds, and the majestic Rocky Mountains in full view. Least attractive elements: The housing crunch and the size of the student body.

Is CU for Everyone?

A tour guide said: "If you do not enjoy living in a young, healthy, natural environment, attending school on a 600-acre campus based at the foot of the Rockies, and do not like to challenge yourself academically while enjoying your surroundings, CU Boulder is not for you. Also, Boulder is not for you if we do not offer your major. But we do offer most."

En Route Perfection, What Should CU Change?

Although the Colorado student body is fairly well balanced, more women are needed in engineering and business; more minority students are needed in all areas. Guaranteed financial aid for all admitted students who demonstrate need would provide greater balance here. And a comforting hand on the shoulder of the freshman who asks, "Is there really an end to this line?" would be very reassuring.

In Summary

CU Boulder has more than the Rockies: A dedicated faculty, impressive facilities (including one of the largest electron microscopes in the country, one of the finest planetariums in the world, a million-volt lightning laboratory, three campus computer centers, six locations of the library), a diverse student body, and good air create a compelling package.

Georgia Institute of Technology

Atlanta

Academics

Importance of the Liberal Arts

Georgia Tech proudly describes its education as "technologically oriented." But there is always the quick reminder that the program is not as technical and/or restrictive as is commonly believed: all undergraduates must take a hefty eighteen quarter hours of humanities and eighteen quarter hours of social studies. In the early seventies, Tech freed the curriculum considerably to relieve the technical rigidities. In fact, the director of admissions reports that some true liberal arts institutions do not require as much immersion in humanities and social studies as Tech does today. Says one undergraduate: "The liberal arts program here is much stronger than what I expected from a technical school. Although Georgia Tech has one of the most strenuous undergraduate technological programs in the nation, traditional liberal arts offerings are of surprisingly good quality." Be that as it may, there are no real majors in the liberal arts—their importance is in meeting early distributional requirements.

Strong Departments

"I'm a ramblin' wreck from Georgia Tech and a hell of an engineer" remains an apt line. Tech claims to have the second largest undergraduate college of engineering in the country and a first-rate one at that. Students complain, however, that chemical engineering is weakening, primarily due to old and overcrowded labs. Chemistry, industrial engineering, and architecture gain the student votes for "best."

Georgia Institute of Technology at Atlanta

1) Size of Student Body

Undergraduate __8,775__ Graduate __2,143__ Total __10,918__

2) 1983 Freshman Class Profile

Class Size __1,589__ % Men __77__ % Women __23__
Percent of Applicants Admitted __58__
Average SATs: Verbal __524__ Math __632__
High School Class Rank: Top Tenth __64__ % Top Quarter __88__ %
    Geographical Distribution (% of class):
In-State __66__% Middle Atlantic __8__ % New England __<1__ %
West __<1__ % Middle West __3__ % South __86__ %
Foreign __<1__ %
Minority Students __10__ % of Class
Financial Aid __57__ % of Class

3) Retention of Students

__33__ % of freshmen graduate in four years
__66__ % of freshmen graduate in five years

4) Ten Most Popular Majors of Graduating Seniors, 1983

1. Electrical Engineering
2. Mechanical Engineering
3. Industrial Engineering
4. Civil Engineering
5. Information and Computer Science
6. Industrial Management
7. Chemical Engineering
8. Aerospace Engineering
9. Architecture
10. Physics

5) The Financial Picture (1982–83)

Annual Campus Budget	$ 164,372,383
Percent of Annual Budget from State Appropriation	32
1983–84 Tuition and Fees for State Residents	$ 1,225
1983–84 Tuition and Fees for Out-of-State Residents	$ 3,625

Class Size and Faculty Accessibility

As at many undergraduate institutions, classes get smaller as one moves closer to the degree. At Georgia Tech all freshmen and sophomores, regardless of major, must take calculus, chemistry, physics, humanities, and social studies. Some examples of class patterns in three required areas:

Calculus:	meets five one-hour periods per week
three periods:	lecture, senior professor, up to 175 students
two periods:	limited to 35 in recitation and discussion
Chemistry:	meets four one-hour periods per week plus one three-hour lab
three periods:	lecture, senior professor, up to 200 students
one period:	limited to 35 in recitation and discussion
lab:	limited to 25 students
Humanities and Social Science:	meets three one-hour periods per week; usually limited to 30 students

Some not-so-popular majors, such as ceramic engineering, enjoy small classes. As in most colleges, faculty enthusiasm for personal advising is uneven at best; there is a genuine desire among some faculty at Tech to counsel—a few even publicize home phone numbers. The greatest gripe among undergraduates, however, is that many on the faculty concentrate on research instead of teaching. The professor who is primarily involved in *teaching* here is rare.

Who Teaches Undergraduates?

Since there are no graduate students in the humanities or social sciences at Tech, all courses in these areas are taught by professors. In the science/technical zones, professors do most of the lecturing. Graduate teaching assistants proctor, supervise laboratories, and lead some entry-level recitations and give a few lectures. Students at Georgia Tech report that "adjunct faculty and grad students do teach some classes. They are of two types: very good or very bad."

Are Most Listed Courses Really Available?

Each quarter, some students are "closed out" of courses during registration. But students at Tech report that the required courses are almost always available, and one can usually juggle a schedule to get everything to fit. Also, changes in the major are easy to transact. Few majors have severe prerequisites for transferring in.

The Library

Tech's library numbers over one million volumes, has over three million patents, and is the largest technical library in the southeast. It is especially strong in its collection of abstracts, indices, and bibliographies for science and engineering. Students complain, however, that resources for liberal arts courses and general reading are restricted.

Honors Program for Freshmen

Students at Georgia Tech are encouraged to "place out" rather than take honors classes. There are freshmen honors courses, however, in mathematics and chemistry.

Campus Life

Housing

Tech can house approximately half of its students in the rather dreary dormitories, fraternities, and married student housing. New students (freshmen and transfers) have top priority. Usually, all freshmen are guaranteed dorm space if they want it. The campus housing situation is about to improve considerably with the completion of a new 560-bed, high-rise dorm. Those who cannot be accommodated on campus fend for themselves in houses or apartments nearby. Obviously, close proximity to a metropolitan area with two million people provides strong housing potential and variety.

The Environs

Georgia Tech is located within one-half mile of Atlanta (which one professor labels "the next international city"), yet the campus does not seem urban. Buildings are well spread out, there are trees and grass and quite limited traffic. One student comments: "Tech is basically a city of 11,000 students that just happens to be within the Atlanta city limits."

Local Hangouts

Everybody goes to the nearby Varsity restaurant, including crowds of tourists. Directly across the street from campus are Chollies, Pippins, Grumpies, and Rickshaws. Everyone, from the nerds to the preppies, inhabits these places. P. J. Haleys is the true beer lover's beat.

The Greeks

Approximately one-quarter of the Tech undergraduates belong to one of the thirty-two fraternities or six sororities. One student reports, "Most of the on-campus social life revolves around the Greeks, at least for men. The sororities are less conspicuous. But recent run-ins with the authorities, both on and off campus, have made the frats suspect."

Athletics

The administration at Georgia Tech claims that "the yellow jacket football team and our school song are known around the world and add immeasurably to our tradition, image, and reputation." But in recent years, the football and basketball teams have been solid losers. Although there is an attempt to correct that situation, particularly among alumni, one student says that losing teams hurt the university's reputation. Perhaps, but it is rare among technical schools for inter-collegiate athletics to excite the crowds.

Drugs/Booze/Sex

Georgia Tech does not have, and cannot recall ever having had, a "drug problem." Lots of beer is consumed—it is *the* drug at Tech, even though a number of teetotalers hold their own. Regarding sex, one undergraduate reports: "With a four to one boy/girl ratio, there is not nearly as much sex here as on other campuses, but enough for those who try hard enough." Some of the men try elsewhere: Emory and the women's colleges scattered through the Southeast.

Student Stereotypes

The nerds are visible, with calculators hanging from their belts and dozens of pens in their shirt pockets, but there are fewer of them than outsiders might think. "Goal-oriented, serious-minded, conservative, and neat" describes Tech's typical student, says one administrator. An Emory coed repeats that the nerds still predominate.

The Tolerance Level

Gays stay in the closet at Tech. "Visibility would probably bring them substantial scorn, or perhaps, avoidance as though they didn't exist," surmises one faculty member. "But conservative religionists are out of the closet and can say whatever they want and find some applause.''

Food

"Nutritious," everyone agrees. The consensus: tolerable to good.

Cars and Transportation

Tech is a walking campus, and all points are accessible within the ten-minute class break. A car is not a liability here, but it is useless for on-campus mobility. Freshmen can bring cars but would probably be better off walking on campus and using Atlanta's superb mass-transit system for venturing out.

Life After College

Post-Bachelor's Placement

This is a strong category for Tech. Although graduate school placement is high, only about 25 percent of the departing undergraduates seek further training immediately. The reason is simple: they are offered top jobs at top salaries as soon as they leave undergraduate school. Most nail a job paying in the mid- to high twenties immediately following college. Remember: well-trained technicians are in demand.

Alumni Stars in the Georgia Tech Galaxy

Space shuttle pilots John Young and Richard Truly graduated from Georgia Tech, as did Jimmy Carter, Senator Sam Nunn, golfer Bobby Jones, and even Arthur Murray, the dance king, not to mention a strong roster of corporate chairmen and presidents: those of Delta Airlines, Boeing Aircraft, Florida Power and Light, General Dynamics, Lockheed Georgia, Atlanta Merchandise Mart, American Express, and Magic Chef.

Admissions-Related Topics

Image versus Reality

The nerdy, bookish Tech image fits some, if not most, but certainly not all. Many students at Tech lead a balanced college life. The image of Georgia Tech as quite competitive and rigorously technical is right on target.

What Elements Most/Least Draw Students?

The proximity to big and bustling Atlanta registers a strong plus or a strong minus, according to the comer. Some fear the danger of the big city and/or the distractions; others view the city as an enormous resource for academic training, not to mention the good life. All have a case.

Is Georgia Tech for Everyone?

No.

En Route Perfection, What Should Georgia Tech Change?

According to the administration, Georgia Tech needs more students majoring in science, management, and architecture and fewer who are determined to enter electrical engineering; more adequate classroom space, laboratories and dormitory facilities; more faculty to create a lower student/teacher ratio; a more streamlined and equitable registration procedure; a *bit* more distance between the campus and downtown Atlanta; winning varsity teams; more money from the state to accomplish all of the above.

The students feel that in addition to a more balanced male/female ratio and more minority students, Tech needs more on-campus parties and distractions.

In Summary

Georgia Tech is one of those institutions the nation labels "private" when, actually, it is indeed public. But it *seems* private in a number of ways: its high SAT averages denote keen selectivity (Georgia Tech claims to enroll more National Merit scholars and National Achievement scholars than any public university in the country); although there are no concentrations in the liberal arts, there *is* concentration on the undergraduate—80 percent of Tech students are seeking the first degree; the Tech alums are zealots, ranking annually among the nation's highest in dollars contributed and percentage of alums supporting; the student body is national—approximately 40 percent are from out of state. The quality and prestige of Georgia Tech are, quite clearly, high. Would that their curriculum and mission were more balanced.

University of Illinois

Urbana-Champaign
Academics

Importance of the Liberal Arts

UIUC is big. And big means a complicated network of many colleges, schools, and institutes which are, in turn, broken into academic departments. The primary undergraduate divisions are the College of Agriculture, the Institute of Aviation, the College of Applied Life Studies, the College of Commerce and Business Administration, the College of Communications, the College of Education, the College of Engineering, the College of Fine and Applied Arts, the College of Liberal Arts and Sciences, and the School of Social Work.

The largest of all these divisions, by considerable margin, is the College of Liberal Arts and Sciences (LAS), which enrolls over 40 percent of the campus undergraduates. LAS offers seventy-five degree programs through thirty-four academic departments and provides the first two years of instruction for other divisions as well. There are campus-wide general education requirements assuring that a liberal arts foundation is basic to all degrees offered by the university.

"Let's face it: some students who are denied admission to our professional colleges with more competitive admissions policies apply to Liberal Arts and Sciences first, then try to transfer later to their preferred colleges. Be that as it may, LAS has an extensive program with diligent students. They set the tone for this whole place," reports one Illinois senior.

University of Illinois at Urbana-Champaign

1) Size of Student Body

Undergraduate __25,989__ Graduate __8,643__   Total __34,632__

2) 1983 Freshman Class Profile

Class Size __5,390__   % Men __50__   % Women __50__
Percent of Applicants Admitted __66__
Average SATs: Verbal __525__   Math __585__
High School Class Rank: Top Tenth __59__ % Top Quarter __87__ %
    Geographical Distribution (% of class):
In-State __97__ % Middle Atlantic ≤ 1 % New England ≤ 1 %
West __<1__ % Middle West __99__ % South __<1__ %
Minority Students __12__ % of Class
Financial Aid __74__ % of Class

3) Retention of Students

__47__ % of freshmen graduate in four years
__65__ % of freshmen graduate in five years

4) Ten Most Popular Majors of Graduating Seniors, 1983

1. Accountancy
2. Finance, Business Administration (tie)
3. Electrical Engineering
4. Biology
5. Psychology
6. Mechanical Engineering
7. Economics
8. Civil Engineering
9. Political Science
10. Architectural Studies

5) The Financial Picture (1982–83)

Annual Campus Budget	$ 461,932,000
Percent of Annual Budget from State Appropriation	52
1983–84 Tuition and Fees for State Residents	$ 1,637
1983–84 Tuition and Fees for Out-of-State Residents	$ 4,055

Strong Departments

Administrators at Illinois like to point to the 1980 *Gourman Report*, which ranked twenty-two Illinois departments among the top seven nationally in their fields. These departments were scattered through the College of Agriculture, Commerce and Business Administration, Communications, Education, Engineering, Fine and Applied Arts, and in the Schools of Humanities and Life Sciences within the LAS. Architecture is certainly a strength here, with approximately one in every twelve practicing architects in America a graduate of Illinois. But students and faculty alike point to engineering and commerce as UIUC's top-of-the-stack. There are a few weak divisions, students say, within the LAS, but even that huge college, as a whole, is demanding.

Class Size and Faculty Accessibility

Students advise that if you want the smallest classes, stick to the study of foreign language. Most departments have large introductory lectures, often followed by small discussion groups. But average "official" registrations per class section for the undergraduate colleges are surprising: Agriculture 25, Applied Life Studies 21, Aviation 10, Commerce and Business Administration 45, Communications 23, Education 15, Engineering 32, Fine and Applied Arts 17, Liberal Arts and Sciences 27, and Social Work 22.

Who Teaches Undergraduates?

Regardless of what the administration claims, underclassmen complain about very large classes and scarce professors. One recent study indicated that over 65 percent of the introductory courses were taught by graduate students (see table).

In response to student complaints regarding large classes, the administration announced recently: "An internal analysis indicates the percentage of instructional hours taught by teaching assistants has not changed significantly since the 1920s." The response was one of loud guffaws.

Are Most Listed Courses Really Available?

About 95 percent of the students who "advance enroll" get the classes they want. For a recent semester's offerings, the areas with the most unfulfilled requests were, in descending order, physical education, classical civilization, health education, and business administration. Popular undergraduate divisions within the university have been forced to raise their entry standards, so dozens of prospective majors are closed out altogether; the Engineering College is the best current example.

TEACHER'S RANK:	Professor	Associate Professor	Assistant Professor	Instructor	Teaching Asst.	Other
Entry-Level Courses	14%	11%	8%	1%	58%	8%
Upper-class Courses	32%	21%	21%	1%	19%	6%

The Library

The library is one of Illinois' greatest assets. It is the largest state university library in America and is third only to Harvard and Yale among public and private universities. A separate undergraduate library has open stacks and satisfies the majority. Although the main library's stacks are closed to undergraduates, marvelous resources are there for the digging. In total, the libraries house over six million volumes.

Honors Programs for Freshmen

There is no freshmen honors program per se at Illinois. There is, however, a university-wide honors program in which freshmen may participate. If a student is named a James scholar, he or she must complete two honors projects per year and maintain a cumulative grade point average of 4.5/5.0 to stay in the program. The James scholars are entitled to certain academic privileges, including special seminars, and individualized research projects.

Illinois is thorough in placement of all beginning freshmen. Through proficiency exam testimony, advanced students can jump to whatever collegiate level is appropriate, even graduate studies for the exceptional scholars.

Campus Life

Housing

Freshmen must live in housing "certified" by the university. There is a broad choice: a wide array of university-owned residential halls (most of which were built in the fifties), fraternities and/or sororities, and twenty-five privately owned "approved" facilities. Some residence halls house libraries and/or computer terminals, and most have food service and lounges. Most students opt for self-regulated twenty-four-hour visitation; however, there are residence hall floors where the opposite sex is not permitted to visit.

Twenty-one percent of the students here live in university residence halls after the freshman year. Many remain in Greek houses, but most drift to nearby private quarters, some of which are more in the mainstream of the campus than remote dorms.

The Environs

This is the heart-of-the-Midwest country, with lots of corn, and endless flats which the university prefers to describe as "the rich farmland of the Illinois prairie." The Urbana-Champaign campus is situated 135 miles south of Chicago in "twin cities" which have 110,000 residents between them. The area is limited unless one enjoys the long drive to the Windy City.

Local Hangouts

Although UIUC is itself socially alive, there are a dozen or so popular watering holes within two blocks of campus, each with a unique clientele. One is for rugby players, another for law school students, one is crammed with Greeks, another is for independents. Music of every taste can be found in one pub or another, from country to New Wave to serious jazz. There are coffee houses, mostly affiliated with church foundations, for those given to sobriety. Even the fast food outlets attract a regular clientele.

Some of the campus hangouts are cultural. The Krannert Center for the Performing Arts has four theaters giving more than 350 performances each year; it passed the 250,000 attendance marks in its first two years. The Center was designed by alumnus Max Abramovitz, the architect of New York City's Lincoln Center for the Performing Arts.

The Greeks

UIUC has the largest number of national fraternities and sororities with residential facilities of any campus in the United States. In all, approximately one-quarter of the student body is actively affiliated with the Greek system. As one student said, "Without a Greek house to call home, this huge place would be a lonely zoo." Another student said: "Every time a house grows weak, the gung-ho alumni step in to bail us out." The Midwest is a traditional Greek stronghold and Illinois is a symbol of that. But the Greeks do more than house students and party; their athletic competitions, philanthropies, and self-governance are all undertaken with vigor.

Athletics

The Illinois administration is quick to comment that neither student tuition nor fees support varsity athletics—the varsity teams are *self*-supporting. Men's football and basketball essentially carry all other men's and women's activities. And Illinois is starting to win again. After a fairly lengthy dormant period, the football team went to the Rose Bowl in 1984, dreary as that performance was. Football creates fervor in Urbana-Champaign, and the basketball season is lively too. There is a bit of controversy on campus, as at all the Big Ten schools, regarding "dumb jocks" who don't meet the regular admissions standards and walk in with full scholarships. But "athletics" to most students here means the super-well-organized intramural and recreational sports, and the Greek and dorm competitions, for both men and women.

Drugs/Booze/Sex

The booze flows at Illinois, especially beer. But the academics are heavy, and serious drinking is fairly well confined to weekends. There is marijuana, but less than there used to be. And, thanks to university housing policies, not to mention the traditional Greek life, students have a high degree of freedom. Virtually all university residence halls are coeducational and "visitation" is common throughout the campus.

Student Stereotypes

The stereotypical Urbana-Champaign student is from Illinois (most often the metropolitan Chicago area), is fairly conservative in political persuasion and dress, and is motivated toward a specific career. UI is a land grant institution, and career/vocational emphasis has been paramount here for generations. There is a touch of variety, but the Illinois Ethic prevails.

The Tolerance Level

With over 500 student registered organizations, most any specific talent or interest or point of view can be accommodated. Religious organizations of all persuasions are visible, not to mention traveling evangelical preachers who regularly visit the Quadrangle in good weather. The gay students' organization has been active but muted for over a decade now. In spite of the general conservatism, students are surprisingly tolerant of the views and individuality of others.

Food

The food is good! Not only is there variety, but the food service and UIUC's residence halls have won one national award after another. If the campus doesn't please, there are over 130 restaurants within fifteen minutes by car, according to the Yellow Pages.

Cars and Transportation

As on other large-population campuses, parking is a severe problem here. Approximately 20 percent of the students have cars, but bicycles are more practical. (The Urbana-Champaign campus was the first in America to have special lanes for bicyclists.) The city bus service is superb and uses the campus as its hub.

Illinois was the first major university in America to provide comprehensive programs and access for the physically disabled. UIUC remains a fine choice for the serious but handicapped student.

Life After College

Post-Bachelor's Placement

Approximately 70 percent of the enrolling freshmen of Illinois anticipate graduate study. The university ranks first in the Big Ten and third among all United States universities in the number of graduates who go on to earn doctoral degrees. In recent years, over 65 percent of the Illinois applicants who applied to medical school gained acceptance; UIUC is the eighth largest supplier of medical applicants in the nation and the fifth largest supplier of *accepted* applicants to M.D.-granting programs.

Alumni Stars in the UIUS Galaxy

More than 275,000 people have graduated from Illinois. The alumni include winners of seven Nobels and sixteen Pulitzers. But they also have scored well in the corporate world: a recent survey shows twenty-three chief executives of the Fortune 500 companies are alumni of UIUC.

Among other distinguished alumni are John B. Anderson, 1980 presidential candidate; John Block, U.S. Secretary of Agriculture; James Reston, Pulitzer Prize–winning *New York Times* columnist; Gene Shalit, television personality; the former U.S. Air Force chief of staff; the retired board chairman of General Motors; the founder of the *Catholic Worker*; ABC News's director of politcal affairs.

Admissions-Related Topics

Image versus Reality

The national image of the University of Illinois is unclear. If anything, UIUC is thought to be large and to have a serious academic atmosphere and an active university town surrounded by flat cornfields.

Illinois seems to *know* it is somewhat without image. As a consequence, UIUC does not exactly hide its candle under a bushel. "This is the only public university in Illinois with the faculty and facilities to develop our future leaders," a recent brochure reports. And there does seem to be just cause for bragging: the largest state university library in the country is here; in a recent survey published in the *Chronicle of Higher Education*, UIUC ranked fourth in overall quality and breadth of its programs among state universities and eighth among all universities in this country; UIUC Professor Emeritus John Bardeen is the only person ever to have won two Nobel Prizes. And consider a random assortment of Illinois' "firsts": the first state-supported school of music in the United States; the first collegiate homecoming celebration; the first discovery of growth rings in teeth(!); the initial development of the pioneering "New Mathematics" curriculum; the first germ-free environment in a laboratory; the first varsity letters awarded to physically handicapped students. And Urbana-Champaign is a major midwestern center for musical and theatrical events. The aforementioned Krannert Center for the Performing Arts is exceptional. The campus supports three museums, one of them second only to the Art Institute of Chicago in size and value of collections in Illinois. Add on the athletic frenzy and the nation's largest Greek system, plus the array of pubs and coffee houses, and you have a more vibrant community than the name somehow suggests.

What Elements Most/Least Draw Students?

Most attractive: the draw of the Colleges of Engineering and Commerce. Also, overall respect for the undergraduate academic offerings.

Least attractive: the size, the perceived academic competition, and some parental concern that UIUC refuses to assume the *in loco parentis* responsibility.

Is Illinois for Everyone?

Almost anyone can find a niche. But it takes a resourceful, well-motivated student to find his or her way in this maze.

En Route Perfection, What Should UIUC Change?

The undergraduate student body is clearly "too Illinois," although there is a sampling of students from around the nation and the world. Minorities are in short supply relative to the population Illinois seeks to serve. Regarding excesses: would that the crowds pushing in to engineering or business scattered throughout the institution's diverse programs. But perhaps the change most needed is expanded faculty (meaning expanded funding) for high demand areas such as business and engineering. And a more vibrant image would help.

In Summary

Somehow, the University of Illinois does not scream out to the nation like a Berkeley or an Ann Arbor or a Chapel Hill. But all the qualities of a world-class university are here. UIUC's faculty is consistently honored by its peers: twenty-two have been elected to the National Academy of Science, twenty-five to the American Academy of Arts and Sciences, twenty-seven to the National Academy of Engineering. From the library on through, the facilities are superb, symbolized perhaps by PLATO, widely recognized as the most advanced computer-based educational system in the world. The quality of the student body is fine, provincial or not. And the graduates seem to regularly climb to considerable heights: a 1982 Standard and Poor's corporation report ranked Illinois third among public institutions and ninth among all universities in the number of undergraduate degrees earned there by the nation's top business executives.

New College of the University of South Florida

Sarasota

Prologue

New College was one of those "noble experiments in higher education" of the 1960s. It opened with considerable hoopla in 1964, moving into the Ringling estate in Sarasota, Florida, designed to include sparkling I. M. Pei–designed quadrangles. But the backers of this innovative college that emphasized tutorials and independent study had more ideas than money. Within a decade, New College had fallen into near-bankruptcy. Through a most unusual agreement with the State of Florida, the avant-garde school was adopted by the University of South Florida in Tampa in 1975. Faculty fears of its unique program being compromised or eliminated proved to be unjustified. New College relies on the state for basic funding, augmented by private donations still solicited by its old board of trustees, now called the New College Foundation. In turn, the public University of South Florida has gained a most attractive branch facility and a showy, progressive program to augment its rather traditional and vocationally oriented main campus concentration.

Academics

Importance of the Liberal Arts

Liberal arts and sciences constitute 110 percent of New College's program. And let us underline *liberal*. There are majors in twenty-two liberal arts departments, although one can also select a divisional concentration instead (social sciences, for example), an interdisciplinary program, or a self-designed major under faculty guidance. "Con-

New College (U. of South Florida) at Sarasota

1) Size of Student Body

Undergraduate __350__   Graduate __0__   Total __350__

2) 1983 Freshman Class Profile

Class Size __113__   % Men __50__   % Women __50__
Percent of Applicants Admitted __60__
Average SATs: Verbal __614__   Math __619__
High School Class Rank: Top Tenth __65__ % Top Quarter __83__ %
  Geographical Distribution (% of class):
In-State __41__ % Middle Atlantic __25__ % New England __4__ %
West _____ % Middle West __11__ % South __56__ %
Foreign __4__ %
Minority Students __6__ % of Class
Financial Aid __75__ % of Class

3) Retention of Students

__70__ % of freshmen graduate in four years
__73__ % of freshmen graduate in five years

4) Ten Most Popular Majors of Graduating Seniors, 1983

Because the New College student body is so small, this chart seems inappropriate. In general, New College students are divided equally among the divisions of humanities, natural sciences, and social studies for their academic majors.

5) The Financial Picture (1982–83)

Annual Campus Budget	$ 2,299,923
Percent of Annual Budget from State Appropriation	69
1983–84 Tuition and Fees for State Residents	$ 1,010
1983–84 Tuition and Fees for Out-of-State Residents	$ 2,890

tracts" are written between students and faculty sponsors regarding what educational activities will be undertaken and completed by the end of each semester. To graduate, a student must arrange seven contracts, three independent study projects, and a final thesis or project, and pass a baccalaureate examination. A final "difference" at New College is the grading system: narrative evaluations replace letter or numerical grades, and each evaluation is marked satisfactory, unsatisfactory, or incomplete. Tutorials abound in this free-wheeling but strenuous academic atmosphere.

Strong Departments

Since departmental and divisional lines are vague here, strengths and weaknesses relate to individual faculty members, not academic areas.

Class Size and Faculty Accessibility

A 10:1 student/faculty ratio keeps classes very small in all three divisions (natural sciences, social sciences, and humanities).

Who Teaches Undergraduates?

The undergraduate is king at New College and all levels of professors teach students seeking the first degree. One freshman reports that faculty and students are difficult to tell apart, given the camaraderie and the small classes.

Are Most Listed Courses Really Available?

The personalized Academic Contract System, and the existence of as many as 300 tutorials per semester, preclude students from being closed out of courses. If you can't get into a course, create another.

The Library

The 150,000-volume library is impressive for a student body of 350, but limited indeed for advanced undergraduates who need broad resources. City libraries are close by, and the University of South Florida's main library in Tampa is accessible by visit or interlibrary loan. The library is not New College's strongest suit.

Honors Program for Freshmen

New College, within the context of the University of South Florida and, indeed, the entire State University System of Florida, *is* an honors college.

Campus Life

Housing

All freshmen live in dormitories, as do 65 percent of the returning students. Others secure housing in the Sarasota community. Most dorm rooms at New College have private entrances and private baths. But students complain that there are no indoor communal areas; palm-treed courtyards provide a good substitute, however.

The Environs

The jewel of New College is the campus itself, on the old Charles Ringling estate, commanding 100 acres of Gulf-front property. There are now twenty-six buildings on the campus, with a new library in the planning. The Sarasota/Bradenton area on Florida's west coast is a resort, catering to the retired and the wealthy. The arts abound, as do activities like boating, fishing, swimming, and golf. The area is growing quickly in population, diversifying both serious and fun off-campus opportunities for students.

Local Hangouts

The Pub in the campus Hamilton Center provides student union–like activity and amenities: pinball, food and beverages, table games. But here is one campus not surrounded by loud beer halls. New College is different, and so are the needs and habits of the people who go there.

The Greeks

None. *Never.*

Athletics

There is a "sail and trail" club at New College, and that's about as organized as sports get here. Soccer and backgammon and chess are organized. But it is not fashionable at New to compete and/or sweat.

Drugs/Booze/Sex

"Indulgence cannot be characterized as excessive here," says a campus official. And the students agree. Although there is an open morality among New College participants, behavior is discreet.

Student Stereotypes

The "hippie" student body that so infuriated the citizens of Sarasota during the early New College days has disappeared, almost. The free spirit is still intact, although the hair is shorter and the jeans well washed. You won't find monograms on shetland sweaters, however.

The Tolerance Level

"Differences" are prized at New College. If you do and/or look like what your brothers and sisters do and/or look like, you're not thinking.

Food

Starchy, but filling.

Cars and Transportation

Although public transportation is accessible, a car is an asset in this rambling resort area. And New College, being so small, can become intense. It is good to have a means of escape now and then. Bicycles on campus abound.

Life After College

Post-Bachelor's Placement

Approximately 40 percent of the students here head to graduate and professional schools immediately following college. The list of accepting institutions is impressive indeed, with heavy emphasis on the private sector. Some students feel the narrative evaluations handicap them in admission to top graduate schools. Be that as it may, most New College students are admissible to graduate and professional schools by means of high standardized test scores. In a recent study, New College ranked ninth in the nation in average LSAT scores. The place is too small to have a formal job placement service, so faculty, staff, and alumni pitch in to assist students in the search.

Alumni Stars in the New College Galaxy

Remember that New College is new indeed. But some of the late sixties and early seventies graduates are already making their mark. Among them, the first daughter of a rabbi to be ordained a rabbi, an advisor to the United States delegation to the SALT talks, a full professor of mathematics at Princeton, a New Hampshire legislator, the screenwriter for the movie *The Black Stallion*, not to mention a young man who entered the college at age twelve, graduated at sixteen, and is now working on his Ph.D. at Cal Tech.

Admissions-Related Topics

Image versus Reality

In its early days, New College was popularly grouped with "alternative colleges" born of the same era and of the same genre: Hampshire in New England, Santa Cruz in California. It was most prominent, perhaps, at its well-publicized founding. As it remained small and grew quarrelsome within its community and its own faculty, the name faded in luster and from public view. Then, at the time of the merger with the University of South Florida, the image became even more blurred. But New College the progressive, liberal, daring institution that was, still is. Unlike Santa Cruz and a few of its early first cousins, the institution has changed very little from its original concept in spite of having been absorbed into the Florida state system.

What Elements Most/Least Draw Students?

Most attractive: low tuition rates for both in-state and out-of-state students, the opportunity to work closely with creative faculty, the lack of tight distribution requirements, the bay front campus, the "feeling of community," and the surprisingly comfortable hybrid of intensity and informality.

Least attractive: the tiny size of the school, the tinier extracurricular offerings on campus. And as one student comments, "Much as we believe in this place, there is a general uneasiness in putting complete confidence in a nontraditional institution during this most traditional era."

Is New College for Everyone?

For those who seek traditional college life, certainly not. For those who want high visibility in seeking and supporting scholarly notions and independence, yes. To cope, individuality is a must at New College.

En Route Perfection, What Should New College Change?

Certainly, New College is not lacking different types of students (except minorities), but it does lack enough students. Although there is pride here in being small, bigger would be better if translated into expanded extracurricular activities and academic facilities.

In Summary

The John D. and Catherine T. MacArthur Foundation recently named New College as one of sixteen "distinguished liberal arts colleges" to receive a $300,000 endowment for visiting professorships. Recognition and the bestowal of one award after another underscores the fact that New College is indeed an elite "private" college at a low public price. In general, the adjective "unique" is overused, but New College, as a public institution, clearly qualifies.

Pennsylvania State University

University Park
Prologue

Penn State is not only huge, it is also complicated. Forgoing a large diagram, suffice it to say that the university is scattered through twenty undergraduate campuses. To confuse matters further, there are ten academic "colleges" which are represented on some campuses and not on others. In all, there are 122 baccalaureate degree programs and 29 two-year associate degree programs. Despite the decentralization, the mother ship is clearly Penn State, University Park. This one campus is huge, all by itself. Each year 4,000 new freshmen and 1,000 transfers from outside the system arrive, in addition to 5,000 new arrivals from Penn State's two-year campuses.

Academics
Importance of the Liberal Arts

Penn State is a land grant institution and as such has always had a strong career orientation. Nonetheless, the College of the Liberal Arts has created academic programs that bridge both liberal arts study and professional training. Two other colleges—the College of Science and the College of Arts and Architecture—also feature Penn State's commitment to a broad and deep liberal education.

In general, liberal arts courses feed the general education program and cut across the ten college boundaries. As one student says, "We have a lot of general ed requirements to fill before we graduate. I guess the strength of this program is that we are exposed to a broad range of subjects, whether we want to be or not. The weakness is that the general education or liberal arts experience is not tied together

Pennsylvania State University at University Park

1) Size of Student Body

Undergraduate __26,000__ Graduate __6,000__   Total __32,000__

2) 1983 Freshman Class Profile

Class Size __4,168__   % Men __47__   % Women __53__
Percent of Applicants Admitted __55__
Average SATs: Verbal __510__   Math __565__
High School Class Rank: Top Tenth _____ % Top Quarter __53__ %
   Geographical Distribution (% of class):
In-State __86__ % Middle Atlantic __95__ % New England __2__ %
West __<1__ % Middle West __2__ % South __<1__ %
Minority Students __7__ % of Class
Financial Aid __75__ % of Class

3) Retention of Students

__53__ % of freshmen graduate in four years
__63__ % of freshmen graduate in five years

4) Ten Most Popular Majors of Graduating Seniors, 1983

1. Accounting
2. Marketing
3. Electrical Engineering
4. Mechanical Engineering
5. Chemical Engineering
6. Finance
7. Computer Science
8. Biology/Premed
9. Speech and Communication
10. Microbiology

5) The Financial Picture (1982–83)

Annual Campus Budget	$ 284,000,000
Percent of Annual Budget from State Appropriation	27
1983–84 Tuition and Fees for State Residents	$ 2,312
1983–84 Tuition and Fees for Out-of-State Residents	$ 4,624

by any structure. It's a buckshot approach. You just hope something hits home."

Strong Departments

Significant departments abound here. Nearly every major in the College of Agriculture and the College of Engineering is absolutely superb. The College of Earth and Mineral Sciences reputedly has the finest meteorology program in the nation, not to mention nonpareil research programs in coal, mining engineering, lubrication research, and nuclear waste disposal. In the College of Science, chemistry, physics, computer science, and astronomy are strong. In the College of Liberal Arts, English, psychology, and speech communication are the best bets. In the College of Human Development, the individual and family studies program is perhaps the nation's best. The College of Health, Physical Education, and Research has received top rankings, and the College of Education, even though facing significant budget cuts, also ranks in the nation's top twenty. The College of Business Administration has been recently ranked in the nation's top twenty and is famed for its accounting program. Penn State's theater arts program is emerging, and the art education department is perhaps one of the nation's best. Also, Penn State has good programs abroad.

Class Size and Faculty Accessibility

The best way to get faculty attention at Penn State is to attend one of the lower-division "Commonwealth campuses" for two years, then transfer to University Park. Two-thirds of Penn State's freshmen do just that. When a student attends Penn State University Park for all four years, he or she can count on very large survey courses (200 to 400 classmates) during the freshman and sophomore years, some of which are taught by closed-circuit television. Most of the large lectures break into once-a-week sections for laboratory or discussion under the tutelage of graduate teaching assistants.

The upper-division sections are, of course, smaller than the lower-division sections. In 1980, for example, the average section size for an upper-division course was twenty-six. Faculty accessibility is not so much a function of a particular discipline, department, or college as it is a function of personality. Faculty members are required to keep office hours and advise students of them at University Park, but the burden of initiating a meeting with a professor remains the student's responsibility. "Even when you dig up a professor in his office," reports one student, "there is little spontaneous interaction."

Who Teaches Undergraduates?

Departmental policy differs from department to department, but full-time faculty are usually on the podium in front of a large introductory class. As at similar multiversities, the grad students take over during discussion. At least Penn State is careful in making certain that foreign teaching assistants hold a fairly high degree of proficiency in English before they attempt to lead discussion.

Are Most Listed Courses Really Available?

Penn State's dean of admissions says, "There is no such thing as truly open, untrammeled access into a particular major here." Most majors at Penn State require certain grade point averages; the more popular the major, the tougher entry becomes. As enrollment pressures build at certain colleges, they're forced to tighten their admission criteria. Even at the freshman admission level, the colleges are uneven in entry requirements.

The Library

An undergraduate reports: "Pattee Library is monstrous. The only disadvantage is that it takes quite a while to track down the material you're seeking. The collection is spread not only throughout one huge building, but parts of it are also housed in smaller libraries around campus. But everything the undergraduate needs is here. And our well-publicized library computerization does speed circulation."

The Association of Research Libraries recently ranked Penn State's library sixteenth among public universities in the nation.

Honors Program for Freshmen

A relatively new University Scholars Program seems quite successful at University Park. Students take one-half of their courses in special honors program sections. Scholars' status confers good benefits: a special, more advanced curriculum in the student's field; the opportunity for greater interaction with faculty; special counseling; special extracurricular programs; and dinner seminars with visiting scholars. The Scholars Program is clearly a lure for some of the Commonwealth of Pennsylvania's brightest teenagers.

Campus Life

Housing

At University Park, about one-third of all students live in college housing, including all freshmen under twenty-one, who are required to do so. After the freshman year, housing is allotted on a first-come, first-served basis. As one student comments: "This means we must stand in line for hours, often camping overnight in weather fair and foul, waiting for the housing office to open. The administration would like us to go to a lottery system, but we students have repeatedly opposed it. By standing in line, we can at least earn a room if we want one." Students who do not make it into campus housing are usually apartment dwellers, if they are not in the Greek system housing. There is an abundance of high rises and apartment complexes near campus, but rents are high.

The Environs

Geographically, University Park is isolated, and getting there is not easy. But once there, the town stands in sharp contrast to the blight of neighboring Appalachian communities. State College, the borough in which the University Park campus is situated, sits in a wide valley between two mountain ridges. Says one tenured faculty member: "One can sit in the upper rows of 85,000-seat Beaver Stadium on a sunny football Saturday in October and fall in love with this place forever by looking out at Mount Nittany and its sister mountains, covered with flaming foliage. It happens! Some students enter graduate school here just to stay in the area, and others seek menial jobs in downtown stores for the same reason. A lot of people want to stay here for a lifetime." A student reports that State College isn't like a small town because there are so many people on campus and such a frenzy of activity.

Local Hangouts

The Wall runs down College Avenue along the south border of campus. It is only a few feet high, and *everybody* sits on it during nice weather to watch the world go by. At night, the partying begins and knows no boundaries. The Hub (student union building) sees a lot of traffic, extracurricular and social, as do the quads of dorm areas. But the bars nearby are the social gathering places for students over twenty-one or those who know the bouncer. Calder Alley is the local "Bourbon Street." The Rathskeller is old and popular and sells more Rolling Rock beer than any other emporium in Pennsylvania. Other prominent watering holes, most of which offer live music every night of the week, include the Phyrst, the Brewery, the Scorpion, the Posthouse, the Shandygaff, Zeno's, and the Saloon. These places are always jammed. And not just on weekends. Every student's one big night of course, is "coming of age" at twenty-one and making the rounds until catatonia sets in.

The Greeks

Penn State has one of the nation's largest Greek systems, with nearly 2,000 men in forty-nine fraternities and over one thousand women in nineteen sororities. The trend is toward even further growth. Beyond numbers, the Greek system is important, says one student, because it is the subject of constant debate. "Fraternities and sororities cause artificial social divisions because people take the distinction between Greek and non-Greek too seriously around here. The Greeks do add a lot to campus life, but too many of their events are restricted to those within. The number of organized groups is so huge, though, that just about anyone who wants to can join."

The fraternities and sororities at Penn State are known for rather phenomenal fund-raising successes for charitable causes such as cystic fibrosis and muscular dystrophy. The Inter-Fraternity Council's annual dance marathon raises $100,000 to ease the financial burden for families of children with cancer. And the Greeks have good fun too. Most of the campus turns out for the infamous Phi Psi 500, a footrace in which hundreds of participants must stop at various bars to chug beer enroute the finish line.

Athletics

A Penn State senior comments, "Football here is mania. Often we don't take the sport that seriously, but the event—the carnival—is a matter of utmost importance. Basketball, gymnastics, wrestling, and soccer also draw good crowds, but nothing like football. Athletics provides us a rallying point. A place this big needs *something* to provide community."

With fifteen men's and thirteen women's intercollegiate sports programs, Penn State offers one of the most comprehensive varsity listings in the nation. Although football is consistently ranked in the nation's top ten, other teams fare well. In 1980, for example, Penn State women won the nationals in gymnastics, lacrosse, and fencing. Football is king, however, and largely because of coach Joe Paterno, a national legend. Paterno believes that student-athletes should not be consumed by college athletics. At University Park, there are no athletic dorms, and "athletic admissions" are the province of the university's dean of admissions.

Drugs/Booze/Sex

Penn State, one must remember, is a fairly conservative outpost. Coed dorms are rare, and so are abuses with drugs. "Having a few beers," however, is a Penn State tradition.

One student summarizes the situation by saying: "Freshmen by no means should worry that they will be sucked into a drug-crazed whirlwind. That is foreign to Penn State. And it is actually very difficult to get into a bar until you are twenty-one. Once there, though, we sure can have fun. Regarding sex—Penn State is no orgy. Many students are disillusioned because there are 17,000 members of the opposite sex on one campus and they still can't get any. A very small percentage of students live with members of the opposite sex. Casual sex connected with parties is not uncommon but is usually restricted to those who would be good at that sort of thing whether they were at Penn State or not."

Student Stereotypes

The stereotypical Penn State student is from the Pittsburgh or Philadelphia area; wears jeans, sneakers, and a T-shirt (a golf shirt for dates); and is not in college to reform society but to join, improve, and rise within it.

As a Penn State senior sees it, "The typical Penn State student sees his studies as the means to an end, and 'good times' as the true end. He/she sobers up a bit during the last two years of college when finding a job becomes the supreme concern. Penn Staters are conservative—they are almost all white, from middle-class suburbia. They flirt briefly with radical politics but only take them seriously if they join the student government. Most of the students here are against big government because they just don't understand it. Yes, there are a few differences here, but students on the whole fit into a few well-worn patterns."

The Tolerance Level

"The student majority here is a pretty homogeneous group, with little tolerance for people who are different. But if a student *is* different, he or she can always find a subculture to feel comfortable in," reports a Penn State student observer.

Penn State looks tolerant when one casually visits the mall. Evangelists "Bro Cope" can be found fulminating from the steps of a classroom building while Krishnas with shaved heads chant their mantras as they pass out literature nearby. No one seems to be bothered. Penn State has an exchange of ideas and political and religious philosophies, but there is a huge status quo–oriented mass in the big middle that spends little time discussing the great issues.

Food

Penn State often grows and/or makes its own. Dining hall dairy and bread products are locally grown and prepared, so, one trusts, they are at least fresh and wholesome. The university's creamery sells about 1,000 cones a day (and *Money* magazine heralded this creamery as one of the nation's ten best).

Students report that the food in the dorms is not bad for institutional fare. "It does not compare with mom's, though, so it draws a lot of complaints. If you don't see any entrees you like, there is always the salad bar," comments one freshman.

Cars and Transportation

Everything a student needs is within walking or commuter bus distance at Penn State except for the parties in town. Be that as it may, it is reported that well over 50 percent of the University Park students, whether living in apartments or on campus, do have automobiles. That excludes freshmen under twenty-one who are not allowed to have cars unless they commute from home.

Life After College

Post-Bachelor's Placement

Penn State is reputed to be a "one-stop shopping center" for job recruiters. The work ethic is strong with this crowd, not to mention specific career goals. A study of a recently graduated class indicated that one year after commencement, 55 percent were employed in their preferred field; 16 percent were employed but not in their preferred field; 12 percent were enrolled in graduate or professional school; and the remaining 17 percent were "in transition." The Career Placement and Counseling Center here reports that Penn State ranks in the top five placement centers of the country in number of job interviews conducted on campus—27,082 in 1982.

Alumni Stars in the Penn State Galaxy

Penn State claims that one out of every thousand Americans is a Penn State graduate! And within that large group are distinguished alumni indeed: Dr. Paul Berg, who won the 1980 Nobel Prize in chemistry; two astronauts, including Guion Bluford, Jr., America's first black astronaut; former U.S. Senator Richard S. Schweiker; several Carter and Reagan administration cabinet and commission members; Dr. Margaret Lindsey of Columbia University, often called "the dean of teacher educators"; and Pulitzer Prize-winning journalist Norman Miller of *The Wall Street Journal.*

Admissions-Related Topics

Image versus Reality

A Penn State coed observes: "Our image and reality are pretty well aligned. This actually *is* a good-time, football school. Perhaps the one surprise is that Penn State is academically more demanding than the world thinks, and you have to do well in your studies without a great deal of supervision. This place is just too big to provide everyone individual attention. On the other hand, the hugeness of Penn State goes away after awhile. The size is only intimidating for the first term or so."

An administrator comments that talking about Penn State's image is something like the blind men trying to describe the elephant according to where each had touched it. Penn State has many different images, many realities.

What Elements Most/Least Draw Students?

The size of Penn State means "opportunity and variety" to some. To others, and particularly parents, the size of Penn State means the possibility of getting lost in the crowd, and dealing with endless bureaucracy. The location and the beauty and the tidiness of the campus seem to appeal to all.

Is Penn State for Everyone?

"No," says one student. "People who want an intensely intellectual environment will be disappointed here. But good students will find plenty to keep them busy. And one can feel isolated or cut adrift here as a result of our size." Penn State/University Park is for *almost* anyone.

En Route Perfection, What Should Penn State Change?

Penn State could relieve its homogeneity with more out-of-state students, more international students, and a better racial mix. Students feel that a good Penn State would be even better with a smaller enrollment so that the overcrowded housing in the fall term and the overcrowded classrooms all year would be relieved. "Ideally," says one student, "there would be no huge auditorium classes and *no* sections would be taught by foreign graduate students who cannot communicate in English." Other students and administrators feel the University Scholars Program could be greatly expanded, and they wish for more local monies to assist needy students without total reliance on state and federal funds.

In Summary

In the words of one administrator: "Penn State is not elitist, but it is quality. We accept thousands of students who need their horizons expanded. We are responsive to the needs of the Commonwealth, but we are clear in our own responsibility to determine an intellectually valid set of missions." A student reflects, "Penn State has not forced a top-quality education upon me, but it has offered me one for the getting. If one wants the best, it's here."

University of Pittsburgh

Prologue

The University of Pittsburgh is a relative newcomer to the "public" roster. Founded in 1787, the university was private until its financial base crumbled in the late 1960s. The Commonwealth of Pennsylvania graciously offered to assume major responsibility for the institution, although private support remains important. Pitt was a sound and respected private institution; it appears to be flourishing under new, or expanded, sponsorship.

Academics

Importance of the Liberal Arts

Contrary to the public perception of Pitt as vocationally oriented, the College of Arts and Sciences, with an undergraduate student body of over 7,000, is easily the largest division of the university. The catalog states Pitt's position clearly: "Indeed, it is arguable that the liberally educated person—literate, intellectually disciplined, intelligently aware of the world—is the one best suited to survive in an age of dizzying technological change and social upheaval. It is also noteworthy that leaders in every field—politics, business, science, law, and the other professions—are nearly all graduates of liberal arts colleges who had the good sense to seek an education for life before pursuing training for a career."

Pitt freshmen have three choices at entry: the College of Arts and Sciences or the Schools of Engineering or Nursing. After one year in CAS, qualified students may transfer into the School of Pharmacy. After two years, qualified students may transfer into the Schools of Education, Library and Information Science, Social Work, or Health Related Professions. Even after transferring to professional programs

University of Pittsburgh

1) Size of Student Body

Undergraduate __19,301__ Graduate __10,124__ Total __29,425__

2) 1983 Freshman Class Profile

Class Size __2,638__ % Men __53__ % Women __47__
Percent of Applicants Admitted __76__
Average SATs: Verbal __480__ Math __530__
High School Class Rank: Top Tenth __23__ % Top Quarter __50__ %
   Geographical Distribution (% of class):
In-State __92__% Middle Atlantic __98__ % New England __1__ %
West _____ % Middle West _____ % South _____ 1 %
Minority Students __14__ % of Class
Financial Aid __59__ % of Class

3) Retention of Students

__72__ % of freshmen graduate in five years

4) Ten Most Popular Majors of Graduating Seniors, 1983

1. Psychology
2. Economics
3. Nursing
4. Computer Science
5. Mechanical Engineering
6. Business
7. Political Science
8. Chemical Engineering
9. Electrical Engineering
10. Information Science

5) The Financial Picture (1982–83)

Annual Campus Budget	$ 313,147,000
Percent of Annual Budget from State Appropriation	26.8
1983–84 Tuition and Fees for State Residents	$ 2,528
1983–84 Tuition and Fees for Out-of-State Residents	$ 4,948

in the junior year, however, Pitt students continue to be exposed to arts and sciences programs and requirements.

In 1981, the College of Arts and Sciences enacted a major curricular reform. Replacing "perfunctory distribution requirements" were "core requirements" of twelve courses: three in literature and the arts; one in philosophy; three in history, social science, and public policy; three in natural science; two in foreign culture or advanced foreign language study.

In short, Pitt's College of Arts and Sciences is the heart of the university.

Strong Departments

Pitt says its Philosophy Department may be the best in the country. Chemistry, physics, statistics, history, and political science are considered very strong also. Computer science is woefully overcrowded, and students say the communications major is considered weak. Other strengths are in foreign area programs: Latin America, East Asia, Russia, and East Europe. Engineering and nursing both draw talented students and are demanding.

Class Size and Faculty Accessibility

Classes here are no larger than at Harvard, says one Pitt administrator. The most obvious overcrowding can be found in computer science and in the opening courses of the natural sciences. But there is a decent student/faculty ratio: nearly 600 faculty members for a student body of 7,500 undergraduates and 1,200 graduate students. With a few exceptions, teachers are considered quite accessible.

Who Teaches Undergraduates?

A good many teaching assistants and part-time faculty can be found in basic composition courses, elementary math courses, opening foreign language courses, lab sections of natural sciences courses, and recitation sections of introductory courses in psychology, economics, and sociology. As an undergraduate moves up the ladder, regular faulty start appearing often.

Are Most Listed Courses Really Available?

Although all majors are available to all students, nabbing the preferred course at the preferred time can be difficult, particularly in math and computer science.

The Library

Pitt's library holds three million volumes, more than adequate for College of Arts and Sciences specialists. And students say nice things about the reading rooms, general facilities, and open stacks of Hilman Library, the main center.

Honors Program for Freshmen

Pitt's Freshmen Seminar Program offers a special repertoire of challenging courses to 200 freshmen recruits who are judged on a combination of high GPA and SATs. Those not invited into the program as freshmen may join later if their grades at Pitt warrant. All seminars in this program are offered by senior faculty members.

In addition, most of the majors offer honors versions, which typically means small seminars, research projects, and the requirement of a senior thesis.

Campus Life

Housing

Housing is not Pitt's strong suit. Approximately 1,500 of the 2,500 freshmen can get university housing, but their comments regarding facilities are anything but lofty. In total, less than one-third of the undergraduates can be accommodated in campus housing, via a lottery system. The balance fend for themselves in the surrounding area of Oakland, at Greek houses, or at home with parents. Although Pitt has a sizable commuter population, there are hundreds of students who would like on-campus housing but are closed out. This is a primary area of student complaint.

The Environs

The city of Pittsburgh suffers a bum rap. Those who remember the grimy industrial center of old would be surprised with the results of massive rehabilitation. And the university is located in the Oakland section of Pittsburgh, the city's cultural center. It is downright attractive. Immediately adjacent to the campus is a huge park and Phipps Conservatory, where a wide collection of exotic plants are displayed and two annual flower shows are held. Within walking distance is the Carnegie Institute Complex, which includes the Museum of Art and History, Carnegie Library, and Carnegie Music Hall. Also adjacent to campus are the Syria Mosque and B'nai B'rith Hallea, both of which host a variety of cultural events. The university is a ten-minute bus ride from downtown Pittsburgh and attractions such as Heinz Hall and Three Rivers Stadium. Also close by are Carnegie-Mellon University, Chatham College, Duquesne University, and Point Park. Students at all these institutions can cross-register. In sum, Pitt is located in a greatly improved city and in the best part of it.

Local Hangouts

The Pitt Student Union hosts the mainstream of campus activities, and certainly the commuters. The dormitory lobbies and patios draw crowds too. In warm weather, the Cathedral lawn and the Law School Grounds are the place to be for sunning, brown bagging, and studying. Beyond the Pitt Union, commuters and others gather at the Burger Chef, oddly placed on the ground floor of the gothic Cathedral.

Near the campus, Greeks congregate at Thirsty's, Mitchell's Pub, and Peter's Pub; the grad students frequent Zelda's; The Decade is the rock and roll center; The Sanctuary is the dance center; The Wooden Keg attracts everyone, as do C. J. Barney's, Gustine's, and The Original for both food and booze.

The Greeks

On a transient downtown campus, Pitt's Greek system provides some social cohesion. Annual Greek Week is a major Pitt tradition, as is Greek participation in support of the varsity teams. Campus "leaders" are often Greek. Housing is also a draw to the Greek system, but providing a base of identity is the major attraction.

Athletics

Football is king here. It all started in 1890 and catapulted into prominence under the direction of "Pop" Warner and Jack Sutherland. At the moment, Pitt football ranks sixth in national championships with nine number-one seasons. Coach Johnny Majors is famous as the architect of the modern Pitt football renaissance with a national championship in 1976 sporting Heisman Trophy winner Tony Dorsett. Panther basketball is big time too, having recently joined the Big East Conference. Although football and basketball for men predominate, there are wide opportunities in athletics, intercollegiate and intermural, for both men and women here.

Drugs/Booze/Sex

Pitt students are widely dispersed and control their own lives. University officials do not feel that drugs present a problem but, as on many other campuses today, there is lots of beer.

Student Stereotypes

Not much homogeneity here. A city university can absorb all types, and Pitt does. The student body is not as sophisticated as the nearby Carnegie-Mellon crowd and not as elegant as the Chatham crowd; Pitt students are basically conservative and casual, with a blue-collar determination to "make it."

The Tolerance Level

Thanks to the urban environment, you can be yourself at Pitt. Chances are no one will notice.

Food

There are plenty of options, so if you don't like what the residence halls serve up, you can easily retreat to a nearby fast-food restaurant. The proximity of the city can be a real benefit in varying the diet.

Cars and Transportation

For the one-third of the students who commute, a car is obviously convenient and parking is available. But parking is a dreadful problem for the one-third of the undergraduates who live in residence halls and the remaining one-third who live in apartments off campus. Public transportation is the way to move in this environment.

Life After College

Post-Bachelor's Placement

A surprising one-half of the Arts and Sciences graduates enroll immediately in a professional or graduate school on securing the B.A., partly because jobs are more difficult to find for this crowd than those with "professional" training. The students who, as undergraduates, major in engineering, computer science, pharmacy, or the health-related fields obtain employment with relative ease and are tempted not to continue graduate training immediately.

Alumni Stars in the Pitt Galaxy

The most famous name on Pitt's lengthy roster of stars is probably Gene Kelly, the song and dance man. But the institution has graduated a long list of judges, presidents of major companies, two White House physicians, several deans of professional schools, at least one Pulitzer Prize winner, and Dr. Moses Bopape, the first black in South Africa to get a Ph.D. in social work and the first black professor of social work in his home country. Peter Flaherty, the former mayor of Pittsburgh; Orrin Hatch, United States senator; Leonard Marks, former head of the United States Information Agency; Eugene Scanlon, majority whip of the Pennsylvania Senate; and Richard Thornburgh, governor of Pennsylvania, all have the Pitt degree.

Admissions-Related Topics

Image versus Reality

"Pitt" connotes a city university in a grimy place with an outstanding football team. Actually, the university's proximity to parks and woods and space makes its (improved) city fairly unobtrusive. The football program *is* strong, but so are the academics. And this is a significant research center.

What Elements Most/Least Draw Students?

Since Pitt's transition from private to public, a big draw is the perception of high-quality education at very low cost. And the "renewed" city of Pittsburgh is a draw too, particularly for Pennsylvanians. On the negative side are the housing problem, the parking problem, and the lack of a bucolic campus. And those who still have not heard of Pittsburgh's renaissance would prefer a college in Philadelphia or Boston.

Is Pitt for Everyone?

There is a broad sweep of programs here and an able student body. But Pitt can be lonely for one closed out of campus housing.

En Route Perfection, What Should Pitt Change?

A senior commented: "Pitt would be perfect if it had even lower tuition, more parking, more housing, and a campus like Cornell's."

In Summary

Pitt is catching hold. Implementation of the new curricular reform, not unlike Harvard's, seems to have created some excitement and continuity throughout the campus. A renewed city and winning ball teams further enhance the contagious spirit.

State University of New York

Binghamton

Prologue

The State University of New York claims to be the largest university system in the world, with nearly 400,000 students and sixty-four campuses. There are four "university centers"—at Binghamton, Albany, Stony Brook, and Buffalo—and a vast array of arts and science colleges, statutory colleges, agricultural and technical colleges, community colleges, and graduate centers. SUNY is a modern phenomenon, created by the legislature in 1948. But its qualitative and quantitative leap came under Governor Nelson A. Rockefeller during the sixties. Because SUNY chose not to establish a flagship campus, such as Berkeley of the California system or Ann Arbor of the Michigan system, it is rarely mentioned when the nation's elite are being named. But with age, strong idiosyncrasies within SUNY are emerging. One campus, with an early liberal arts bent, has become a strong and highly selective undergraduate center. It is Binghamton. Although most SUNY campuses accommodate undergraduates in a liberal arts program, Binghamton now soars in reputation above the others.

Academics

Importance of the Liberal Arts

Binghamton *is* liberal arts and always has been. Its seed was Harpur, a small liberal arts college. At the time Harpur was absorbed by SUNY in 1950, it was the only public liberal arts college in the entire state. By the end of the decade, when the Binghamton campus was designated for development as a university center, Harpur had already established a strong reputation for liberal arts and selective admissions. Today, Harpur maintains its name as the undergraduate unit

State University of New York at Binghamton

1) Size of Student Body

Undergraduate __8,650__   Graduate __2,700__   Total __11,350__

2) 1983 Freshman Class Profile

Class Size __1,600__   % Men __41__   % Women __59__
Percent of Applicants Admitted __48__
Average SATs: Verbal __532__   Math __590__
High School Class Rank: Top Tenth __57__ % Top Quarter __92__ %
   Geographical Distribution (% of class):
In-State __96__ % Middle Atlantic __98__ % New England __2__ %
West _____ % Middle West _____ % South _____ %
Minority Students __8__ % of Class
Financial Aid __85__ % of Class

3) Retention of Students

__60__ % of freshmen graduate in four years
__65__ % of freshmen graduate in five years

4) Ten Most Popular Majors of Graduating Seniors, 1983

1. Psychology
2. Political Science
3. Biological Science
4. Accounting
5. Management (School of Management)
6. Mathematics
7. English
8. Economics
9. History
10. Chemistry

5) The Financial Picture (1982–83)

Annual Campus Budget	$ 77,300,000
Percent of Annual Budget from State Appropriation	60
1983–84 Tuition and Fees for State Residents	$ 1,350
1983–84 Tuition and Fees for Out-of-State Residents	$ 2,650

of the School of Arts and Sciences at Binghamton and enrolls 65 percent of the students at the university center. The other undergraduate schools—Nursing, Management, and General Studies in Professional Education—share the basic liberal arts philosophy which Harpur embodied from the start. (They also share classrooms, faculty, and facilities.) There are strong liberal arts distributional requirements at Binghamton for all undergraduates, regardless of major. And that's good: with Binghamton's goal-oriented, intense get-to-the-best-grad-school-quickly New York syndrome, there is danger of narrow specialization in the final two years.

Strong Departments

Students at Binghamton rush to gain admission to medical school and law school. And they are well prepared to do so, particularly the premeds. Health sciences are strenuous here. Other popular and demanding majors are psychology, political science, and English. Within the psychology major alone are 300 students. Other popular but smaller departments include geography, geology, anthropology, and cinema. Music and theater have extensive programs but less of a following here than at SUNY-Purchase. There are substantial cross-disciplinary programs: Judaic studies, medieval studies, linguistics, law and society. Nursing remains popular, but women have their eye on many careers now and are spread rather evenly throughout the curriculum. If anything, it is the technical side that needs bolstering at Binghamton. With interest in computer science booming and in engineering growing, Binghamton is under considerable pressure to meet these student interests of the late eighties and nineties.

Class Size and Faculty Accessibility

Freshmen who are good enough to be chosen for the Integrated Semester Program get the small classes. For others, the usual big lecture/small discussion groups syndrome prevails. A Binghamton administrator says, "Faculty sometimes are able to add a small seminar here and there." Most often, though, students have to wait for upper-level courses to become visible and active in the classroom.

Who Teaches Undergraduates?

With a relatively small graduate school (approximately 2,000 students) TAs are not as common here as at the larger public universities. Teaching assistants do handle a good many of the recitation sections, with full-time faculty up front for the lectures.

Are Most Listed Courses Really Available?

Most of the traditional liberal arts areas at Binghamton are quite accessible to students at registration, now that there is a crush for business and computer courses. The School of Management remains relatively small, so nonmajors find access to individual courses nearly impossible. Beyond the fad subjects of the moment, any course with a popular instructor fills early.

The Library

A couple of years ago the library catalogued its millionth volume, and it continues to grow quickly. Residential college library annexes are scattered throughout the campus, and the science library is separate. The main library, Bartle, features huge picture windows with outstanding views of the surrounding wooded hills.

Honors Program for Freshmen

Binghamton is experimenting with an honors program for new students. Also, five freshmen each year are lured by a merit scholarship labeled the SUNY Honors Program, providing full tuition, room and board, and access to top courses.

Campus Life

Housing

Just over half of the undergraduates live on campus, including 92 percent of the freshmen. Housing is in four residential college clusters, each with its own dining hall, library, and social, recreational, and laundry facilities. Dorms look a bit different here, as students are permitted to paint murals in rooms or along corridors, to personalize their quarters at will. But the place is tidy: Binghamton has won five consecutive annual awards for the best-maintained SUNY campus. The students themselves are key to that recognition.

The Environs

Binghamton is three and a half hours northwest of New York City and one hour from Ithaca, home of Cornell and Ithaca College. The 600-acre wooded campus is on a rolling hillside overlooking the Susquehana River Valley, with the towns of Endicott and Johnson City nearby. One would have to categorize this setting as "rural." And looking at the high percentage of students from New York City and

"The Island," (meaning Long Island) the geographic tranquility is a welcome balance to the on-campus achievement effort.

Local Hangouts

The "UU," or University Union, is the hub for activities emanating from 160 organized student groups. Downstairs is a pub serving beer and pizza, and there is a nearby, much-criticized mini-mall for those who want fast foods. The Food Co-op, the Kosher Kitchen, and others are all within the UU. Students also hang out at the residential colleges' snack bars and game rooms and around the two gyms. Since most students remain near campus during the weekends, close-by pubs with beer and Pac-Man prosper.

The Greeks

Fraternities and sororities just haven't gained a footing here, although a few struggle with small numbers.

Athletics

Intercollegiate sports are as unimportant to SUNY-Binghamton as the Greeks, but intermurals prosper. If someone wants "the big game," Syracuse and Cornell are not far away. Binghamton does putter in NCAA Division III, fielding varsity teams in men's soccer, wrestling, and baseball, as well as women's volleyball and softball.

Drugs/Booze/Sex

Drug use seems low here, but the beer flows freely. With the male/female ratio fairly even, either side can find companions. "It's 'The Island Removed,' socially," says one student. "We all crave greater variety, but that will just have to wait for graduate school."

Student Stereotypes

This place is very New York, and stereotype-labeling is probably fair. Clearly, the students are bright and liberal, wear high-fashion casual gear, and have their eyes on graduate school and a job in "the City" (New York). There are differences, but not many.

The Tolerance Level

SUNY-Binghamton, like the City, can be friendly to all types. The admissions director says: "Computer freaks, gays, farmers, and even serious intellectuals are able to find a reasonably comfortable niche here." Those on the left seem more comfortable than those on the right, but studies uniformly capture all.

Food

The UU allows considerable variety and an escape from the residential college dining halls. On balance, one can eat fairly well here.

Cars and Transportation

Thanks to an efficient student-managed campus bus system, a car makes little sense on campus. And the county bus system for off-campus traveling is not bad. Parking is limited, so a car can present problems (but would be handy for intermittent escape). A bicycle is much more useful.

Life After College

Post-Bachelor's Placement

Ah, SUNY-Binghamton's placement statistics are impressive. As one young lady says: "Success is the name of the game here, and we are an ambitious lot. We *get* into graduate school." Fully 85 percent of the entering freshmen say they plan to go on to graduate or professional school, and the tradition to do so is strong. Local authorities claim 70 percent of Binghamton's applicants to medical school find a place, as do 98 percent of the law school aspirants and over 90 percent of the dental school applicants. "Accounting, actuarial, and computer science graduates just about write their own tickets, as do some geology majors," comments one placement officer. The nurses fare well also. Post-B.A. plans *are* realized by Binghamton students— and an impressive array of ivy-coated names top the list.

Alumni Stars in the SUNY-Binghamton Galaxy

Famous alums wearing the SUNY-Binghamton label are few and far between, since the institution is so young. But graduates of the sixties and seventies are accomplishing nonetheless: the director of the art gallery at the University of Notre Dame is a Binghamton graduate, as are the screenwriter for *Blazing Saddles*, a Nader-raider project head and author, the owner of the *New York Times* building at One Times Square, and the publisher of *USA Today*.

Admissions-Related Topics

Image versus Reality

Binghamton's image is fairly on target and most positive in New York circles. But for some reason, out-of-staters just don't catch on. A campus visit promotes enthusiasm, but not many non–New Yorkers show up. SUNY-Binghamton overlaps in admissions with some very selective private institutions, as well it should. Although its positive image is consistent with the product, its visibility remains provincial.

What Elements Most/Least Draw Students?

Most attractive: the graduate/professional school placement record, the no-nonsense academic reputation, the idyllic campus, and the general friendliness.

Least attractive: the grind-it-out academics with little intellectual flair, the weather, the homogeneity of the student body, the crowded dorms, and the limited number of majors-of-the-eighties.

Is SUNY-Binghamton for Everyone?

Those who crave intercollegiate sports and a heavy Greek scene should look elsewhere. But SUNY-Binghamton can definitely accommodate the others. There is tolerance and space here, and a solid program for the nontechnical.

En Route Perfection, What Should SUNY-Binghamton Change?

Repeat: there are too many New Yorkers on the fast lane to graduate school and the professional job market. Minority students would add balance, not to mention students from elsewhere in the nation and a few who are just "laid back." It would be nice if SUNY could change the weather in Binghamton; a bit more sun, particularly in the late winter, would boost morale. More zip in a handful of spectator sports would help, and a handout from the state or private sources to expand teenagers' new infatuation with computers and business.

In Summary

The SUNY system has yet to find its way to the top of the nation's college pecking order. The "discovery," particularly of the four university centers, is long overdue. For the undergraduate interested in a tough general program and a well-paved path to success thereafter, Binghamton is a top-flight sleeper.

University of Washington

Seattle

Academics

Importance of the Liberal Arts

The University of Washington is prominent in academic circles for leadership in research funded by huge federal grants. International fame for graduate-level research has, unfortunately, eclipsed its reputation for strong undergraduate offerings. And although a complicated conglomerate of sixteen colleges and schools offers instruction at UW, the undergraduate College of Arts and Sciences is by far the university's largest division, with more than sixty departments enrolling 20,285 undergraduate students. As the director of admissions says, "There is an increasing commitment to the idea that general and distributed studies in the arts and sciences are the essential component of undergraduate education, for those who take professional degrees such as business or engineering, or for those who remain in the College." Although an array of strong undergraduate majors aligns with Washington's prominent graduate and professional divisions, the liberal arts curriculum in general is a force at the University of Washington.

Strong Departments

A good many of Washington's undergraduate programs have been ranked among the top ten to twenty in the country by professional surveys in recent years: the departments of zoology, comparative literature, drama, Slavic languages, Asian studies, forest resources, business administration, English, mathematics, nursing, romance languages, and several areas of engineering.

Regrettably, a severely cut budget due to a weak state economy

University of Washington at Seattle

1) Size of Student Body

Undergraduate __23,529__ Graduate __10,779__ Total __34,308__

2) 1983 Freshman Class Profile

Class Size __3,877__ % Men __52__ % Women __48__
Percent of Applicants Admitted __79__
Average SATs: Verbal __497__   Math __566__
   Geographical Distribution (% of class):
In-State __86__% Middle Atlantic __1__ % New England __1__ %
West __95__ % Middle West __1__ % South __1__ %
Foreign __1__ %
Minority Students __25__ % of Class
Financial Aid __33__ % of Class

3) Retention of Students

__18__ % of freshmen graduate in four years
__42__ % of freshmen graduate in five years

4) Ten Most Popular Majors of Graduating Seniors, 1983

1. Business Administration
2. Engineering (all)
3. Economics
4. English
5. Psychology
6. Communications
7. Political Science
8. Art
9. History
10. Mathematics

5) The Financial Picture (1982–83)

Annual Campus Budget	$ 458,869,259
Percent of Annual Budget from State Appropriation	31
1983–84 Tuition and Fees for State Residents	$ 1,302
1983–84 Tuition and Fees for Out-of-State Residents	$ 3,618

is taking a toll on the university's academic programs. Some programs will be eliminated altogether and others cut back. It will take a few years to know where the true shortfalls linger.

Class Size and Faculty Accessibility

UW labels itself "the largest single-campus university in the western United States." With an enrollment of nearly 35,000 students, it is not surprising to find large classes, particularly in introductory courses. Departments reputed to assemble huge lecture audiences in freshmen or sophomore courses are psychology, economics, sociology, political science, and biology. Some esoteric subjects muster only seminar-size groups; the more popular disciplines, however, have large classes throughout. Classes at the junior and senior levels average twenty-five students. As students move up, the classes grow smaller.

Who Teaches Undergraduates?

Even the lectures in large introductory courses are sometimes taught by graduate students, particularly in English, mathematics, and social sciences. But that is the exception, not the norm. Most undergrads are taught by full-time Washington faculty. And the faculty members here have a good reputation for after-class accessibility.

Are Most Listed Courses Really Available?

Students must jump hurdles to gain access to the most popular majors and courses at UW. Engineering, business administration, architecture, communications, computer science, physical therapy and other health-related fields all have stiff grade cutoff points for entry. In most other areas of study, one generally finds unrestricted access.

The Library

UW's library system gains high marks. It holds the thirteenth largest collection in the United States, with over four million volumes and three million items in microform. There are branch libraries scattered throughout the campus for easy access. The strongest collections are reputedly in engineering, fisheries, forestry, health sciences, and in area studies dealing with East Asia, South Asia, Scandinavia, Slavic regions, and Pacific Northwest.

Honors Program for Freshmen

The College of Arts and Sciences has an Honors Program for exceptional students who enroll in "honors everything": honors seminars, honors sections of regular courses, and so on. The bachelor's degree of the successful student is designated, of course, "Graduated with Honors."

A unique offering of the University of Washington is the Early Entrance Program. Intended for youngsters of junior high school age or even younger, this program enrolls the students in university courses, one at a time, until they can assume a full load; or through the Transition Component, a year-long program that bridges the gap between their junior high or high school work and university-level competency.

Campus Life

Housing

Housing policies at the University of Washington are not mainstream Americana. For example, freshmen are not given priority to live in the seven campus residence halls (some of which have stunning views of Portage Bay). Those who have resided in the halls longest have highest priority. New students are assigned housing by lottery, first come, first served. Oddly, candidates for admission are urged to make housing applications immediately upon receipt of the application, whether admitted to the university or not. In all, 4,400 students live in campus residence halls; approximately 90 percent of them are undergraduates.

The fraternities and sororities offer another 3,500 beds. The availability of housing alone makes the Greek system strong here. Those who are not accommodated in residence halls or fraternities/sororities fend for themselves in neighborhoods close by. More and more students are choosing to commute from home. Related to the "live at home" preference is the fact that many UW undergraduates are well beyond their teens.

The Environs

If you can tolerate dampness, the University of Washington's locale offers a high quality of living. The 260-acre campus is parklike, is close to shops selling international wares and an array of ethnic restaurants, and has a lively atmosphere. Seattle is only four miles away, easily accessible by bus. The old World's Fair Center is now a seventy-four-acre civic complex containing everything from amusement sections to sporting event facilities to the Art Museum, the Seattle Opera and Repertory Theater, the Pacific Science Center, and the dominant and oft-pictured Space Needle. Mount Rainier and the Olympic and

Cascade mountain ranges are within a short drive, and Canada's border to British Columbia is only 150 miles away. This is an attractive and scenic area, particularly for the outdoorsperson and anyone who loves water (in the air as well as in the lakes and seas).

Local Hangouts

The Student Union Building (Hub) is the central gathering place. On the whole, though, UW's academic types can be found in the library, in the computer center, or in the labs; the postpone-the-paper-until-tomorrow types (who are also the soap opera buffs) can be found in the Hub's television room or the residence hall lounges; the fraternity and sorority types stay home on Greek row and wander out now and then to class; the video fanatics jam the game room of the Hub; the commuters congregate at the campus food facilities (By George, Terry Cafe) or the espresso bars. *All* types converge on a wealth of taverns in the University District, particularly on weekends.

The Greeks

Given the heavy commuter traffic to UW and the paucity of dormitory rooms, the fraternities and sororities provide some social continuity. Housing almost as many students as the residence halls, the Greeks also get high points for a variety of educational and cultural activities, placing particular emphasis on study programs for new students. And they are, of course, the campus party centers. Even the administration has considerable admiration for the Greeks here. As one dean said, "The Greeks are surprisingly good citizens considering the latitude they have in developing their own programs and standards of conduct. Fraternities and sororities clearly add to the high quality of life on this campus."

Athletics

UW's football team has graced the Rose Bowl television screen more than once during the past few years, signifying serious business in intercollegiate athletics here. The men's and women's crews, and women's gymnastics and volleyball teams have also been prominent in national rankings. And, as everywhere else in America today, intermurals and club sports are on the upswing.

Drugs/Booze/Sex

Says one administrator tersely, "The University of Washington does not concern itself with the private lives of individuals on this campus." The students are, quite obviously, on their own. In this diverse society, you can find anyone doing most anything. But one must remember that the Pacific Northwest is not known for overt displays, and this campus is 92 percent Washingtonian.

Student Stereotypes

Again, there is a taste of it all. The Greeks are the trendy ones, sporting Izod shirts and Sperry Topsiders, being politically conservative, and leading a rather homogeneous life. The commuters and dormies are a mixed bag, from Greek facsimiles to punks to hippies. As one student said, "Although people here may *look* different, 'moderate' is in."

The Tolerance Level

This is an accepting place. There is little evidence, if any, of racism, bigotry, or intolerance of unusual life-styles. Although moderation is in vogue, a few assertive groups are visible: minorities, women's groups, gays, and a handful of ultraconservatives.

Food

The university is proud of its "flexible meal system," which allows residence hall students broad choices among the facilities on campus. It is fashionable to complain about the coffee and burgers at the Hub. Nonetheless, UW brags that it has among the greatest variety of eateries of all the campuses in America.

Cars and Transportation

Because the campus is so close to the city, a car is more a bother than a blessing. Hundreds of commuters and carpools eat up the parking spaces. The university says it has "no available data on cars owned by UW students," but the percentage of resident students with cars seems very low. Public transportation is good here, even to the sea and the slopes.

Life After College

Post-Bachelor's Placement

The University of Washington stresses the practical in preparing students for the future. An administrator reports: "Our graduates with baccalaureate, master's, and doctoral degrees are highly successful in their job search, *especially* if they have technical degrees. Students pursuing nontechnical degrees are encouraged to become involved in internships in career-related employment while still at the university so they can focus on skills that will make them good job candidates if they are not proceeding on to graduate study."

Alumni Stars in the UW Galaxy

Some who wear the UW ring: Edward Carlson, chairman of United Airlines/Westin Hotels; Imogen Cunningham, one of the nation's foremost women photographers; Carolyn Dimmick, the first woman on the Washington Supreme Court; Bonnie Dunbar, the astronaut; John Fery, chairman of the Boise Cascade Corporation; Donald Peterson, president of Ford Motor Company; Rob Weller, host of *Entertainment Tonight.*

Admissions-Related Topics

Image versus Reality

The University of Washington is thought to be urban, research-oriented, and in financial trouble. These are all in large part correct, but one must remember that Seattle is a splendid city and the environs are appealing, the undergraduate program is very strong despite the graduate-and-research tilt, and the financial problems have not *yet* made a noticeable dent on the institution's quality.

What Elements Most/Least Draw Students?

Most attractive: the location and the campus itself, the wide range of academic offerings, the strong library and research facilities, and the overall academic reputation.

Least attractive: the intimidating size and the seemingly complex internal structure for those who wonder if the undergraduate "might get lost."

Is UW for Everyone?

From the search for housing on through, UW is for the capable person who can fend for him or herself. There is little hand-holding here. But there is plenty of academic rigor available, along with a lively, multifaceted community—if the student is willing to search for what is comfortable and appealing.

En Route Perfection, What Should UW Change?

The university should try to get more money, more space, and more students from outside Washington.

In Summary

Proud and regionally secure, the University of Washington does provide a cultural difference for those from any other part of America, as well as quality academics not limited to its frenzy of upper-level research. But this is a sophisticated and sometimes stiff environment, and an undergraduate without a fierce streak of independence can be lonely.

University of Wisconsin

Madison

Academics

Importance of the Liberal Arts

There are over 152 undergraduate majors available at UW-Madison, among a seemingly endless variety of schools, programs, and interdisciplinary configurations. But amidst the variety and confusion, the College of Letters and Science (the largest liberal arts college in the state of Wisconsin) offers the broadest range of course offerings and educational opportunities.

The importance and mission of the liberal arts is captured through well-rehearsed lines from a university administrator: "Madison's College of Letters and Science provides (1) competence in communication, (2) competence in utilizing the modes of thought characteristic of the major areas of knowledge, (3) a knowledge of man's basic cultural heritage, and (4) a thorough understanding of at least one subject area. The purpose is not to constrain the individual student but rather to ensure the probability that the student will have a meaningful and valuable educational experience." Virtually all of the professional programs at Madison require some courses from the several hundred offered in the College of Letters and Science.

There are staunch supporters among the University of Wisconsin's faculty for the liberal arts program; this is particularly worth noting in this era of careerism. As one professor states, "I cannot recall a classics major being rejected by a law school ever. The literacy and self-disciplined qualities of the classics major are highly valued by many graduate programs."

Madison integrates everything. Students studying premed, for example, may select to live at the French House; and prospective en-

University of Wisconsin at Madison

1) Size of Student Body

   Undergraduate _29,268_ Graduate _10,884_   Total _40,152_

2) 1983 Freshman Class Profile

   Class Size _5,110_   % Men _52_   % Women _48_
   Percent of Applicants Admitted _84_
   Average SATs: Verbal _504_   Math _579_
   High School Class Rank: Top Tenth _33_ % Top Quarter _67_ %
      Geographical Distribution (% of class):
   In-State _77_____% Middle Atlantic _3_ % New England _1_ %
   West ___1_____ % Middle West ___88_ % South _____1_ %
   Foreign _6_____ %
   Minority Students _5_ % of Class
   Financial Aid _43_ % of Class

3) Retention of Students

   _55_ % of freshmen graduate in four years
   ____ % of freshmen graduate in five years

4) Ten Most Popular Majors of Graduating Seniors, 1983

   1. Electrical and Computer En-   6. Communication Arts
      gineering   7. Pharmacy
   2. Mechanical Engineering   8. Elementary Education
   3. Journalism   9. Economics
   4. Nursing   10. Civil and Environmental En-
   5. Chemical Engineering   gineering

5) The Financial Picture (1982–83)

Annual Campus Budget	$ 584,853,649
Percent of Annual Budget from State Appropriation	34
1983–84 Tuition and Fees for State Residents	$ 1,199
1983–84 Tuition and Fees for Out-of-State Residents	$ 4,079

gineers or health professionals may spend a year abroad studying a wide variety of liberal arts courses to complement their demanding professional program requirements.

Strong Departments

Many departments at Madison are ranked nationally among the best; these consistently include chemical engineering, Spanish, mathematics, agriculture, psychology, and business. But to name only a few departments may be splitting hairs. When departmental weaknesses appear at Madison, attention is paid to quick recovery. The overall standard is very high.

Class Size and Faculty Accessibility

Madison is typical of big universities: students in the freshmen and sophomore years are exposed to a string of lectures with 300 to 400 students. Typically, however, weekly discussion sections, led by graduate students, contain approximately twenty students. As one advances from introductory to more specialized courses, class size diminishes and more full-time professors appear.

All teaching faculty must announce a schedule of office hours. The complaint here is the reverse of what one often hears: faculty members are irked that more students do not seek individual advice.

Who Teaches Undergraduates?

The most distinguished faculty are supposed to teach at all levels of the undergraduate program, but students complain that the most famous rarely come out of their research cubicles to appear at the podium. Teaching assistants "under the direction of a senior faculty member" regularly teach introductory courses that are in high demand—English, chemistry, and mathematics, for example.

Are Most Listed Courses Really Available?

Engineering, business, and health-related majors are exceedingly popular here, as elsewhere. Students admitted to the freshmen class do not easily slip into these crowded areas. "Established selection requirements" to enter the major must be met by the beginning of the junior year.

Aside from high demand programs, there are some high demand courses in such fields as chemistry and foreign language where students are often closed out. The course can usually be taken in the following semester with limited disruption.

The Library

The library system at Madison is awesome, considered "a national and international resource," and highly decentralized. The central library is supplemented by five professional school libraries and thirteen branch libraries (with a total of 3.5 million items), including an undergraduate library, an art library, and departmental libraries scattered through the campus. In addition, the library of the Wisconsin Historical Society is located on campus and houses nearly 1,300,000 items available to students.

Honors Program for Freshmen

There is no identifiable honors program for freshmen, but students of particularly high ability can "place" into advanced courses easily.

Campus Life

Housing

Although two-thirds of all students live within one mile of the campus at Madison, only one-fourth reside in university housing. Not even all the freshmen squeeze in—under three-fourths of the new class can be accommodated each year. Room assignments are made according to date of application, and that's that. A Wisconsin law favors citizens, so nonresidents are almost always closed out of campus housing and are forced to fend for themselves. Coops and private dorms, apartments and rooming houses, and fraternities and sororities dot the environs of the campus. The university does not inspect or evaluate private facilities and quality is erratic.

The Environs

Madison, the state capitol, is an all-American city (that means clean) of 170,000. The 900-acre campus is situated on rolling hills atop a prehistoric Indian site that overlooks Lake Mendota, the largest of four lakes adjoining the town. Milwaukee is one hour away.

Local Hangouts

Wisconsin's two student unions are often called "the living rooms of the university." They offer everything, from eating facilities to cultural and recreational opportunities. But students are hardly limited to the campus: a mile-long mall connecting the university with the state capitol offers a host of pubs, restaurants, and fun spots.

The Greeks

As one non-Greek said: "Fraternities and sororities are very important to the people in them, and not at all important to the rest of us. They are small in number and small in population." Although the fraternities and sororities declined in the sixties and seventies, membership is growing again and several chapters are making a bid for a comeback. But as one administrator has commented: "Major campus happenings are not dependent upon our Greeks."

Athletics

Intercollegiate athletics do not create the level of frenzy at Wisconsin that the other Big Ten schools experience. And there is strong talk among faculty here regarding the place of the athletic program: players are students first and athletes second. As for those who attend events, they are often beer-guzzlers first and spectators second. In short, intercollegiate athletics at Madison are in proper perspective. Beyond the 900 men and women involved in the intercollegiate program are scores who take advantage of the very decent intermural and club opportunities.

Drugs/Booze/Sex

Beer is back and, to a lesser extent, so is hard liquor. Other "substances" are available but are no longer as visible as they once were. As one student says, "Marijuana, Quaaludes, and cocaine are done to some extent in subgroups, but unobtrusively to avoid notoriety or attention by authorities."

Regarding the sex life at Madison, one senior reports: "There is probably more sex here than a lot of parents would like to believe, and considerably less than the popular media would have you believe. The arrival of coed dorms at Madison is perhaps responsible for a greater sense of mutual respect between the sexes." There is considerable cohabitation at Wisconsin. "But a great many of these arrangements are asexual," says one administrator. "Others represent long-term monogamous commitments, many of which outlast more formal marriages."

Student Stereotypes

No doubt about it, Wisconsin is a multidimensional campus where a student can try on and discard a number of different styles and identities en route to the degree, finding company in each incarnation.

The Tolerance Level

> A freshman reports: *"Differences* here present no problem. You can always find buddies who will understand if not accompany you. *Proselytism*, on the other hand, will almost always be challenged."

Food

> This is another campus where the food is labeled "nutritious." There is a variety of meal contracts, so one is not stuck in one place and/or paying for food not eaten. Fast-food eateries and ethnic restaurants abound nearby.

Cars and Transportation

> Bikes and mopeds are popular here, and they make sense. An automobile can be handy but, as always, parking is a problem. Approximately 35 percent of the undergraduates have cars in Madison, but fewer than 15 percent of them actually drive to class.

Life After College

Post-Bachelor's Placement

> Wisconsin reports: "Although we have no studies which provide data on the acceptance of our graduates to graduate and professional schools, we have no reason to believe that most of them are not accepted by first-rate graduate programs across the country." Well-developed career counseling facilities are available, and a comprehensive network of alumni contacts to assist graduates in placement has also been developed. But Madison professors and students seem less interested in the job than the learning en route.

Alumni Stars in the UW-Madison Galaxy

> UW-Madison has graduated over a quarter of a million students. The well known are in many fields. In arts and entertainment: Frederic March, Don Ameche, David Susskind, Edwin Newman, McDonald Carey, author Zona Gale, and showman John Ringling. Five former or current faculty members are winners of the Nobel Prize, as are six alumni. Pulitzer Prize winners also dot the faculty and alumni ranks. Among corporate presidents and board chairmen are the heads of Whirlpool, Revere Copper, Kimberly-Clark, Outboard Marine, Con Edison, Western Electric, Republic Airlines, General Electric, AT&T, Campbell Soup, Ralston Purina, and Kraft Foods. Badgers have also made their mark in education not just as college presidents or deans:

economist Walter Heller was the economic advisor to Presidents Kennedy and Johnson; two-time Nobel winner John Bardeen is considered one of America's greatest physicists. Madison alums in publishing include the exeutive editor of *Reader's Digest,* a *Newsweek* bureau chief, the managing editor of *US News & World Report,* and the vice-president of UPI. And there are politicians: former Senators Gaylord Nelson, Wayne Morse, Robert LaFollette, for example. Others who share a Madison heritage are John Savage, who designed the Grand Coulee and Hoover dams, and world-renowned architect Frank Lloyd Wright.

Admissions-Related Topics

Image versus Reality

> One small-town Wisconsinite reports: "Madison was always considered different, just different. It was the one place in the state that was truly cosmopolitan, politically aware, ultraliberal, and a retreat for the real intellectuals." The old image may well remain close to the mark. Madison certainly has more in common with Berkeley than with Urbana or Bloomington.

What Elements Most/Least Draw Students?

> Most attractive: the reputation of the educational program; the liberal intellectual atmosphere.
> Least appealing: the size, the location ("too far from home"), the dreary housing situation, the "too liberal" atmosphere, and the weather.

Is UW-Madison for Everyone?

> Students in Madison must cope with relative anonymity in large crowds and a decentralized system. In this complex environment, a student must be smart and well disciplined and have considerable self-confidence. There is a graduate school mentality here that many undergraduates find uncomfortable. For some, UW-Madison may not be the best place to start as a freshman. Since approximately 4,000 students enter each year as transfers, entering Madison after gaining basic college experience elsewhere becomes a worthy option.

En Route Perfection, What Should UW-Madison Change?

> "UW-Madison has an excess of prospective engineers and business majors, and too many students who need remedial help in writing and computational skills," says one administrator. And the same administrator agrees with students that the student body, although var-

ied, would be even more interesting with more returning adults, more minority and disabled students. Overall, though, this is a self-satisfied group.

In Summary

"Diversity" is a key word at Wisconsin—in academic programs, facilities, activities, student body. But "liberal" is key too—Wisconsin is not liberal in the Midwestern context alone, but in the national context as well. And there is certainly academic quality here. National polls always rank Wisconsin high, but locals push even further in a school song: "When you say Wisconsin, you've said it all."

Appendix

The Writing on the Walls

There are those who say that the *real* way to tell colleges apart is by analyzing their graffiti. Following this sage advice, the author, assisted by local students, pursued this provocative study on the eight Public Ivy campuses. It is true—the graffiti "tone" differed markedly from campus to campus. On the whole, the "liberal" institutions kept the graffiti inside the public johns; the graffiti itself was rather academic, clever-off-color, rarely dirty. In the more "conservative" institutions with a tendency toward homogenous student bodies and more rules and regulations, the graffiti came out of the johns and onto the study tables; the graffiti itself was rarely academic or thoughtful or fun, and often disgustingly base.

A potpourri of institutional graffiti, highly censored, is presented here:

University of California

On a number of UC campuses, there were "grout wars." Johns throughout the system are glaze-tiled, so the graffiti can be quickly removed. But maintenance people cannot remove what is written in miniscule letters in the grout *between* the tiles. A sampling:

"Congroutulations!" "Sourgrout" "The Grouton School" "Rainbow Grout" "Ulysses S. Grout" "The Grout Gatsby" "Grout-o-Marks" "This graffiti is just grout!"

Writer #1:   "If you believe in the Unmoved Mover, you believe in God. It is a contradiction to think that a thing can move without being moved.

Writer #2: "Oh, come on—the result of an immovable object being hit by an unstoppable force is simply ORGASM!"

Miami University

"I search for reverse but there is none
No changing what's already been done, no
editing what's already been said
All that's left is onward, with memories,
      good and bad, in my head . . .
Better off dead?"

"Q: Why did the little Beta run away from his frat home?
  A: He didn't like the way he was being reared.
  Q: Why did he come home?
  A: He couldn't leave his friends behind."

"No longer will you roam
  forever as master of this planet
  because only the rocks live forever.
  Note: Acid 'dissolves' rain."

Writer #1: "I'm proud that no fags defame walls at Miami."
Writer #2: "Surprise!! Contact Dennis at 4-6600."

University of Michigan

Writer #1: "Ronald Reagan is a prune-faced cowboy."
Writer #2: "Hey, why take it out on cowboys?"
"Reality is for those who can't handle drugs."
"Bring Back Carter!! (Billy)"

University of North Carolina (Winner of the author's Grand Graffiti Award)

"I have found reality. It's on my ankle and sparkles."
"Oral Roberts is God's #1 mouthwash."
"I dream of giving birth to a child who will say, 'Mother, what was war?' "
"Gay women stay women."
"Give your children mental blocks this Christmas."
"An elephant stood looking at a naked man and said, 'How does he breathe through that little thing?' "

University of Texas

"Profanity is the linguistic crutch of the inarticulate."
"Frat boys are just God's way of letting us know He can make mistakes too."
"*Repeat* your sins before it is too late!"
"I'd rather be gay and rich than poor and straight."
"ROTC: Retarded Officers Training Corps"

University of Vermont

"Whatever happened to the good old days of domination?"

"There once was a mathematician named Hall
Who had a dodecahedron ball;
The length of his beam
Times 4, divided by 16,
Is his number—give him a call!"

"Beef Lives! . . . and reigns at Sigma Nu."

"UVM: The Golden Age High School."

Writer #1: "Try Christ!!"
Writer #2: "OK, OK—what time is his seminar?"

"*We* are the people our parents warned us about!"

University of Virginia

"Long Island rules!"

"To do is to be . . . Socrates
To be is to do . . . Sartre
Ob-be-do-be-do . . . Sinatra"

"Rugby players eat their dead."

William and Mary College

Writer #1: "Why is it that William and Mary chicks won't do it on the first date?
Writer #2: " 'Cause all you frat boys are better at defacing public places than seducing women."

"Physics majors die young."

Writer #1: "What is love, what is freedom?
                      God is love—in His spirit is liberty."
Writer #2: "Hey, could you please be more specific? And was He a Beta?"

"I go to the College of S and M in Williamsburg."

Index